CAMPAIGNS OF THE CIVIL WAR

SHERMAN'S MARCH
TO THE SEA

HOOD'S TENNESSEE CAMPAIGN
&
THE CAROLINA CAMPAIGNS OF 1865

BY

JACOB D. COX, LL.D.,
LATE MAJOR-GENERAL COMMANDING TWENTY-THIRD ARMY CORPS

WITH A NEW INTRODUCTION

BY

BROOKS D. SIMPSON

DA CAPO PRESS
NEW YORK

Library of Congress Cataloging in Publication Data

Cox, Jacob D. (Jacob Dolson), 1828-1900.
[March to the sea]
Sherman's march to the sea: Hood's Tennessee Campaign &
the Carolina Campaigns of 1865 / by Jacob D. Cox; new in-
troduction by Brooks D. Simpson.—1st Da Capo Press ed.
     p.   cm.
Original title: The March to the sea: Franklin and Nashville.
Includes index.
ISBN 0-306-80587-1
   1. United States—History—Civil War, 1861—1865—Cam-
paigns. 2. Sherman's March to the Sea—Personal narratives. 3.
Cox, Jacob D. (Jacob Dolson), 1828-1900. I. Title.
E477.7.C69 1994   94-11263
973.7′3—dc20   CIP

First Da Capo Press edition 1994

This Da Capo Press paperback edition of
Sherman's March to the Sea is an unabridged republication
of the edition published in New York in 1882 under the title
The March to the Sea—Franklin and Nashville.
It is here supplemented with a new introduction
by Brooks D. Simpson.

Published by Da Capo Press, Inc.
A Subsidiary of Plenum Publishing Corporation
233 Spring Street, New York, N.Y. 10013

SHERMAN'S MARCH
TO THE SEA

INTRODUCTION

——————

With the reelection of Abraham Lincoln as President of the United States on November 8, 1864, the American Civil War entered its final stage. Gone were whatever hopes the Confederacy had of ousting the Lincoln administration by fostering war-weariness in the Northern electorate. But the war was not yet over, and the Union high command knew it. No sooner had Atlanta fallen in September than Ulysses S. Grant wanted more. "We want to keep the enemy constantly pressed to the end of the war," he told William T. Sherman. "If we give him no peace whilst the war lasts, the end cannot be distant." If the Confederacy was doomed, its leaders showed no sign that they recognized it. "Our cause is not lost," Jefferson Davis, on a visit to John Bell Hood's Army of Tennessee, declared in late September. "Sherman cannot keep up his long line of communication; and retreat sooner or later he must. And when that day comes, the fate that befell the army of the French Empire in its retreat from Moscow will be reenacted." So long as Confederates believed Davis, the war would continue. To crush the Confederacy, Union armies would have to destroy both its ability and will to keep fighting.[1]

Jacob D. Cox's account of these final six months is best divided into three stories. The first tale is of Sherman's decision to break loose from his supply tether and march through the interior of Georgia to the Atlantic coast. Capturing Atlanta, while in itself of great political as well as military significance, was only half of Sherman's original assignment, for Hood's Army of Tennessee remained a force to be reckoned with. After rebuilding his army, Hood planned to turn Sherman's victory to his advantage by striking at the Union supply line extending back to Chattanooga along a lone rail line. At worst, he reasoned, such a strategy would pin Sherman in place. Unable to corner the Confederate, Sherman cast about for alternatives and hit upon the idea of dividing his command, leaving part of it under George H. Thomas to keep Hood in check while he set out with the remainder on a march to the Atlantic coast. With ill-concealed enthusiasm, he declared, "I can make this march, and make Georgia howl!" He was far more restrained in explaining the impact of such a march on the Confederacy. "If we can march a well-appointed army right through his territory, it is a demonstration to the world . . . that we have a power which Davis can not resist," he told Grant. "This may not be war, but rather statesmanship. . . . If the North can march an army right through the South, it is proof positive that the North can prevail in this contest." His target was enemy morale: "I propose to demonstrate the vulnerability of the South and make its inhabitants feel that war and individual ruin are synonymous terms."

Initially Grant demurred, arguing that the destruction of Hood's army remained Sherman's foremost priority; however, he too had always entertained the notion of a column cutting through the Confederate heartland, and after several exchanges of correspondence with Sherman, he gave his approval. In later years, when some of Sherman's detractors suggested that the March to the Sea was Grant's idea, the general-in-chief responded that the question of credit "is easily answered: it was clearly Sherman, and to him also belongs the credit of its brilliant execution." With some sixty thousand hand-picked veterans, Sherman took his leave of a still-smoldering Atlanta on November 16 and made his way southeast into the interior.

Much has been made of the resulting march, especially about how the Union soldiers behaved and how much they destroyed, with stories of indiscriminate destruction and pillage winning great favor with advocates of the Lost Cause. In fact, Sherman's men, although they foraged liberally on local farms, on the whole demonstrated good discipline and restraint; however, deserters from both armies, fugitive slaves, Confederate cavalry, and the so-called "bummers" of Sherman's army were less scrupulous in their behavior toward white civilians. This as much as anything else brought the war home to supporters of the Confederacy, achieving Sherman's goal of shattering their will to persist in rebellion. Nor did the advancing Yankees feel much sympathy for Confederate civilians when they came across the shrunken bodies of comrades who had escaped from Andersonville prison. "These people made war on us, defied and dared us to come south to their country, where they boasted they would kill us and do all manner of horrible things," Sherman later remarked. "We accepted their challenge, and now for them to whine and complain of the natural and necessary results is beneath contempt."[2]

By early December, Sherman's forces were within sight of Savannah, Georgia. Supplies landed by Grant awaited them. On December 21 the Confederate garrison escaped across a road Sherman had left open—shades of Hood's escape from Atlanta!—and on the next day Sherman entered the city. He wired Lincoln: "I beg to present you as a Christmas gift the city of Savannah, with one hundred and fifty heavy guns and plenty of ammunition, also about twenty-five thousand bales of cotton." The March to the Sea thus passed into history and myth.

Sherman's march eroded Confederate morale, but by itself it could do little. Of equal importance was the fate of the Rebel field armies. In Virginia, Grant maintained what Lincoln called "a bull-dog grip" on Robert E. Lee and the Army of Northern Virginia in the entrenchments east and south of Richmond and Petersburg, depriving the Confederacy of its most able offensive general. Hood and the Army of Tennessee were a different matter. As Sherman mapped out his march, Hood pondered his next move. His army was too weak to attack; to sit in a defensive posture did no good; and thus in the end Hood was drawn to a third alternative, that of launching his own invasion of Tennessee.

On November 20, just days after Sherman left Atlanta, Hood commenced his offensive with an army 40,000 strong. He crossed the Tennessee River at Florence, Alabama and headed north to Tennessee, targeting Nashville. Confronting him was John M. Schofield and two infantry corps (one of which was commanded by Jacob D. Cox) with orders to delay the Confederate advance while Thomas gathered reinforcements at Nashville. At Spring Hill confusion between Confederate commanders deprived the Rebels of an excellent chance to block Schofield's retreat by securing a turnpike; instead the Yankees continued on their way to Franklin under cover of darkness. In years to come Hood and others would debate who was to blame for this blunder, overlooking the fact that alternative routes to Franklin and Nashville remained available to Schofield. The next day Hood picked up the pursuit, marching toward Franklin, where the Yankees had entrenched in preparation for an encounter. Cox himself had supervised the erection of fortifications; his headquarters, at a farmhouse owned by the Carter family, became a focal point of Confederate assaults, as Hood ordered his men forward in an attempt to smash Schofield. Through the late afternoon and into the evening the butternuts charged. Federal fire proved so heavy that one Confederate private remarked that as his regiment advanced, "we instinctively pulled our hat brims down as though to protect our faces."[3] Still the Rebels came on, meeting their foes in hand-to-hand combat. "Blood actually ran in the ditch and in places saturated our clothing where we were lying down," remarked one Confederate.[4] Some 6,000 Confederates fell killed or wounded. Six generals were killed; five more were wounded; one fell prisoner. Fifty-five regimental commanders were among the casualties. Schofield managed to withdraw across the Tennessee under cover of darkness.

Several days later Hood drew up his damaged command south of Nashville. There George H. Thomas methodically prepared to crush the Confederate force. Both generals would come under fire for their actions over the next two weeks. What did Hood think he would accomplish by waiting south of Nashville? Why did Thomas take so long to attack? The harsh weather had much to do with answering both questions. In fact, Hood had very little idea of what to do next, and before long his men were struggling with an abundance of cold and a shortage of food, clothing, and high spirits. In such circumstances Hood later claimed that he decided to await Thomas's next move with the aim of shattering any assault. It is just as likely that he had little idea of how outnumbered he was, for Thomas's force of 70,000 men might well overwhelm Hood's suffering 25,000, and there were far better locations to establish defensive positions. Finally, it is difficult to assess Hood's state of mind during this critical period, for he soon detached over 6,000 men to attack a Federal garrison at Murfreesboro.[5]

Thomas planned to assault Hood with such devastating force that it would be the Confederates who would be destroyed. The cold made it difficult to gather sufficient cavalry and to position men south of the Tennessee, while ice storms rendered nearly impassable the ground over which the soldiers would advance. These difficulties were all too apparent to Thomas and his generals, but elsewhere the high command grew uneasy. "The President feels solicitous about the disposition of General Thomas to lay in fortifications for an indefinite period," Secretary of War Edwin M. Stanton informed Grant. "This looks like the McClellan and Rosecrans strategy of do nothing and let the rebels raid the country." What if Hood swung north to the Ohio River? What if he replicated Sherman's march in reverse? Grant did what he could to reinforce Thomas, but before long his dispatches began to betray impatience at Thomas's failure to take the offensive. Others agreed: Sherman was "somewhat astonished" that Thomas had not already advanced, while Stanton scoffed, "Thomas seems unwilling to attack because it is hazardous, as if all war was anything but hazardous."

Under pressure from Washington, and well-acquainted through first-hand experience with Thomas's tendency to dawdle, Grant's dispatches became ever more insistent in their calls for action. Thomas's responses first spoke of the weather, then promised action, and finally reported postponements. At last Grant ran out of patience. At first he planned to replace Thomas with either Schofield and then John A. Logan; then he elected to go to Nashville to take command personally, leaving his headquarters at City Point, Virginia, on December 14.

As Grant travelled to Washington, Thomas finally moved, striking the Confederate left on December 15 with a sledgehammer blow of 40,000 men. By dusk the Confederate position had collapsed, in part because Hood failed to dispatch sufficient reinforcements in a timely manner. The Confederates withdrew to a second position anchored on what would become known as Shy's Hill. On December 16, after Union cannon bombarded the hill for hours, Thomas's infantry smashed the Rebel lines. In the melee that followed, Lieutenant Colonel William M. Shy, commanding several consolidated Tennessee regiments, fell on the hill that now bears his name. Some 113 years later his body was unearthed; the embalming had been so skilled that at first police thought he had been a recent murder victim.[6] Those Confederates who did not fall with Shy soon broke and fled, and the entire Rebel position collapsed. What followed was a rout; what remained of the Army of Tennessee came close to disintegrating altogether. Fortunately for the Confederates, bad weather slowed the Union pursuit.

* * *

The third and final phase of campaigning described by Cox commenced with Sherman's decision to march north through the Carolinas toward Richmond—a decision reached only after Grant learned that his initial inclination to transfer Sherman's force to Richmond via water would take up too much time and place an unnecessary burden on Union naval transport. Once more Grant gave in to his subordinate; at the same time, intending to close down the last Confederate port at Wilmington, the general-in-chief ordered an expedition against Fort Fisher, which guarded approaches to that city. An initial effort, directed by Benjamin F. Butler, failed ignominiously; but Grant ordered a second attempt, replacing Butler with Alfred H. Terry. Under cover of a naval bombardment Terry's troops landed opposite the fort on January 13. Two days later they captured it with the assistance of a brigade of marines and seamen. Although it took until February 22 for Union forces to enter Wilmington, the Confederacy was now sealed from Europe. Grant hurried Schofield's Army of the Ohio eastward by rail and water to North Carolina; Cox's account is one of the few that exist of this oft-overlooked campaign.

Four days after the fall of Fort Fisher, Sherman commenced his march northward. By the beginning of February his columns had reached South Carolina, a state Sherman's men held in special contempt as the birthplace of secession—and acted accordingly. Feinting toward Charleston, South Carolina, and Augusta, Georgia, Sherman instead drove between these two cities toward Columbia, the capital of South Carolina. There Confederate general Wade Hampton had assembled a small force that offered but token resistance. On February 16 Sherman bounced artillery shells off the walls of the state house (today stars mark the damage); the next day his men entered the city. In their haste to evacuate, Hampton's men set fire to bales of cotton to prevent their capture; unfortunately, these burning bales helped set fire to a significant portion of Columbia. Some Yankees did what they could to contain the blaze; others showed no remorse for the conflagration, deeming it just revenge. To this day the image of Sherman as a destroyer is rooted in large part in the myth that he torched Columbia, although he failed to submit Savannah to the same treatment. Such an image had its uses: Confederate soldiers, afraid for the safety of their homes and families, deserted in ever-increasing numbers.

To stop Sherman, Jefferson Davis finally turned to Joseph E. Johnston. Named commander of the Army of Tennessee on February 23, Johnston gathered his scattered forces, including many veterans of Franklin and Nashville, for one last stand against Sherman in North Carolina. Grant and Sherman feared that Lee would abandon Richmond and Petersburg and march south to join Johnston, whereupon the united Confederate forces would first attempt to destroy Sherman, then turn on Grant. Johnston had hoped for just this to occur; when it did not, he attacked part of Sherman's force at Bentonville in an almost forlorn effort to stop the Yankee advance. After sweeping back the Rebels, Sherman moved on and joined forces with Schofield at Goldsboro on March 23. Several weeks later, when word arrived at Johnston's headquarters of Lee's surrender to Grant at Appomattox, the Confederate commander commenced negotiations with Sherman, culminating in his surrender on April 26 at Durham Station, North Carolina.

These negotiations proved controversial, in large part because Sherman's initial offer of terms was rejected by the authorities at Washington. Sherman, convinced that it was of the utmost importance to secure the surrender of Confederate forces in the field before they broke up into roving bands of guerrillas, wanted to forestall such a calamity. (In breaking the news of Lincoln's assassination to his men, he warned them to prepare themselves for the war's "last and worst shape, that of assassins and guerrillas.") The previous month he had visited City Point to confer with Grant and Lincoln about how best to close out the war. Sherman was impressed with Lincoln's desire for a lenient peace; although he had assured Grant that he would "be careful not to complicate any points of civil policy," his terms did exactly that. The North, still reeling from the impact of Lincoln's assassination, was in no mood for such terms. Critics claimed that Sherman had stepped out of bounds in prescribing conditions for the restoration of civil rule in the defeated Confederacy; in guaranteeing Southern whites their "rights of person and property," he had possibly revived slavery's tenuous existence. The damage was soon undone, as Grant travelled to Sherman's headquarters to oversee a new agreement based on the Appomattox terms. For all intents and purposes, the conflict east of the Mississippi thus ended. Cavalry raids under James H. Wilson and George Stoneman as well as the long-awaited capture of Mobile helped complete the Confederate collapse, although Grant observed that these operations had little impact on the close of the war and destroyed lives and property "at a time when we would have liked to have spared them."

* * *

When Charles Scribners' Sons of New York commenced its landmark series, *The Campaigns of the Civil War,* the publishing house declared its intention to present accounts "by a number of leading actors in and students of the great conflict of 1861-'65, with a view to bringing together, for the first time, a full and authoritative military history of the suppression of the Rebellion." Of the sixteen volumes that eventually appeared, nearly all were prepared by participants in the conflict (all members of the Union forces); indeed, the civilian military historian John C. Ropes remarked in his preface to *The Army Under Pope* (1881) that "it may be presumptuous in a civilian to attempt a history of a campaign."

Cox's selection as the author of this volume of Charles Scribner's Sons *Campaigns of the Civil War* series was most appropriate, for he had seen action under both Sherman and Thomas during the last six months of the war. Left with Schofield and Thomas to keep Hood in check, Cox led his men northward through the night at Spring Hill; at Franklin he had supervised the construction of the field fortifications which proved so effective against Hood's assaulting columns; at Nashville his division joined in the attack on the anchor of the Confederate defense at Shy's Hill. He accompanied Schofield to North Carolina, advanced toward New Bern and Goldsboro, and helped close out the war.

Afterwards, Cox entered politics. Elected governor of Ohio in 1865, four years later he joined Ulysses S. Grant's cabinet as secretary of the interior. A supporter of civil service reform and an opponent of so-called Radical Reconstruction measures, Cox became an irritant to the President, who once growled, "The trouble was that General Cox thought the Interior Department was the whole government, and that Cox was the Interior Department." Eventually Cox resigned; while he later served a single term in Congress as a representative, his political fortunes never quite recovered from his break with Grant, and he had to rest content with offering political advice to others while practicing law in Ohio.

During these years Cox developed an interest in the military history of the Civil War. As the military book critic of *The Nation*, he became embroiled in a debate over the accuracy and fairness of Sherman's *Memoirs*, as he chose to defend his old chief's account. Almost as notable, especially in light of his continuing criticism of Grant as president, was his dispassionate, insightful, and fair review of Grant's *Memoirs*. Obviously Cox possessed just the qualities that Scribners' sought—a participant who could prepare a comprehensive and concise history—when the publisher approached him to contribute two volumes, *Atlanta* (also available from Da Capo Press) and *The March to the Sea*, to its campaign series. As one reviewer put it, *The March to the Sea* possessed "the charms of historic narrative which comes from his graceful and expressive style."[7]

Cox's assessments did not always pass uncontested. An anonymous reviewer chided Cox for his criticisms of George H. Thomas, which he termed "not only unjust but abominably ungrateful." Schofield and David S. Stanley took particular umbrage at Cox's insistence that he had commanded the fortified line at Franklin, and Schofield did not speak highly of Cox's performance at Nashville. Stanley labelled Cox "a reckless inventor of lies," declaring, "All his writings are full of the spirit of falsehood."[8] Stanley also feuded with

Schofield, and Schofield, who was critical of Thomas's generalship, had to defend himself from charges that he had connived to secure Thomas's removal at Nashville. But victory has a way of tempering such disputes. It was the Confederate debate over Hood's generalship and the incident at Spring Hill that has attracted more attention from historians. Cox's evaluation of Thomas's generalship also came under criticism from defenders of the Rock of Chickamauga, yet to the modern reader it seems a rather balanced assessment. To be sure, Cox did not always comprehend the broader issues at stake. His account shows little sympathy for fugitive slaves, describing them as "ignorant" and "uneducated" without pausing to ponder why that might be so. As he had attended Oberlin College, a hotbed of abolitionist sentiment, such remarks appear especially surprising, although less so when one recalls that after the war Cox called for the colonization of blacks along the Atlantic coast.

Despite these shortcomings, Cox's account provides a concise, thoughtful discussion of these three critical campaigns, of interest to scholar and buff alike. Whether well-read in the literature of military operations or just becoming interested in these climactic campaigns, the reader will profit from a perusal of what follows.

Brooks D. Simpson
Chandler, Arizona
February 1994

NOTES

[1] The best accounts of the campaigns covered in this volume include Joseph T. Glatthaar, *The March to the Sea and Beyond: Sherman's Troops in the Savannah and Carolinas Campaigns* (1986); Wiley Sword, *Embrace an Angry Wind: The Confederacy's Last Hurrah* (1992); Stanley F. Horn, *The Decisive Battle of Nashville* (1956); Thomas L. Connelly, *Autumn of Glory: The Army of Tennessee, 1862-1865* (1971); Steven E. Woodworth, *Jefferson Davis and His Generals: The Failure of Confederate Command in the West* (1990); Richard M. McMurry, *John Bell Hood and the War for Southern Independence* (1982); Freeman Cleaves, *Rock of Chickamauga: The Life of General George H. Thomas* (1948); Francis F. McKinney, *Education in Violence* (1961); Craig L. Symonds, *Joseph E. Johnston* (1992); and John F. Marszalek, *Sherman: A Soldier's Passion for Order* (1993).

[2] Marszalek, *Sherman*, 316.

[3] Sword, *Embrace an Angry Wind*, 208.

[4] Woodworth, *Jefferson Davis and His Generals*, 300.

[5] Connelly, *Autumn of Glory*, 507.

[6] Sword, *Embrace an Angry Wind*, 442.

[7] *The New York Times*, December 24, 1882.

[8] Sword, *Embrace an Angry Wind*, 441.

PREFACE.

THE class of readers which has been most in the author's mind in preparing the two volumes assigned him in the series, is that which includes the surviving officers and men who served in the late war. His aim has been to supplement their personal knowledge by the facts which are within the reach of recent research, and to give unity and symmetry to the history of the campaigns here told, by examining each in the light of the plans and purposes of the leaders on both sides.

The limits assigned to the volumes have made it necessary to choose between the narration of incidents which would enliven the story, and that fulness of strictly military detail which seemed necessary to make the several campaigns clearly intelligible, and to enable the reader to judge, with some degree of satisfaction, the character of the operations. The former course would perhaps have made the work more popular, but the latter has seemed likely to make it more useful and to meet the wishes of those for whom it has been chiefly written. It is still hoped, however, that the general reader will not find it difficult to follow the movements described, and that the effort to do so will give to such a broader understanding of what the great game of war really is.

The maps in both volumes are, with two exceptions, reduced copies of the official surveys made by the engineers of the army. For the originals the author is indebted to the courtesy of General Poe, U. S. Engineers. In reducing them it has not been possible to preserve all the details of the originals; but the effort has been to give accurately what is most essential. The reader is presumed to make reference to an ordinary hand-atlas for the relations of the special theatre of operations to that of the whole war. To have illustrated the text by larger and more elaborate maps would have thwarted the purpose of the publishers to put the series within the reach of all.

To General Drum, Adjutant-General, and to Colonel Scott, of the War Records Office, the author is greatly indebted for access to unpublished archives, and for official information without which it would have been impossible to reach the degree of accuracy which he hopes will be found to mark the more important parts of the narrative : it would be vain to expect to escape all error with our present means of investigation. A still greater debt of obligation, if possible, is due to Major E. C. Dawes, late of the Fifty-third Ohio, who has not only given the use of his valuable collection of books and documents relating to the war, but has thought no personal trouble too great in assisting to verify facts and trace events, and whose zeal in investigation has been a constant aid and stimulus.

CINCINNATI, September, 1882.

CONTENTS.

CHAPTER VII.

CHAPTER VIII.

CHAPTER IX.

CHAPTER X.

CHAPTER XI.

CHAPTER XII.

CHAPTER XIII.

APPENDIX A.

APPENDIX B.

APPENDIX C.

APPENDIX D.

APPENDIX E.

APPENDIX F.

LIST OF MAPS.

THE MARCH TO THE SEA.

CHAPTER I.

PLANNING THE CAMPAIGN.

WHEN Sherman stood upon the border of Alabama, at the close of October, 1864, looking toward Gadsden, and following in his mind's eye the retreating forces of Hood who was marching westward, he had an undoubting conviction that the true counter-movement was to turn his back upon his adversary and march away for Savannah and the sea. He had formed the opinion at the beginning of the month, but the campaign of October made him sure of it. The mobility of Hood's army was such that there was little hope of coming up with it till accident, or the exhaustion of the country, should force him to come to bay. The delays to a pursuing column may be indefinitely increased by an active and well-handled rear guard, and the moral effect of allowing the war to be transferred again to Tennessee would be every way bad. Still, if Hood had crossed the Tennessee anywhere between Stevenson and Guntersville, in the bend of the river, Sherman would have pursued him; but when he marched to Decatur, and, upon General R. S. Granger

showing a bold front there, moved still further west to Tuscumbia, nearly at the Mississippi line, it was clear as day to
the National Commander that the only way to preserve the
moral superiority and the initiative, was to put in operation
his previous plan.   He thought it probable that Hood
would be forced to follow him, especially since the latter
had been made, by a recent order of the Confederate Government, subordinate to General Beauregard, who had been
invested with the military command of all the territory between Middle Georgia and the Mississippi River.   He was
not mistaken in his forecast of Beauregard's judgment in
this respect, as will soon be seen; but Beauregard did not
feel authorized to take actual control of Hood's movements
under the somewhat peculiar orders given by President
Davis.   To try whether an indication of his counter-movement would call Hood back from the west, Sherman marched
again into Georgia in the first days of November, and concentrated his army at Rome and Kingston.   There, upon
the second of the month, he got from Grant the final assent
to his plan, and put all the capacity of the railroad, now repaired, to the utmost strain to remove surplus stores and
material of war from Atlanta and other posts in Georgia to
Nashville.

No military operation of the war has been so commonly
misunderstood as the campaign on which Sherman was now
entering.   The brilliancy of its design and the immense results which followed, have captivated the popular imagina-
tion and deeply impressed students of military history every-
where; but there has been a singular tendency to treat the
conception of a march from Atlanta to the gulf or to the
ocean as if that were an invention or a discovery.   People
have disputed the priority of idea, as if it were a patent
right; and, besides the military claimants of the honor of

the invention, non-combatants of both sexes have entered the lists and claimed to have given expression to the thought of such a movement before Sherman had captured Atlanta. General Badeau, the historian of Grant's campaigns, must be held responsible for a good deal of this misapprehension, which he seems to have shared himself; for he treats Grant's earlier indications of Mobile as an objective point, as if these contained the essential parts of the campaign as actually conducted. For the matter of that, we have seen, in a former volume, that Sherman gave a sufficiently clear outline of the movement in his letter to the General-in-Chief before the campaign of Atlanta had opened in the spring. In that, not only the march to the coast was foreshadowed, but the subsequent campaign through the Carolinas, which was to make, as he said, "short work" of what was left of the Confederate Government and cause.

Whoever will reflect a little, will see, however, that not even in this fuller anticipation of the outward form of the movement are found the essential features which gave to Sherman's decision and plan in October their peculiar military character. Unless the campaign just closed had been an aimless thing, we must suppose that both Grant and Sherman had reflected upon what should be done when Atlanta fell. Every intelligent person in the country, in or out of the army, must have seen that the successful march of a great army from Chattanooga southward, meant not only the capture of Atlanta, but more. The problems of war are not matters of occult science, and while it was hoped that in some decisive engagement Johnston's army might be routed before it reached the Chattahoochee, it took no genius to see that if its retreat to Atlanta should leave it with a still formidable organization, further opera-

tions would be necessary. These would naturally be such
as would turn to good use the auxiliary efforts which Canby
and the Navy were making to reduce Mobile, and, by reaching a hand to Sherman from the South, put the whole of
Alabama and Mississippi behind a wall of national bayonets
moving Eastward, and driving the Confederate Army before
them. This was the course of events which would be the
natural sequence of what had gone before, if no disaster
befell us; and had things worked in this way, we should
never have had the almost absurd debate upon the question
of intellectual authorship.

It was Hood's audacious movement upon Sherman's communications that changed all that. His design was to carry
back the war from Central Georgia to Tennessee, as, once
and again, Lee had carried it back from Central Virginia to
the Potomac. A weak general would have made haste to
put the National Army on the north side of the Tennessee
to cover and protect his communications; and Hood's purpose would have been successfully accomplished. It would
have been much better than this to have followed Hood
across Alabama, striving to get between him and his own
dépôts of supply, though this might have had no really decisive results. To provide for a sufficient force to keep him
from reaching the Northern States before the rapidly collecting recruits should swell Thomas's army to a size fully
able to deal with him, and with sixty thousand veterans
strike for the very heart of the Confederacy, was completely
to turn the tables upon the enterprising Southern general,
and make his very audacity prove at once his own ruin and
the ruin of the cause for which he fought. This was what
Sherman did, and the determination to do it, in the actual
situation, before any base upon the distant seacoast had been
secured, called for the very highest qualities in a commander.

The moral courage which decides upon a daring course, when failure must involve terrible and far-reaching consequences, is far greater in kind and in degree than that which the subordinate or the soldier in the ranks is called upon to show. The cool-headed, practical skill which carries out such a plan, through the vicissitudes of a campaign where the circumstances are always the unexpected, is only possible to one who unites physical hardihood to mental grasp and unbending will.

In thus fixing his purpose, Sherman had no assistance. He had heard nothing from Grant in reply to his proposal of the movement, though the latter had sent, on October 11th, a conditional approval, which the interruption of communications had prevented Sherman from receiving. Thomas advised against his plan,[1] and on November 1st Grant suggested to him to resume that of following Hood.[2] But Sherman was immovable in his judgment, unless Hood should try to cross the Tennessee somewhere near him, and on the second of the month Grant gave formal and final consent. Grant's sympathies were never lacking for a bold and decided course, but in this instance he had less faith than Sherman that all would go well in Tennessee in the interval. Lincoln, as he himself said a little later, " was anxious, if not fearful," but did not interfere.

So long as it seemed probable that he would force his adversary to follow him, Sherman's purpose had been to

---

[1] Despatch of October 17th.

[2] Despatch of that date: " Do you not think it advisable, now that Hood has gone so far North, to entirely ruin him before starting on your proposed campaign." Badeau says, vol. iii., p. 62: " Sherman declared Hood would follow him; Grant was certain that the rebel army would go North." Neither statement is quite accurate. He wrote this, forgetting that in the despatch of November 1st (which he himself quotes on page 157) Grant said : " I believed, and still believe, that if you had started South while Hood was in the neighborhood of you, he would have been forced to go after you." There was no real difference of opinion on this point.

leave only the Fourth Corps (Stanley's) in addition to the troops already stationed in Tennessee, and these, with the recruits which were rapidly enrolling, would have given Thomas very soon an army quite large enough for all probable needs. When Hood had passed Decatur, however, Sherman determined to send back Schofield with the Twenty-third Corps also, reckoning that the two corps, together with that of Major General A. J. Smith, which was ordered to join Thomas as speedily as possible, and the garrisons and posts in Tennessee, would make an army equal to Hood's at the opening of the new campaign. The recruits which would be added to this would soon give it a decided superiority, the real risk being limited to the time within which Thomas should be concentrating his forces.

Three divisions of the Sixteenth Corps were at this time under General A. J. Smith in Missouri, near the Kansas border, but on October 29th, General Rosecrans, who commanded that department, was directed from Washington to send Smith's troops to Nashville, and promptly put them in motion for the Mississippi River. Sherman had hoped that steamboats might meet them at Booneville on the Missouri and transport them directly to Paducah on the Ohio; but the Missouri was so low that navigation could not be depended upon, and Smith's troops were obliged to move by land to St. Louis from Warrensburg, where they were on November 2d.

Sherman had the most implicit confidence in General Thomas's ability to bear the great responsibilities to be imposed upon him, writing to Halleck that he was better suited to the emergency than any man he had. The very differences in temperament between the two men seemed to adapt them to the work each was to do. The task before Thomas was to conduct a cautious and purposely dilatory campaign till his reinforcements should be well in hand, and then, resuming the aggressive, to drive Hood southward and follow him wherever he should go. His whole career had borne witness to the unflinching courage with which he would meet the impetuosity of his opponent, and the tenacity with which he would stick to the contest even if the odds should be against him. Yet he would have been glad to avoid the task, and had said to Sherman, when the plan was first opened to him, that the one thing he did not wish was to assume the part allotted to him, unless Sherman and the authorities at Washington deemed it absolutely necessary. With the addition to his forces of Schofield's Twenty-third Corps he believed he would be strong enough to drive Hood back, but this increase he urged as indispensable, and as soon as Grant's definitive consent to the new plan of campaign was received, Schofield was ordered to march to Resaca and Dalton, where his troops were to meet the trains and be transported by rail to Nashville. The burden of taking to the rear the surplus material at Atlanta and of carrying to that place the stores Sherman intended to take with him, was overtaxing the railway, and it was not till November 7th that the last of Schofield's command procured transportation, though he had gone on to Nashville upon the 4th, for the purpose of arranging with Thomas the details of the operations committed to them.

This assignment of the Twenty-third Corps to duty under General Thomas had been at Schofield's own suggestion, and was agreeable, therefore, to both officers. Schofield's departmental command covered East Tennessee and part of Kentucky, and his presence saved the necessity of any change in the organization there. But still stronger motives were found in the fact that the strength of the Twenty-third Corps had been reduced below ten thousand men present for duty, by the casualties of the campaign, and the opportunity would thus be given it to recruit the two divisions already belonging to it, while a third division of new troops was ordered to join it when the new levies should reach the front. Schofield also believed that the campaign in Tennessee was to be an important one, full of varied military problems and contingencies, and that he could be quite as useful there as in any other field of operations.

For a full understanding of the situation in the Confederate army, and of the motives which controlled Hood's subsequent plan of campaign, we must go back to the beginning of September. The fall of Atlanta had been followed by differences between Confederate leaders as to the policy which should now be pursued. Governor Brown of Georgia had assumed the responsibility of giving a general furlough to the Georgia militia, ostensibly for the purpose of gathering the autumnal crops. Against this the President of the Confederacy protested, as well as against the claim of Governor Brown that the militia of the State were in the field under State authority for the defence of the State, and that as Governor he had the right to appoint and assign the officers to these State forces, and to keep them within the State boundaries. This assertion by the State executive of a very mild form of the doctrine of State rights, was looked upon as hardly less than treason by the Confederate Government. A war begun to assert the doctrine that every State was itself the judge of its rights under the Constitution and of the measure of redress when it considered those rights violated, had resulted in a centralization of which no Northern statesman had ever dreamed.

On September 8th, Hood telegraphed to General Bragg, at Richmond, suggesting that all the reserves of Georgia, under General Cobb, be ordered to his army, and that General Taylor be ordered to relieve Hardee in the command of his corps, bringing with him all the troops which could be spared from the department Taylor was then commanding, and which included Alabama and Mississippi. No immediate notice seems to have been taken of this at Richmond, and, on the 13th, Hood repeated the request to Davis himself, charging Hardee with being the cause of all the defeats his army had suffered, except that of July 28th at Ezra Church. A week later, still apparently without a reply, he sketched his proposed movement upon Sherman's communications, and he now learned that the Confederate President would immediately visit his camp. Accordingly, on September 25th, Davis reached Hood's headquarters at Palmetto, and a couple of days were spent in conference not only with Hood, but with his principal subordinates. The general plan of Hood's new campaign was approved, with the understanding that if he should succeed in drawing Sherman away from Atlanta, the new invasion of Tennessee should be made by crossing the river near Guntersville, not far from the Georgia line. The decision upon Hood's demand for Hardee's removal from his corps was a more troublesome question than the approval of the plan of operations. The great injustice of Hood's charges has been shown in the story of the Atlanta campaign; but the dissatisfaction of a commanding general with a subordinate is so strong a reason for a change that it will rarely do to ignore it. Lieutenant-General Richard Taylor, whom Hood suggested as Hardee's successor, was the brother-in-law of Mr. Davis, and the latter very well knew that this relationship would complicate the difficulty and be seized upon by many as proof

of personal motives on his part if he should give Hood his
wish. He seems, besides, to have had a real respect for
Hardee, and to have been driven to very serious doubts of
his own wisdom in giving Hood the command from which he
had hoped so much. The solution he reached was perhaps
the best the situation allowed. He determined to transfer
Hardee to a departmental command, including Eastern
Georgia and the adjacent territory in South Carolina and
Florida, a promotion in form, while he combined Hood's
and Taylor's departments in one military division and assigned General Beauregard to the command, with the understanding that Hood's army organization should not be disturbed, though Beauregard was expected to assume the
personal control whenever he might deem it necessary to be
with the troops.

Hood learned of the intended changes by a communication from Davis on September 28th or 29th, and the formal
orders followed in a day or two. Davis met Beauregard at
Augusta, in the first week of October, explained to him
Hood's plan of operations, which he had already begun to
execute, and no doubt impressed upon him the policy of
making no unnecessary interference with Hood's purposes.
Certain it is that it must have been in deference to some
such instructions that Beauregard carefully avoided establishing his headquarters with the army in the field, though
he kept near enough to Hood to have frequent conferences
with him, until the latter crossed the Tennessee, some six
weeks later. Hood was already across the Chattahoochee on
his northward march when the formal order placing Beauregard over him was issued, and as it had no influence upon
the campaign till the Confederate army reached Gadsden
at the close of October, no mention was made of these
changes in the narrative of operations in the last volume,

Beauregard had indeed overtaken Hood on October 9th, at Cave Spring, near Rome, before the crossing of the Coosa, but the conference does not appear to have had any significance. At Gadsden, however, on the 20th and 21st, the two generals fully discussed the situation, and Hood's proposal to march on Guntersville and cross the Tennessee there, was approved by Beauregard. It was arranged that Wheeler's cavalry corps, consisting of twelve brigades (to be increased by another sent from Jackson's division) should closely watch Sherman's movement, opposing and harassing his advance, whatever way he turned; and if he should march for the sea, Governor Brown and General Cobb held out expectations that, in the emergency, seventeen thousand Georgia troops could join Wheeler, and throw themselves across Sherman's path. Beauregard also expected in this event to draw some five thousand men from the Carolinas, making, as he reckoned, an army of twenty-nine thousand to oppose the eastward march of the National forces.[1]

In the invasion of Tennessee, Hood would be accompanied by part of Jackson's division of cavalry, and Forrest, who was between Tuscumbia and Corinth, was ordered to join him with all his mounted force. At Florence, on November 6th, and before beginning his movement against Schofield, Hood had present with him 41,185 infantry and artillery, and 3,544 cavalry, making an aggregate of 44,729. About No-

---

[1] Beauregard's Official Report. In this, however, he has underestimated Wheeler's cavalry. That corps reported at Lovejoy Station, August 1st, an " effective " total of enlisted men of 6,283, and it does not appear to have suffered notably between that time and the opening of the new campaign. It was joined by a brigade from Jackson's division, and a Kentucky infantry brigade, which was mounted. These made about two thousand seven hundred enlisted men, and adding the usual proportion of officers to the whole list of "effectives," it gives Wheeler an actual force, in round numbers, of 10,000, instead of 7,000, as estimated by Beauregard. Hood puts the number at 10,000 (Advance and Retreat, p. 310).

vember 15th he was joined by Forrest with his cavalry corps, numbering 9,209 present, and increasing the aggregate to 53,938 officers and men present.[1]

After his conference with Beauregard, Hood had gone but one day's march from Gadsden toward Guntersville when he suddenly turned his columns to the west, making first for Decatur. He learned that Forrest had started upon a raid northward into West Tennessee, and that it was uncertain how long it might be before that cavalry could join him. On October 7th, and before seeing Beauregard, he had asked General Taylor to send Forrest a second time into Tennessee to break the Nashville and Chattanooga Railway, if he could, or at least to occupy Thomas's forces so as to create a diversion in his favor. Forrest was at Cherokee Station, where he had been refitting and resting his command, and both Taylor and he misapprehended Hood's wish to have a strong cavalry force with his moving column as

---

[1] These figures are taken from the official returns in the Adjutant-General's office at Washington, and are distributed as follows :

Infantry.		Artillery.		Cavalry.	
S. D. Lee's corps	11,784	Lee's	909	Jackson's division	3,152
A. P. Stewart's corps	11,524	Stewart's	958	Buford's "	3,857
B. F. Cheatham's corps	14,325	Cheatham's	880	Chalmers's "	2,841
Engineers	484	Jackson's	321	Roddey's "	2,511
				Escorts	392
Totals	38,117		3,068		12,753

This is exclusive of Forrest's artillery, and of about one thousand men made up of the Fifth Mississippi Cavalry and several battalions of State reserves which joined Forrest. Roddey's division was left in Alabama to hold the line of the Tennessee River. The "present sick" were reported at 2,000, and the present on "extra duty" at 8,267, but these last were, when necessary, put into action by the Confederates. Beauregard's estimate of the "effective" force (deducting officers, etc.) was 27,285 infantry and artillery, and 7,700 cavalry, or an aggregate of 35,000. This is less than two-thirds of the number shown to be present by the official returns. See also Appendix A, 2.

soon as possible. They conceived the idea that a strong diversion in his favor west of the Tennessee would be of most use to him, and Forrest accordingly started northward on the 18th and was at Jackson, Tenn., on the day Hood left the Guntersville road to move westward. But Hood's statement that this news from Forrest was the reason for his change of plan is more specious than sound. Forrest remained at Jackson till the 28th, when Beauregard and Hood were in conference near Decatur, and the orders which apparently stopped him there could have brought him back to Tuscumbia, or to any other place where the Tennessee could be more easily crossed and a junction with Hood more speedily made. It is more probable that Hood's real motive was to get rid of Sherman, who would have been close upon his heels at Guntersville. He hoped that when he should cross the river at Decatur or at Tuscumbia, Sherman would hasten to concentrate in front of Nashville to meet him, and that his brilliant strategy would thus undo all that had been done since the battle of Stone's River. After his disappointment and defeat, it was natural that he should seek plausible reasons for what had proven so disastrous a movement. There certainly was no excuse for making so radical a change in plans without consulting his superior, and his doing so shows that he was determined to treat his subordination to Beauregard as only a nominal thing, while he sought to regain his own prestige by a brilliant stroke.[1]

Beauregard, amazed at the sudden change of movement, hastened after Hood and overtook him at Decatur, where he had expected to cross the river, but where the vigorous defense of the post satisfied both the Confederate officers that

---

[1] Beauregard's Report ; also, Taylor's Destruction and Reconstruction, pp. 207, 208, and Jordan and Prior's Campaigns of Forrest, pp. 589, 590.

it would be quite too costly to force a crossing there, if it
could be done at all. The post was commanded by Colonel
Doolittle, of the Eighteenth Michigan, whose bold and
judicious use of the garrison promptly repulsed the first
efforts to carry the place. General R. S. Granger arrived with
reinforcements at the close of the first day. A brisk sortie
from the garrison captured over a hundred prisoners from
Cheatham's corps, spiking a couple of guns, and inflicting
considerable loss in killed and wounded. Hood now marched
to Tuscumbia, and by the last day of October secured an
unobstructed crossing, occupying the town of Florence on
the northern bank of the river. At this point the navigation of the Tennessee is interrupted by Muscle Shoals above
and Colbert Shoals below, so that it was only in the highest
water that even light gunboats could pass. Croxton's brigade of cavalry was in observation near Florence, but was
unable to make any serious opposition, and pontoon bridges
were soon laid. Could Hood then have marched at once
upon Pulaski he would have found but little opposition
south of Duck River. It was necessary, however, to rear-
range his lines of communication and accumulate at Florence supplies for the campaign. He had left Gadsden with
twenty days' rations, but when soldiers' haversacks are overloaded there is always a great waste of food, and his wagons
had been unable to keep up with the troops. The prisoners
taken by Granger at Decatur reported that the men were
half mutinous at the scanty issue of supplies, and when
Tuscumbia was reached the sustenance of the army had become the problem demanding first attention. Hood pro-
fesses to believe he had reason to expect supplies to meet
him at Tuscumbia; but the superintendent of the railway
reported the road in no condition to furnish the requisite
transportation, and in spite of the most earnest efforts of

Beauregard and Taylor to put it speedily in repair, the greater part of the three weeks' delay at Florence must probably be attributed to its half ruined and decayed condition. Stores were collected at points on the Mobile and Ohio Railroad in Mississippi, carried to Corinth and thence east to Cherokee Station upon a piece of the Memphis and Charleston Railroad which Forrest had been able to protect. But from Cherokee Station to Tuscumbia was a gap of fifteen or sixteen miles where the road had never been rebuilt, and here the army stores must be hauled in wagon trains over a wretched country road, which became a quagmire as soon as the rains began.

Beauregard does not seem to have ventured upon any peremptory interference with Hood at their meeting at Decatur, but acquiesced in what was done, sharing, no doubt, the hopes of the latter that the news of their crossing at Florence would be quickly followed by that of the return of Sherman to Middle Tennessee. But it had become evident that there would be delays; and Forrest, who had been waiting at Jackson, resumed his expedition with a purpose of attracting Thomas's attention to the west and rear of Nashville, so as to draw troops in that direction and prevent the concentration in front of Hood, where alone was any serious danger. He struck the river on the 29th, a few miles above Fort Henry, and his batteries disabled and brought to three transports and a "tin-clad" gunboat, the Undine. The latter, after a stout defence, was injured in her machinery and was run ashore and abandoned. Two of the transports were burned, but the gunboat and the other transport were in the possession of Forrest's "horse-marines" for a couple of days, when the transport with her lading of stores was recaptured and the Undine was run ashore and burned. Forrest's first appearance on the river was at the most north-

ern point he reached, and he returned, making demonstrations to assist his purpose at various places along the western bank. On November 4th he appeared opposite Johnsonville, eighty miles directly west of Nashville, and by
a noisy cannonade caused a panic in the garrison. Three
gunboats, eight transports, and some barges were moored to
the river bank, and great quantities of stores were in warehouses at the landing. All these were abandoned and
burned by the crews and garrison, and the troops fled
toward Nashville, the commandant telegraphing Thomas
that Forrest was across the river and marching in pursuit.[1]
But Forrest had not crossed, and continued his march up
the river. At Perryville he put over part of Rucker's brigade, but kept the body of his troops on the western side,
reaching Cherokee Station on the 15th and joining Hood at
Florence next day. The dates which have been given and
the character of Forrest's movement, which came in contact
with no National forces west of the river, plainly prove the
purposes of the Confederate generals. Time was needed to
repair the railway and collect supplies at Tuscumbia, and
this was the easiest way to get it.

Sherman's attitude, however, was not without its influence upon his adversaries. They knew that the Twentieth
Corps was still at Atlanta and that Sherman with three
others was observing them at Rome or Kingston. It was
quite among the possibilities that he might march westward
across Alabama, destroying all railway lines and close in
upon the rear of Hood's army, while Thomas delayed him
in the " barrens " of Tennessee, where the country could do
but little to sustain such an army. The desire to see Sher-

---

[1] The garrison consisted of about 1,000 men, of the Twelfth United States colored troops, Forty-third Wisconsin Infantry, and Eleventh Tennessee Cavalry
all under command of Colonel C. R. Thompson, of the first-named regiment.

man begin some definite movement undoubtedly worked upon Hood, and after the expected preparation for his advance was made he still delayed till Beauregard spurred him anew to his work by urgent despatches of a kind to which he was not used. It is not unreasonable to suppose that he was bitterly disappointed in finding that Sherman did not hasten back to Tennessee, and was oppressed with the foreboding that if this part of his plan failed and Sherman turned eastward, he would be in no small measure responsible for the impending ruin of the Confederate cause.

Returning to the preparations Sherman was making to give Thomas forces enough to cope with Hood in Tennessee, we find that on October 30th Wood's division of Stanley's (Fourth) corps was moving by rail from Chattanooga, and by November 3d the whole corps was concentrated at Pulaski, eighty miles south of Nashville and forty-four north of Decatur, upon the railway connecting those places. Decatur and Athens were held by General Granger, who commanded the District of Northern Alabama, which also included Huntsville and Stevenson; but the bridges and trestles on the railway between Pulaski and Athens at the crossing of Elk River had been destroyed by Forrest in the latter part of September and had not been rebuilt, and Pulaski was therefore the terminus of the direct railway line south from Nashville. When it was definitely known that the Confederate army was at Tuscumbia and Florence, Thomas had ordered Stanley to get together his corps at Pulaski, but he did not put Granger under his command, and the latter continued through the whole campaign to receive his orders direct from Nashville.

On November 3d, Schofield started Cooper's division of the Twenty-third Corps upon the railway trains for Nashville, leaving Cox's division for several days at Dalton till transportation could be got for it. Schofield himself went

forward with the advance, and when he reached Nashville
next day, Thomas had just received the first alarming news
from Johnsonville, and hurried Schofield in person with Gallup's brigade (the first of the Twenty-third Corps to arrive)
to Gillem's Station, on the railway from Nashville to the
abandoned post. Finding no enemy near Gillem's, Schofield marched to Johnsonville on the 6th, and was able to
give Thomas the truth as to the disgraceful affair. General
Cooper, with Gallup's and Moore's brigades of his division,
were placed at Johnsonville for a time, with orders to fortify
it in accordance with a general plan prepared by the engineers. Schofield returned to Nashville, whence he was sent
on the 11th by Thomas to Pulaski, to assume command of
the forces assembling there. The remainder of the Twenty-
third Corps reached Nashville on the 9th, and went forward
by easy stages. On the 15th, Schofield had at Pulaski the
Fourth Corps and Cox's division of the Twenty-third, Strickland's brigade of the latter corps was at Columbia, and the
cavalry under General Hatch was covering the front and
right, toward Florence and Waynesboro.

When the Fourth and Twenty-third Corps reported to
Thomas, and even before the arrival of A. J. Smith with the
divisions of the Sixteenth Corps, his official returns showed
a force present for duty just about equal to that of Hood,
though differently divided, being stronger in infantry and
weaker in cavalry. The latter numbered 5,591, being less
than half Hood's strength in that arm, but the infantry and
artillery were 48,975.[1] When this force should be increased

---

[1] These figures give the "present for duty" on October 31st, and were distributed as follows: Fourth Corps, 12,331; Twenty-third Corps, 10,624; cavalry,
5,591; District of Tennessee, 18,661; unassigned detachments, 7,359—total,
54,566. This does not include the District of Etowah under Steedman, which
first appears in Thomas's report for November 20th, and which numbered 6,421.
The official returns for subsequent dates will be found in Appendix A.

by Steedman's garrisons in Northern Georgia and at Chattanooga, by A. J. Smith's corps, and by detachments which
Thomas was authorized to draw from Schofield's department, Sherman estimated the army in Tennessee easily able
to cope with Hood.   When he should leave his base of supplies in Georgia, the necessity for guarding a long line of
railway would cease, and Chattanooga would be the only
place in Thomas's department east of Nashville which it
would be necessary to garrison.   The supplies in store at
Chattanooga were all that would be needed for the posts
maintained in East Tennessee.   Thomas could therefore
concentrate nearly everything to meet Hood, and when the
latter should be defeated and driven southward, the lines of
operation would necessarily be rearranged.   As soon as it
seemed probable that Hood intended to make Florence and
Tuscumbia his base, Sherman wrote Thomas, "You must
unite all your men into one army, and abandon all minor
points if you expect to defeat Hood."   The long delay of the
Confederate general in making his advance from the Tennessee gave the needed time for preliminary arrangements;
and when, on November 12th, parting messages were exchanged between them, Thomas was able to say to Sherman
that he believed he should have "men enough to ruin Hood
unless he gets out of the way very rapidly."   Thomas was
empowered, in the absence of his superior, to exert all the
authority of Sherman himself in the Military Division of the
Mississippi, and the new campaign was begun.

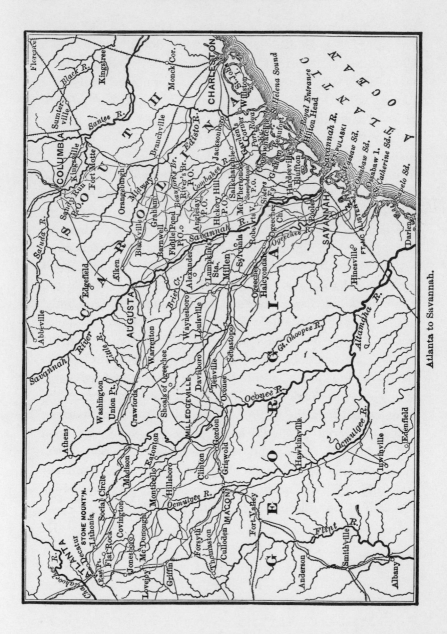

Atlanta to Savannah.

CHAPTER II.

THE MARCH THROUGH GEORGIA.

AT Rome, when parting with one of the officers he was sending back to Tennessee, Sherman said, "If there's to be any hard fighting, you will have it to do." He perfectly understood that there was no sufficient force in Georgia to thwart his plan or even to delay his march. Before leaving Atlanta he pointed out to one of his principal subordinates that a National army at Columbia, S. C., would end the war unless it should be routed and destroyed. Deprived of the material support of all the States but North Carolina, it would be impossible for the Confederate Government to feed its army at Richmond, or to fill its exchequer. The experience it had with the country west of the Mississippi proved that a region isolated from the rest of the Confederacy would not furnish men or money, and could not furnish supplies; while anxiety for their families, who were within the National lines, tempted the soldiers from those States to desert, and weakened the confidence of the whole army. In such a situation credit would be destroyed, the Confederate paper money would become worthless, its foreign assistance would be cut off, and the rebellion must end. The one chance left would be for Lee to break away from Grant, overwhelm Sherman, and re-establish the Confederate power in a central position by the abandonment of Virginia. But this implied that Lee could break away from Grant, who, on the

south side of Petersburg, was as near Columbia as his opponent, and would be close upon his heels from the moment
the lines about Richmond were abandoned.

If Sherman, therefore, should reach Columbia with an
army that could resist the first onslaught of Lee, the last
hope of the Confederacy would be crushed between the
national forces meeting from the east and west. Of course,
this implied that Thomas should, at least, be able to resist
Hood till the Eastern campaign should be ended, when, in
the general collapse of the Richmond Government, Hood
must as certainly abandon the hopeless cause, as Johnston
was in fact forced to do after Lee's surrender in the following spring.

To establish a new base upon the sea was a necessary part
of such a plan, for the old base at Chattanooga must be
abandoned from the start, and the practical separation of
the Carolinas from the Gulf States could only be accomplished by a great and thorough destruction of railway lines
in Georgia. The army could live upon the country while
marching, but it must have the ordinary means of supply
within a very few days from the time of halting, or it would
starve. The country through which it moved was hostile, no
local government could be made to respond to formal requi-
sitions for subsistence, and the wasteful method of foraging
itself made a necessity for moving on into new fields. A
rapid march to the sea, the occupation of some harbor capable of becoming a fortified base, and the opening of lines of
ocean communication with the great dépôts of the North must
therefore constitute the first part of the vast project. Beyond this Sherman did not venture to plan in detail, and
recognizing the possibility that unlooked-for opposition
might force a modification even of this, he kept in mind
the alternative that he might have to go west rather than

east of Macon. He requested that the fleets on the coast might watch for his appearance at Morris Island near Charleston, at Ossabaw Sound just south of Savannah, and at Pensacola and Mobile. If he should reach Morris Island, it would naturally be by the way of Augusta and the left bank of the Savannah River. Ossabaw Sound would, in like manner, indicate the route by way of Milledgeville, Millen, and the valley of the Ogeechee. The Gulf ports would only be chosen if his course to the east should be made impracticable.

On November 12th communication with the rear was broken. The railway bridge at Alatoona was taken to pieces and carried to the rear to be stored; but from the crossing of the Etowah, southward to Atlanta, the whole line of the road was thoroughly destroyed. The foundries, machine-shops, and factories at Rome were burned, lest they should be again turned to use by the enemy, and on the 14th the army was concentrated at Atlanta. Sherman's force now consisted of two corps of the Army of the Tennessee under General Howard, and two of the Army of the Cumberland under General Slocum, which were respectively designated as right and left wing. Logan was absent, and his corps (the Fifteenth) was in command of Major-General P. J. Osterhaus. The division of General J. E. Smith, which had been distributed along the railroad in Northern Georgia, had joined that corps, which now consisted of four divisions, commanded by Generals Woods, Hazen, Smith, and Corse. Blair's corps (Seventeenth) had three divisions, viz., Mower's, Leggett's, and Giles A. Smith's. The assignment of Slocum to the command of the wing left the Twentieth Corps under Brigadier-General A. S. Williams, with Geary, Ward, and Jackson as division commanders. Davis's (Fourteenth) corps retained the organization it had at the close of the Atlanta campaign, and consisted of Carlin's, Morgan's, and Baird's divisions. The cavalry was under Kilpatrick, and was but a single division, composed of the two brigades of Murray and Atkins. The numerical force of the whole, according to the returns of November 10th, only two days before communication with the North was broken, was a little over fifty-nine thousand, but furloughed men and recruits hurried so fast to the front in those last days that the muster at Atlanta showed a total of over sixty-two thousand.[1] No pains had been spared to make this a thoroughly efficient force, for an army in an enemy's country and without a base cannot afford to be encumbered with sick, or to have its trains or its artillery delayed by weak or insufficient teams. The artillery was reduced to about one gun to a thousand men, and the batteries usually to four guns each, with eight good horses to each gun or caisson. Twenty days' rations were in hand, and two hundred rounds of ammunition of all kinds were in the wagons. Droves of beef cattle to furnish the meat ration were ready to accompany the march, and these grew larger rather than smaller as the army moved through the country.

The determination to abandon Atlanta involved also the undoing of much work that had been done there in the early autumn. As the town could not be used by the National forces, the defences must be destroyed, the workshops, mills, and dépôts ruined and burned. This task had been given to Colonel Poe, Chief Engineer, and was completed by the time the army was assembled and ready to march southward.

---

[1] Fifteenth Corps, infantry, 15,894; Seventeenth Corps, 11,732; Fourteenth Corps, 13,962; Twentieth Corps, 13,741; artillery, 1,812; cavalry, 5,063—total, 62,204.

On the morning of November 15th the movement began. The two corps of each wing were ordered to march upon separate roads, at first diverging sharply, and threatening both Macon and Augusta, but having the neighborhood of Milledgeville, the capital of the State, for their place of rendezvous at the end of the first stage. Sherman himself accompanied the left wing, which followed the line of railway leading from Atlanta to Augusta; for, by doing so, he could get the earliest and best information of any new efforts the Confederate Government might make for the defence of the Carolinas. In this way he could best decide upon the proper direction for his columns after he should reach the Oconee River.

After leaving the mountainous region of Northern Georgia, the topography of the country is determined by the river courses, which run in radiating lines from the highlands a hundred miles northeast of Atlanta. The Savannah River, which separates the State from South Carolina, flows nearly southeast in a very direct general line to the sea. Augusta is on the right bank like a half-way house, and Savannah, on the same side of the stream, is near its mouth. The Ocmulgee and Oconee Rivers rise near Atlanta, and flow in parallel valleys about forty miles apart in the same southeasterly direction nearly two hundred miles, when they unite to form the Altamaha, which enters the ocean a little north of the Florida line. Macon is on the west bank of the Ocmulgee, about a hundred miles from Atlanta, and Milledgeville, thirty miles northeast of Macon, is on the same side of the Oconee, which, however, has a direction more nearly north and south above the city. The only other stream of any importance in this part of the State is the Ogeechee, which rises midway between Milledgeville and Augusta, but gradually approaches the Savannah, so that for fifty or sixty miles from the ocean these rivers are nearly parallel and from fifteen to twenty miles apart.

The general line of Sherman's march was between the Ocmulgee and Oconee Rivers, though he sent his right wing at first along the Macon Railroad by more westerly routes, for the purpose of deceiving the enemy, and to drive off Wheeler's cavalry and some three thousand Georgia militia, under General G. W. Smith, which had been assembled at Lovejoy Station for some days. Howard's right (Fifteenth Corps) marched by way of Jonesboro, McDonough, and Indian Spring to the crossing of the Ocmulgee at Planters' Factory, the Seventeenth Corps keeping a little farther east, but reaching the river at the same place. Kilpatrick, with most of the cavalry, was upon this flank, and drove the enemy's skirmishers before him to Lovejoy's. Smith had retired rapidly upon Macon with his infantry, but the old lines at Lovejoy's were held by two brigades of cavalry with two pieces of artillery. Kilpatrick dismounted his men and charged the works on foot, carrying them handsomely. He followed his success with a rapid attack by another column, which captured the guns and followed the retreating enemy some miles toward Macon. The cavalry continued its demonstrations nearly to Forsyth, creating the impression of an advance in force in that direction; then it turned eastward and crossed the Ocmulgee with the infantry.

A section of pontoon train was with each corps, and Howard put down two bridges;[1] but though his head of column reached Planters' Factory on the 18th, and the bridges were kept full day and night, it was not till the morning of the

---

[1] The pontoons used by Sherman, both in the Atlanta campaign and the present one, were those of canvas, of which the frames could be disjointed. Their lightness and serviceability left little to be desired, and they proved thoroughly satisfactory in hard and constant campaign use.

20th that the rear guard was able to cross. The bank on the eastern side of the river was steep and slippery from rain, making it tedious work getting the trains up the hill. His heads of columns were pushing forward meanwhile, and reached Clinton, a few miles north of Macon, by the time the rear was over the river. Kilpatrick now made a feint upon Macon, striking the railway a little east of the town, capturing and destroying a train of cars, and tearing up the track for a mile. Under cover of this demonstration and while the cavalry were holding all roads north and east of Macon, Howard's infantry on the 22d closed up toward Gordon, a station on the Savannah railroad, twenty miles eastward. Woods's division of the Fifteenth Corps brought up the rear and was approaching Griswoldville.

Returning to the left wing, which Sherman accompanied, we find that it had applied itself in earnest to the destruction of the railway from Atlanta to Augusta, making thorough work of it to Madison, seventy miles from Atlanta, and destroying the bridge over the Oconee River, ten or twelve miles further on. Here, the divergence between the wings was greatest, the distance from Slocum's left to Kilpatrick, on the right, being fifty miles in a direct line. Sherman, however, did not cross the Oconee, but directed Slocum to turn southward along the right bank of the river with Williams's (Twentieth) corps, while Davis's (Fourteenth) took the interior line by a more direct route to Milledgeville, where the left wing assembled on the 23d, the advance of the Twentieth Corps having entered the city the day before, driving out a small force of the enemy, which retreated rapidly across the river, leaving the bridge uninjured. Slocum immediately threw out Jackson's division to the east, covering and securing the bridge for further operations.

Sherman's advance from Atlanta drew from Beauregard a

rattling volley of telegraphic despatches to all the Confederate officials, civil and military. In these he made much of the fact that he had ordered General Taylor in Alabama to move with his available forces into Georgia; but Taylor had no available forces, and could only go in person to Macon, where he arrived on the 22d, just in time to meet Governor Brown with his Adjutant, Toombs, escaping from the State Capitol on the approach of Slocum's columns. The only organized troops were Wheeler's cavalry, Smith's division of Georgia militia, and a couple of battalions of local volunteers. General Howell Cobb was nominally Confederate commander of "reserves," but there seems to have been no reserves to command. Hardee had been there the day before, coming up from Savannah, and judging rightly that the spread of Sherman's wings from Oconee Bridge to Planters' Factory argued a course toward Augusta or Savannah, he declared that Macon was in no danger and directed Smith to move his division rapidly eastward, to interpose, if possible, between Sherman and Augusta, delaying his march and obstructing the roads. Wheeler, under orders already given, would continue to harass the flank and rear of the National forces. Orders from Richmond had extended Hardee's authority over the theatre of operations in Georgia, and having given the best directions the circumstances allowed, he hastened back to Savannah to strengthen its means of defence and to be in direct communication with Augusta, Charleston, and Richmond.

Beauregard issued from Corinth, Miss., a proclamation to the people of Georgia, calling upon them to arise for the defence of the State, and to "obstruct and destroy all roads in Sherman's front, flank, and rear," assuring them that the enemy would then starve in their midst. He strove to raise vague hopes also by announcing that he was hastening to join them in defence of their homes and firesides. A more practical step was his order to Hood to begin the Tennessee campaign, the only counter-stroke in his power. At Milledgeville, the approach of Sherman was met by an Act of the Legislature to levy *en masse* the population, with a hysterical preamble, picturing the National general as an ogre, and exhorting the people "to die freemen rather than live slaves." The act, to have been of any use, should have been passed a month before, when Hood was starting west from Gadsden. It was now only a confession of terror, for there was no time to organize. Any disposition of the inhabitants along his route to destroy roads was effectually checked by Sherman's making it known that the houses and property of those who did so would be destroyed. Such opposition to a large army can never be of real use; its common effect is only to increase by retaliation the miseries of the unfortunate people along the line of march, and in this case there was, besides, no lack of evidence that most of them were heartily tired of the war, and had lost all the enthusiasm which leads to self-sacrifice. Even in such a panic the strife of political factions was not stilled, and the opponents of Governor Brown's States-rights policy took advantage of the flight from the Capital to perpetrate a novel absurdity. The Lieutenant-Governor, Wright, was also a general in the Confederate army, and on the 21st, the day before our occupation of the Capital, issued a proclamation from Augusta, declaring himself *ex-officio* Governor of the part of the State east of the Oconee, and ordering the people under the levy *en masse* to report to him, by reason of what a Confederate historian calls the "territorial disability" of the Governor.[1] The proclamation had no result, but

---

[1] Jones's Siege of Savannah, etc., p. 18.

the ridiculousness of it is shown by the fact that the Georgia militia under Smith were moved by Brown's orders to Savannah, reaching there on the 30th, and General Taylor returned from Savannah to Macon after that time, as will be seen. In truth, communication by courier from Augusta to Macon was only interrupted while the army was passing.

While Taylor, Brown, Toombs, and Cobb were conferring at Macon on the 22d, the division of Georgia militia under Brigadier General Phillips was marching toward Gordon in the effort to obey Hardee's order. At Griswoldville, about eight miles out, they ran into Walcutt's brigade of Woods's division, which was the rear guard of the right wing, and attacked it with more courage than discretion. Walcutt had been making a reconnoisance toward Macon, driving back Wheeler's cavalry, and was recalled by General Woods to a position on the Duncan Farm, a little east of the town. Here his flanks were protected by swampy ground, his line was on the crest of a hill, with open ground in front, on which the enemy must attack. This Phillips did with a great deal of vigor, putting in all four of his brigades, and striving hard also to turn the flanks of Walcutt's position. He was superior in artillery, as Walcutt had only two guns with him, and was obliged to withdraw these early in the engagement. But the infantry attacks, which were renewed several times, were repulsed with severe loss, and Phillips retreated, after several hours' fighting, having lost over six hundred in killed and wounded. On the National side, General Woods, who was present, reports a total of ninety-four casualties. Walcutt was severely wounded in the leg, and the command of the brigade devolved upon Colonel Catterson (Ninety-seventh Indiana) during the latter half of the combat. Both officers distinguished themselves by their conduct and courage.

Nothing could be more useless than this engagement, for Phillips had before him two corps if Walcutt had been driven off; but he had been ordered to move along the railroad, and thought he was obliged to do so till he should be recalled. This was done as soon as Smith at Macon heard of the fight, and the division, at the instance of Taylor, was sent southward by rail to Albany, which was the end of the railway in that direction. Thence they marched sixty miles to Thomasville on the Savannah and Gulf Railroad, where Toombs hectored the railway officials into furnishing transportation with unwonted promptness, and they reported to Hardee in Savannah on the last day of the month. Hardee's orders to Wheeler now directed him to get in front of Sherman's forces and cover all the roads by which he might move. Wheeler accordingly marched south of the Central Railroad, swam the Oconee River, and reached Sandersville on the 26th, just before the National columns. The change of position of the Confederate cavalry was followed by Kilpatrick, who moved, by Sherman's direction, to the front and left of the infantry, there being no enemy whatever on the right flank after crossing the Oconee.

Sherman had not delayed at Milledgeville, but had marched again on the 24th. Davis's (Fourteenth) corps now became the flanking column on the left. The Twentieth Corps (Williams's), after passing Sandersville, reached the Central Railroad at Tennille and marched to Davisboro, destroying the track as they went. From Davisboro both corps of the left wing moved by the same road to Louisville, crossing the Ogeechee River before reaching that place, where they camped on the 29th. The work of destroying the railway was begun by the right wing at Griswoldville, and of the hundred miles between that station and Millen very little of the road was left. Howard found the crossing

of the Oconee near Ball's Ferry a difficult operation, for the
river was up and the current so swift that the ferry could
not be used. Wheeler's cavalry made some resistance from
the other side. A detachment of Blair's corps, directed by
the engineers, succeeded in constructing a flying bridge
some two miles above the ferry, and getting over to the left
bank, moved down to the principal road, which had been
cleared of the enemy by the artillery on the hither side.
The pontoons were then laid and the march resumed.

On leaving Milledgeville, Sherman ordered Kilpatrick to
make a considerable detour to the north, feinting strongly on
Augusta, but trying hard to reach and destroy the important
railway bridge and trestles at Briar Creek, near Waynesboro,
half way between Augusta and Millen. He was then to
move rapidly on Millen in the hope of releasing the National
prisoners of war who were in a prison camp near that place.
Kilpatrick moved by one of the principal roads to Augusta,
giving out that he was marching on that city. After he had
passed the Ogeechee Shoals, Wheeler heard of his movement, and rapidly concentrated his force on the Augusta
road, where it debouches from the swamps of Briar Creek.
Kilpatrick, however, in obedience to his orders, turned the
head of his columns to the right, upon the road running
from Warrenton to Waynesboro, and they were well on
their way to the latter place before Wheeler was aware of
it. Murray's brigade was in the rear, and two of his regiments, the Eighth Indiana and Second Kentucky, constituted the rear-guard. These became too far separated
from the column when they camped at evening near a
place called Sylvan Grove. Wheeler heard of their where-
abouts, and attacked them in the middle of the night.
Though surprised and driven from their camps, the regiments stoutly fought their way back, and were only gradu-

ally driven in on the rest of Murray's brigade. Wheeler
followed up persistently with his superior forces, harassing
the rear and flank of the column, and causing some confusion, but gaining no important advantage, except that
Kilpatrick was obliged to abandon the effort to burn the
Briar Creek bridge and trestles, and to turn his line of
march southwesterly from Waynesboro, after destroying a
mile or two of the railroad. He reported that he here
learned that the Millen prisoners had been removed, and
determined to rejoin the army at Louisville. On the 27th
Murray's brigade passed through that of Atkins, which now
became the rear-guard, and on the 28th this order was
reversed, each brigade taking, alternately, the brunt of the
continuing fight with Wheeler. Early in the morning of
the 28th Kilpatrick himself narrowly escaped capture, having improperly made his quarters for the night at some
distance from the body of his command, the Ninth Michigan being with him as a guard. The enemy got between
him and the column, and it was with no little difficulty he
succeeded in cutting his way out, and saving himself from
the consequences of his own folly. The long causeway and
bridge at Buckhead Creek was held while the division
passed, by Colonel Heath and the Fifth Ohio, with two howitzers, and Wheeler there received a severe check. The
bridge was destroyed, and Kilpatrick took a strong position
at Reynolds's plantation. Wheeler here attacked in force,
but was decisively repulsed, and Kilpatrick effected his
junction with the infantry without further molestation.
Wheeler's whole corps, consisting of Dibrell's, Hume's, and
Anderson's divisions, was engaged in this series of sharp
skirmishes, and he boasted loudly that he had routed Kilpatrick, causing him to fly in confusion with a loss of nearly
two hundred in killed, wounded, and captured. Chafing

at this rebuff, Kilpatrick obtained permission to deliver a
return blow, and after resting his horses a day or two,
marched from Louisville on Waynesboro, supported by
Baird's division of Davis's (Fourteenth) corps. He attacked
Wheeler near the town, and drove him by very spirited
charges from three successive lines of barricades, chasing
him through Waynesboro, and over Briar Creek. Wheeler
admits that it was with difficulty he "succeeded in withdrawing" from his position at the town, but seeks to take
off the edge of his chagrin by reporting that he was attacked by the Fourteenth Corps, as well as by Kilpatrick's
cavalry. Baird's division was not actually engaged, but its
presence and close support no doubt assisted Kilpatrick, by
enabling him to make more decisive movements than he
could otherwise have ventured on, as he could freely use his
horsemen on the flanks of a solid body of advancing infantry.

Millen was reached on December 3d, by Blair's corps,
which Sherman accompanied, and the direct railway communication between Savannah and Augusta was cut. Three
corps now moved down the narrowing space between the
Savannah and Ogeechee Rivers, while Osterhaus, with
the Fifteenth, marched on the right bank of the latter
stream in two columns some miles apart. Howard was in
person with this corps and met with no resistance. Indeed
from Millen onward the march of the whole army was a
methodic progress with no noticeable opposition, for even
Wheeler's horsemen generally kept a respectful distance,
and soon crossed to the left bank of the Savannah. The
country became more sandy, corn and grain grew scarcer,
and all began to realize that they were approaching the low
country bordering the sea, where but little breadstuffs or
forage would be found. On the 9th and 10th the columns
closed in upon the defences of Savannah, Davis's corps rest-

ing its left upon the Savannah River, Williams's, Blair's, and Osterhaus's continuing the line toward the right, near the Ogeechee. Cavalry detachments, and skilful infantry scouts were sent out to open communication with the fleet and to cut the Gulf Railway, thus severing the last connection of the city with the south. But before tracing these operations farther, some of the characteristic features of the march just made are worthy of a little more attention.

The destruction of railway communication between the Confederate Army at Richmond, and the Gulf States, had been a very important part of Sherman's purpose, and he spared no pains to do this thoroughly. A battalion of mechanics was selected and furnished with tools for ripping the rails from the cross-ties and twisting them when heated, and these were kept constantly at work ; but the infantry on the march became expert in methods of their own, and the cavalry also joined in the work, though the almost constant skirmishing on the flanks and rear of the army usually kept the mounted troops otherwise employed. A division of infantry would be extended along the railway line about the length of its proper front. The men, stacking arms, would cluster along one side of the track, and at the word of command, lifting together, would raise the line of rail with the ties as high as their shoulders ; then at another command they would let the whole drop, stepping back out of the way as it fell. The heavy fall would shake loose many of the spikes and chairs, and seizing the loosened rails, the men, using them as levers, would quickly pry off the rest. The cross-ties would now be piled up like cob-houses, and with these and other fuel a brisk fire would be made ; the rails were piled upon the fire, and in half an hour would be red hot in the middle. Seizing the rail now by the two ends, the soldiers would twist it about a tree, or interlace and twine the whole pile together in great iron knots, making them useless for anything but old iron, and most unmanageable and troublesome, even to convey away to a mill. In this way it was not difficult for a corps marching along the railway to destroy, in a day, ten or fifteen miles of track most completely; and Sherman himself gave close watch to the work, to see that it was not slighted. Then all machine-shops, stations, bridges, and culverts were destroyed, and the masonry blown up.

The extent of line destroyed was enormous. From the Etowah River through Atlanta southward to Lovejoy's, for a hundred miles nothing was left of the road. From Fairburn through Atlanta eastward to Madison and the Oconee River, another hundred miles, the destruction was equally complete. From Gordon southeastwardly the ruin of the Central road was continued to the very suburbs of Savannah, a hundred and sixty miles. Then there were serious breaks in the branch road from Gordon northward through Milledgeville, and in that connecting Augusta and Millen. So great a destruction would have been a long and serious interruption even at the North; but the blockade of Southern ports and the small facilities for manufacture in the Confederate States made the damage practically irreparable. The lines which were wrecked were the only ones which then connected the Gulf States with the Carolinas, and even if Sherman had not marched northward from Savannah the resources of the Confederacy would have been seriously crippled. The forage of the country was also destroyed throughout a belt fifty or sixty miles in width. Both armies cooperated in this; the Confederate cavalry burning it that it might not fall into the hands of the National Army, and the latter leaving none that they could not themselves use, so that wagon transportation of military supplies across the belt might be made more difficult.

As the campaign progressed, great numbers of negroes attached themselves to the columns and accompanied the march. This was contrary to the wish of Sherman, who felt the embarrassment of having thousands of mouths added to the number of those who must be fed from the country as he moved. Those who had less responsibility for the campaign did not trouble themselves so much with this consideration, and the men in the ranks generally encouraged the slaves to leave the plantations. The negroes themselves found it hard to let slip the present opportunity of getting out of bondage, and their uneducated minds could not estimate the hope of freedom at the close of the war as having much weight against the instant liberty which was to be had by simply tramping away after the blue-coated soldiers.

The natural result was that the regular bivouacs of the troops were fringed by numberless gipsy camps, where the negro families, old and young, endured every privation, living upon the charity of the soldiers, helping themselves to what they could glean in the track of the army foragers. On the march, they trudged along, making no complaint, full of a simple faith that "Lincoln's men" were leading them to abodes of ease and plenty.

When the lower and less fruitful lands were reached, the embarrassment and military annoyance increased. This was more particularly felt in the left wing, which was then the only one exposed to the attacks of the enemy. Losing patience at the failure of all orders and exhortations to these poor people to stay at home, General Davis (commanding the Fourteenth Corps), ordered the pontoon bridge at Ebenezer Creek to be taken up before the refugees who were following that corps had crossed, so as to leave them on the further bank of the unfordable stream and thus disembarrass the marching troops. It would be unjust to that officer to believe that the order would have been given, if the effect had been foreseen. The poor refugees had their hearts so set on liberation, and the fear of falling into the hands of the Confederate cavalry was so great, that, with wild wailings and cries, the great crowd rushed, like a stampeded drove of cattle, into the water, those who could not swim as well as those who could, and many were drowned in spite of the earnest efforts of the soldiers to help them. As soon as the character of the unthinking rush and panic was seen, all was done that could be done to save them from the water; but the loss of life was still great enough to prove that there were many ignorant, simple souls to whom it was literally preferable to die freemen rather than to live slaves.

When Savannah was reached, the great number of colored refugees with all the columns were placed on the Sea Islands, under the care of government officers, and added largely to the colonies already established there. The Freedmen's Bureau was afterward, in great measure, the necessary outgrowth of this organization.

The subsistence of the army upon the country was a necessary part of Sherman's plan, and the bizarre character given it by the humor of the soldiers has made it a striking feature of the march. It is important, however, to distinguish between what was planned and ordered, and what was an accidental growth of the soldier's disposition to make sport of everything that could be turned to amusement. The orders issued were of a strictly proper military character. The supplies in the trains were to be treated as a reserve to be drawn upon only in case of necessity, and a systematic foraging upon the country for daily food was the regular means of getting rations. Each regiment organized a foraging party of about one-twentieth of its numbers under command of an officer. These parties set out first

of all, in the morning, those of the same brigades and divisions working in concert, keeping near enough together to
be a mutual support if attacked by the enemy, and aiming
to rejoin the column at the halting place appointed for the
end of the day's march. The foragers became the *beau
ideal* of partisan troops. Their self-confidence and daring
increased to a wonderful pitch, and no organized line of
skirmishers could so quickly clear the head of column of
the opposing cavalry of the enemy. Nothing short of an
intrenched line of battle could stop them, and when they
were far scattered on the flank, plying their vocation, if a
body of hostile cavalry approached, a singular sight was to
be seen. Here and there, from barn, from granary and
smoke-house, and from the kitchen gardens of the plantations, isolated foragers would hasten by converging lines,
driving before them the laden mule heaped high with vege-
tables, smoked bacon, fresh meat, and poultry. As soon as
two or three of these met, one would drive the animals, and
the others, from fence corners or behind trees, would begin
a bold skirmish, their Springfield rifles giving them the advantage in range over the carbines of the horsemen. As
they were pressed they would continue falling back and
assembling, the regimental platoons falling in beside each
other till their line of fire would become too hot for their
opponents, and these would retire reporting that they had
driven in the skirmishers upon the main column which was
probably miles away. The work of foraging would then be
resumed. It was of the rarest possible occurrence that
Wheeler's men succeeded in breaking through these enterprising flankers and approaching the troops of the line, and
as the columns approached the place designated for their
evening camp, they would find this ludicrous but most
bountiful supply train waiting for them at every fork of the

road, with as much regularity as a railway train running on
"schedule time."

They brought in all animals that could be applied to army
use, and as the mule teams or artillery horses broke down
in pulling through the swamps which made a wide border
for every stream, fresh animals were ready, so that on reaching Savannah the teams were fat and sleek and in far better
condition than they had been at Atlanta.

The orders given these parties forbade their entering occupied private houses, or meddling with private property of
the kinds not included in supplies and munitions of war,
and in the best disciplined divisions these orders were enforced. Discipline in armies, however, is apt to be uneven,
and among sixty thousand men there are men enough who
are willing to become robbers, and officers enough who are
willing to wink at irregularities or to share the loot, to make
such a march a terrible scourge to any country. A bad emi-
nence in this respect was generally accorded to Kilpatrick,
whose notorious immoralities and rapacity set so demoralizing an example to his troops that the best disciplinarians
among his subordinates could only mitigate its influence.
His enterprise and daring had made his two brigades usually
hold their own against the dozen which Wheeler commanded, and the value of his services made his commander
willing to be ignorant of *escapades* which he could hardly
condone, and which on more than one occasion came near
resulting in Kilpatrick's own capture and the rout of his
command. But he was quite capable, in a night attack of
this kind, of mounting, bare-backed, the first animal, horse or
mule, that came to hand, and charging in his shirt at the head
of his troopers with a dare-devil recklessness that dismayed
his opponents and imparted his own daring to his men.

Then, the confirmed and habitual stragglers soon became

numerous enough to be a nuisance upon the line of march. Here again the difference in portions of the army was very marked. In some brigades every regiment was made to keep its own rear guard to prevent straggling, and the bri-, gade provost guard marched in rear of all, arresting any who sought to leave the ranks, and reporting the regimental commander who allowed his men to scatter. But little by little the stragglers became numerous enough to cause serious complaint, and they followed the command without joining it for days together, living on the country, and shirking the labors of their comrades. It was to these that the name "bummer" was properly applied. This class was numerous in the Confederate as in the National Army, in proportion to its strength, and the Southern people cried out for the most summary execution of military justice against them. Responsible persons addressed specific complaints to the Confederate War Secretary, charging robbery and pillage of the most scandalous kinds against their own troops. Their leading newspapers demanded the cashiering and shooting of colonels and other officers, and declared their conduct worse than the enemy's. It is perhaps vain to hope that a great war can ever be conducted without abuses of this kind, and we may congratulate ourselves that the wrongs done were almost without exception to property, and that murders, rapes, and other heinous personal offences were nearly unknown.[1]

The great mass of the officers and soldiers of the line worked hard and continuously, day by day, in marching, in bridging streams, in making corduroy roads through the swamps, in lifting the wagons and cannon from mud-holes, and in tearing up the railways. They saw little or nothing

---

[1] For a few extracts from Southern newspapers corroborating what is here stated see Appendix C.

of the people of the country, and knew comparatively little
of the foragers' work, except to enjoy the fruits of it and the
unspeakable ludicrousness of the cavalcade as it came in at
night. The foragers turned into beasts of burden, oxen and
cows as well as the horses and mules. Here would be a
silver-mounted family carriage drawn by a jackass and a
cow, loaded inside and out with everything the country pro-
duced, vegetable and animal, dead and alive. There would
be an ox-cart, similarly loaded, and drawn by a nondescript
tandem team, equally incongruous. Perched upon the top
would be a ragged forager, rigged out in a fur hat of a
fashion worn by dandies of a century ago, or a dress-coat
which had done service at stylish balls of a former genera-
tion. The jibes and jeers, the fun and the practical jokes
ran down the whole line as the *cortege* came in, and no mas-
querade in carnival could compare with it for original humor and rollicking enjoyment.[1]

The weather had generally been perfect. A flurry of snow
and a sharp, cold wind had lasted for a day or two about
November 23d, but the Indian summer set in after that, and
on December 8th the heat was even sultry. The camps in
the open pine-woods, the bonfires along the railways, the
occasional sham-battles at night, with blazing pine-knots for
weapons whirling in the darkness, all combined to leave
upon the minds of officers and men the impression of a vast
holiday frolic ; and in the reunions of the veterans since the
war, this campaign has always been a romantic dream more
than a reality, and no chorus rings out with so joyous a
swell as when they join in the refrain,

"As we were marching through Georgia."

---

[1] For details and incidents of all the phases of the march, see Colonel Nichols's
Story of the Great March ; Reminiscences of the War, by Samuel Toombs; The
Ninety-second Illinois Volunteers, by Gen. Atkins, etc., etc.

CHAPTER III.

SAVANNAH.

SAVANNAH was then a city of about twenty-five thousand inhabitants, on the Georgia side of the Savannah River, and had been the home of a well-to-do people who had made it one of the pleasantest towns of the South. It is built upon a sandy plateau some forty feet above the water, and though fifteen miles distant from the ocean, it is the nearest point to the harbor entrance where a city could be built. A little below, the land sinks almost to the level of the sea; the whole coast is low and cut into islands by deep sinuous natural canals or creeks. These are widely bordered by the salt marsh which is all awash at high tide. The upland on which the place is built is almost like an island in the swamps, and has a width of six or eight miles. Other upland knolls are found here and there through the region, and these were usually the places of plantation homesteads, in the midst of broad rice-fields which had been reclaimed from the surrounding marsh.

The Savannah and Ogeechee Rivers approach each other at the ocean, as has already been stated, so that the tongue of land which separates them is scarcely more than ten or fifteen miles in width for a distance of nearly fifty miles from the sea. Both rivers are bordered by the rice swamps which make a natural barrier around the city on the north-west, about three miles away, and which, in their original condition, were the savannahs from which the early navigators gave the name to the river. Besides these, the Little Ogeechee flows between the greater stream of the same name and the Savannah, skirting the city or the adjoining plantations on the southwest. The natural line of defence for the town on the north, therefore, was also a series of suburban plantations with their rice-fields in front : these, beginning on the Savannah, were known as Williamson's, Daly's, Lawton's, and the Silk Hope plantations, and beyond them the Salt Creek marshes and the Little Ogeechee continued the line of defence to the railway bridge of the Atlantic and Gulf Railroad. The roads into the city were narrow causeways, heaped high enough to be out of water when the rice-fields were overflowed, as they often were, to a depth of from three to six feet. Extensive dams, canals, and flood-gates were part of the system by which the artificial inundation necessary for rice tillage was made, and these works were easily modified so as to become an essential part of the military defence.

The Savannah River, from the city to the sea, is a broad estuary with small, scattered islands. Immediately in front of the town is Hutchinson Island, much larger than those below, being about five miles long and dividing the river into two narrower channels. Nearly half of this island is above Williamson's plantation, and therefore was outside of the natural line of defence above described. The lower half of it, however, was held by the Confederate troops, as its occupation was necessary not only to holding the city, but to the preservation of a line of retreat toward Charleston. Immediately above Hutchinson Island was Argyle Island, ten miles long, with a smaller one (Onslow Island) on the west of it, so that for some distance there were three channels for the river.

Before Sherman's appearance in Eastern Georgia the sea defences of Savannah had been the only ones of impor-

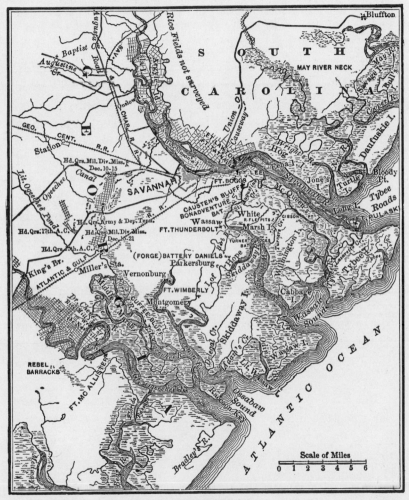

Savannah and Vicinity.

tance, and after the fall of Fort Pulaski, in the spring of 1862, these had been somewhat contracted, and now con-

sisted of a line of redoubts and strong detached forts along
the interior channels connecting the Savannah River with
the Great Ogeechee, from Fort Jackson to Fort MacAllister.
These, with the fortified islands in the river and a work or
two on the South Carolina side, had been sufficient for the
protection of the town from expeditions by sea and naval attacks. They were armed with heavy ordnance, ranging
from ten inch columbiads to smooth thirty-twos, with some
howitzers to be used in case of a direct assault. The ex-
pansion of the mouths of the Ogeechee into the sea is known
as Ossabaw Sound ; that at the mouth of the Savannah is
Tybee Sound, and Warsaw Sound [1] is an indentation half
way between the two. These, with other entrances along
that part of the shore, were anxiously watched by the fleet
under Rear-Admiral Dahlgren, so that no time might be
lost in opening communication with Sherman when he
should reach the coast.

The principal naval rendezvous and military post of the
National forces, however, was at Port Royal, twenty miles
farther to the northeast, at the mouth of Broad River ; and
Major-General J. G. Foster, whose headquarters were at
Beaufort, had collected large quantities of supplies ready to
be shipped to Sherman's army as soon as it could be
reached.

But Hardee was unwilling to make his defence of Savannah upon the interior line of fortifications, if he could avoid
it. To do so would involve the abandonment of the Charleston Railroad near the city, for it crossed the river fifteen or
eighteen miles above. If this part of the road were given
up, his only connection with Charleston and the North

---

[1] Many of our best maps call this name Wassaw. I follow the authority of
Colonel Jones, author of The Siege of Savannah, and a long time resident of the
city.

would be by the Union Causeway to Hardeeville, a station about six miles from the river in South Carolina, which would become the terminus of the railway. This causeway, which became a little later Hardee's way of escape from Savannah, starts at a ferry near the lower end of Hutchinson Island and runs northward for a long distance through rice swamps, which protect it from lateral approach. It had been impossible for Hardee to accumulate supplies enough for any protracted siege, even if he had been willing to allow himself to be invested; and the difficulties of his situation would be greatly increased, if fifteen or twenty miles of waggoning over a single road were necessary to the introduction of provisions for his troops and for the citizens. His first purpose, therefore, was to make and hold a line between the Savannah and the Ogeechee, far enough out to cover the Charleston railway bridge. An excellent position had been selected and entrenched, running from a point above the bridge, southwest behind Monteith Swamp to the Great Ogeechee River. Detached works had been built along this line, and infantry and artillery had been put in them, but Sherman had made them of no avail by marching Howard with the Fifteenth Corps down the right bank of the Ogeechee, flanking and turning them, so that Hardee had no choice but to destroy the railway bridge and fall back to his interior works at the city.

But let us return a moment to the last days of November, when General Richard Taylor, by the aid of Toombs as State Adjutant, was bringing to Savannah the militia derisively called Governor Brown's army, but which was now proving almost the sole resource of the Confederacy. Never was energy more timely in a pinch than that which now brought this division to the critical point. Taylor had hastened to Savannah in advance of it, and while consulting with Hardee

on November 29th, news came that a division of National
troops under General Hatch had landed that morning at
Boyd's Neck, on Broad River, and was marching on Grahamville and the Charleston Railroad, about twenty miles from
the Savannah crossing. General Foster had ordered this
movement as one likely to be of use to Sherman whether he
arrived at Beaufort or at Savannah, and had Hatch succeeded in establishing himself on the railway, it is hard to
see how Hardee could have extricated himself from his difficulties. The Georgia militia were enlisted on the condition
that they were not to be ordered out of the State, but Taylor and Toombs laid their heads together and delighted Hardee by arranging with General G. W. Smith to switch off the
trains upon the Charleston road before reaching Savannah,
and in the night, so that the State troops awoke at the station near Grahamville in South Carolina, having been made,
as Taylor humorously tells the story, " unconscious patri-
ots."[1] But the vigor of the Confederates had been lacking
on the National side. Hatch delayed advancing on the 29th,
when there was nothing between him and the railway but a
handful of cavalry, and intrenched a position near his landing place, though Grahamville was less than ten miles away.
When he advanced next day, Smith with his Georgia troops
was ready to meet him, and taking advantage of the swamps,
which gave him, near Honey Hill, a position that could only
be approached by a causeway, the advance of the National
column was checked by artillery. Hatch attempted a flanking movement, but the Confederates set fire to the broom-
sedge, which was dead and dry in the late autumn, and this
prairie fire sweeping down before the wind upon our troops
forced them to seek cover of some watercourse. Hatch,

---

[1] Taylor's Destruction and Reconstruction, p. 215. Jones's Siege of Savannah, p. 36.

however, advanced again, and drove the enemy back a mile and a half upon an intrenched line which had been previously made. Here several courageous assaults were made, but they were repulsed, and in the night Hatch retired upon his own fortifications near Boyd's Neck. The Confederates report their loss as less than fifty, while ours was over seven hundred. It was only a fresh instance of the manner in which irresolute leadership in war wastes the lives of men by alternating between an ill-timed caution and an equally ill-timed rashness. No maxim is supported by more abundant proof than that which enjoins audacity and speed in the earlier steps of such expeditions, of which the essential feature is that they should be in the nature of a surprise.

The result of the consultation between Hardee and Taylor was that the latter sent a report to the Richmond Govern-ment which contained a very just estimate of the situation. They rightly thought that Sherman would not attempt to enter South Carolina before establishing a new base of supplies upon the coast, and that the greater ease in following the upland roads between rivers would prevent him from moving at once upon Charleston, where his route would be across numerous deep rivers and swamps. They assumed, therefore, that he would continue to move on Savannah, and advised that Hardee should prepare to abandon that place before he should be completely invested. Then, Hardee's troops should be united with those which Bragg was now assembling at Augusta, and with the garrison of Charleston, and all the scattered detachments in the Carolinas, the whole should be vigorously used to oppose the march north-ward which Sherman must be expected to make as soon as he had established a base on the ocean. No sounder military judgment could be made, and the subsequent errors of Beauregard and Bragg grew out of their departure from it

when Sherman's skilful demonstrations threw them into
doubt as to his purpose. Writing of it later, Taylor expressed his own sense of the crisis by saying it was plain
that "unless a force could be interposed between Sherman
and Lee's rear, the game would be over when the former
moved."[1]

Hardee assigned troops and commanders to his lines of
defence as follows. From the Savannah, at Williamson's
plantation, to the Central Railroad crossing, the Georgia
militia under General G. W. Smith held the lines with
twenty guns in position. The batteries at the Central Railroad and on the Louisville road with the lines to the head
of Shaw's Dam were held by the troops of General McLaws
with twenty-nine pieces of artillery. General Wright commanded the left, reaching from Shaw's Dam to the bridge of
the Gulf Railway over the Little Ogeechee, and had thirty-
two guns in position on his front. The artillery above referred to was the heavier armament, besides which the light
artillery, consisting of eleven batteries of forty-eight guns
in all, under Colonel Jones, was distributed as the necessity
of the moment demanded.

The forts and fixed batteries on the side toward the sea
were under the command of Colonel E. C. Anderson. Of
these, Fort McAllister was the only one within the scope of
the National attack, and is, therefore, the only one which
need be described. It was situated at Genesis Point on the
right bank of the Great Ogeechee River, commanding the
channel of approach from Ossabaw Sound and covering the
important bridge of the Gulf Railway across the river. It
was a heavy earthwork with its principal front toward the
river it was intended to command; but the gorge had also

---

[1] Destruction and Reconstruction, p. 218.

been closed by a straight infantry line with works for the protection of artillery at intervals in it. The armament consisted of seven heavy guns in permanent position, and eight light field guns, all mounted in barbette. The river was planted with torpedoes, and before the arrival of Sherman, sub-terra shells had also been placed along the land face, where the ditch was further protected by palisades and a fraise. As it was possible this fort would become isolated, it had been supplied with about fifty days' rations. Its garrison was about two hundred men under command of Major G. W. Anderson. Immediately above the fort the river makes a double loop, the straight line across either neck being less than a quarter of a mile, while the course by the stream is nine miles. In nearly a direct line across the broader part of the loop above the fort is the Cheves plantation with its rice-mill, two miles away, upon the other bank of the river. The fort was at the edge of the higher ground, and south of it the land fell away to the broad salt marshes over which the Sound and the sea could be seen in the distance.

Hardee's whole force consisted of about eighteen thousand men, from which must be deducted about one thousand sick in hospital. The garrisons for the forts on the sea front were small, though these, of course, could not be evacuated, as the navy was likely to make some efforts at co-operation with Sherman.[1] The inhabitants would also be available, to some extent, under the *levy en masse* which

---

[1] Jones's Siege of Savannah is the chief authority for the details of the situation within the Confederate lines. He says (p. 91) that the rations issued by the Commissary on December 16th were as follows : viz., to Confederate troops, 11,-291 ; to Militia, 3,249 ; to hospitals, 1,282 ; total, 15,822. Assuming that officers either commuted their rations, or bought from the Commissary, about 2,000 must be added to these. Colonel Jones says that only 10,000 men were available for active duty on the western line, but this would depend on the judgment of the general in command.

the Legislature had ordered, and which was enforced by Hardee under a proclamation of the Mayor issued on November 28th.

Such was the situation in Savannah when, on December 10th, the National army closed in on the works around the city. A day or two was spent in bringing the several corps into position, but on the 12th the investment was complete from the Savannah River to the Ogeechee. Jackson's division of Williams's (Twentieth) corps rested on the river at the extreme left, and the other divisions of that corps extended the line to the Central Railroad. Here Davis's (Fourteenth) corps joined it and reached somewhat beyond the Ogeechee Canal, near the Lawton plantation, where it united with the left of Blair's (Seventeenth) corps. Osterhaus's (Fifteenth) corps completed the line to the Great Ogeechee River, near King's Bridge, a structure a thousand feet long, which the enemy had destroyed; but the posts were still standing, and under the direction of Howard's chief engineer, Captain Reese, the bridge was rebuilt and fit for use by the 13th. On the Central Railroad Slocum's pickets were close to the three-mile post, the Confederate entrenched line being a quarter of a mile nearer to the city; but the works were farther from the town in front of Howard.

During the last few days breadstuffs had been very scarce in the country, and foraging was not bringing in the bountiful supply which had been usual. The bread ration was drawn from the train, and rice was nearly the only thing the country now furnished the troops. Sherman's first task, therefore, was to open communication with the fleet and establish a base of supplies by means of transports plying between Ossabaw Sound and Port Royal. Howard had sent a skilful scouting officer, Captain Duncan, with two men to pass Fort McAllister in the night in a canoe, and Duncan had succeeded in reaching Admiral Dahlgren, though it was not known till a day or two later. Kilpatrick also was pushing light parties' of horse along the coast for the same purpose. To make use of the Ogeechee River, however, would be impossible till Fort McAllister was taken, and no sooner was King's Bridge passable than Sherman ordered Howard to send a sufficient force to attack and carry the fort by storm, believing that the more promptly this should be done the less the loss would be in doing it. Howard assigned Hazen's division of the Fifteenth Corps to the duty, and this command crossed the bridge at daybreak of the 13th, and moving down the right bank of the river, reached the vicinity of the fort before noon.

General Howard had established a signal station at Cheves's rice-mill on the left bank of the river, which has already been referred to, and there a section of DeGres's battery of twenty-pound Parrotts had been intrenched, covering the rear of the investing line. Sherman and Howard were both at the signal station on the roof of the mill, communicating with Hazen, and watching for boats from the fleet.

Hazen's men had captured a picket about a mile from the fort, and had learned of the position of a line of torpedoes in the road; these had been removed, and the advanced brigade under Colonel W. S. Jones had approached within half a mile of the fort early in the afternoon. Jones was anxious to attack at once, but Hazen thought it wiser to make the assault with portions of each of his three brigades, and delayed the attack till they could be brought into position. The reserve was placed where the torpedoes had been found, and three regiments from each brigade were detailed to make the assault. Colonel Wells S. Jones's brigade was on the left, Colonel Oliver's in the centre, and Colonel

Theodore Jones's on the right. The latter of these found
considerable difficulty in getting into position, and it was
nearly five o'clock before the signal for the attack could be
given. The garrison of the fort had recently added an abattis
to their defences on the land side, but had not had time to
remove the large trunks of the trees from which the branches
for this use had been taken. These trunks gave good cover
to the skirmish line, which was pressed so close to the fort
as to pick off the gunners and prevent the effective use of
the artillery.

Meanwhile Sherman and Howard, full of impatience, were
watching the declining sun from the top of Cheves's mill,
and signalling their orders to hasten. A tug-boat from the
fleet had come in sight, and approached as close as it was
safe ; and to its captain's question whether the fort had been
taken, which reached Sherman just as Hazen's signal to his
troops to advance had been given, he answered, "Not yet,
but it will be in a minute." The gallant dash of the line
fulfilled the promise. A short, sharp struggle ensued, and
the parapet was crowned on all sides by the detachments, at
nearly the same moment. The attack had been in a thin
line concentrating as they reached the fort, and the men
passed the abatis, the palisades, and the ditch with scarce
a perceptible halt. Their greatest loss was from the torpedoes which exploded under their feet just before the ditch
was reached. Part of the troops on the extreme flanks got
around the palisading, where the angle of the works at the
river's edge was not so well protected, and were helped by
the fact that the tide was out, the abatis not extending below high-water mark. It was all over in fifteen minutes,
and the National flag floated on the staff from which the
Confederate ensign was pulled down, while the victors fired
a *feu-de-joie.* Hazen's loss was 24 killed and 110 wounded·

that of the garrison was 48. There was no formal surrender, but officers and men ceased the struggle when they found that they were overpowered. Colonel W. S. Jones fell severely wounded as the assault began, and the command of that brigade devolved on Colonel Martin of the One Hundred and Eleventh Illinois.

The capture of the fort had an importance to Sherman far out of proportion to its military strength. The Great Ogeechee was now open and vessels could reach King's Bridge in rear of the right of his line. So the question of a base on the sea was already solved, and the opportune presence of the tug which Sherman had signalled from Cheves's mill enabled him to send despatches that same night to Admiral Dahlgren's flag-ship in Warsaw Sound, for General Foster at Port Royal and General Grant at City Point. Before morning he heard of General Foster's arrival in the river, though unable to reach Fort McAllister because of the torpedoes planted below it. Thereupon Sherman again took a small boat and joined Foster upon his steamer, when he decided that the best economy of time would be found in proceeding at once to find Admiral Dahlgren in Warsaw Sound. The admiral entered earnestly into the plans for co-operation, undertook to find light-draught vessels for the transportation of supplies to King's Bridge, and to remove the obstructions from the Ogeechee.

Foster reported the efforts he had made to reach the Charleston railway, and that although he had not succeeded in getting actual possession of any point of the road, he had, about a week before, intrenched a position near Coosawhatchee from which his guns commanded the railroad. He was unable to be in the saddle owing to the breaking out of an old wound, and this was a serious misfortune, for the juncture was one in which the presence of the responsible commander is the only guaranty for thorough work at the front. The truth was, that although the position referred to was within a mile of the railway, the enemy continued to operate the road without serious interruption as far as Hardeeville, from which point the connection with Savannah was made by the Union Causeway. Within the range of the guns at Foster's position the railway was used chiefly at night, and the trains were kept running till the evacuation of Savannah, a week later.

Foster, however, was directed to establish himself upon the railway, if possible, and Sherman returned on the morning of December 15th to Howard's headquarters. Strong reconnoissances had meanwhile been made by the corps commanders, the approaches to Hardee's works had been carefully studied, and the preliminary steps taken to drain off the overflow from portions of the rice-fields in front of the city. By mending some of the breaks in the causeways and canals, and especially in the Ogeechee Canal, and by rearranging the flood-gates within our lines so that they should shut out the water from the rivers instead of shutting it in, the depth of the inundations began to be sensibly diminished. Till the water should be a good deal reduced an assault could hardly be thought of, for narrow columns along the causeways and dykes would have little chance, and in the overflowed fields the certainty of all wounded men being drowned would make an unjustifiable waste of human life.

On the night of the 11th, General Williams of the Twentieth Corps had put over part of the Third Wisconsin upon Argyle Island, and next morning the rest of the regiment. While these troops were crossing, three armed steamers of the Confederates attempted to descend the river, but were fired upon by Winegar's rifled battery, two of them were driven back, and one, the Resolute, was driven ashore upon the island and captured with its crew by Colonel Hawley and the Wisconsin regiment. Hardee had other gunboats below, and the presence of these in the river made it seem unadvisable to lay pontoon bridges till some thorough means of protecting them could be arranged. By an unfortunate mistake the Resolute was burned by her captors, when she would have been of inestimable value in ferrying troops and supplies. The Confederates had carefully removed all flat-boats and barges from the river, and the great exposure of detached troops on the South Carolina side, with no as-sured means of communication or of supply, made it seem better to trust to Foster's ability to complete the invest-ment on the east by seizing the railway to which his troops were so near.

Large quantities of rice were found on the island, and for some days this was the only breadstuff the men could pro-cure, while the rice-straw was the only forage for animals. On the 16th, Colonel Carman with the remainder of his bri-gade joined Hawley on the island, while at the same time Wheeler began a concentration of the Confederate cavalry opposite, to contest any landing on the Carolina shore.

At the right, Howard was making corduroy roads to con-nect the camps with the new dépôt that was preparing at King's Bridge, and was hurrying the operations which were expected to drain the rice-fields. His divisions and Slo-cum's were also arranging earthworks to receive some heavy rifled guns which Sherman had directed Foster to send from Port Royal, as the light artillery brought with the army could not cope with the armament of the Confederate forti-fications. In many places a fringe of pine woods protected the camps of the National troops, and it was noticed that when this was half a mile deep, the shot from even the heaviest of the enemy's guns failed to pass through it. Around the plantation houses were groves of giant live-oaks festooned with the tillandsia, the long moss of the South, and the headquarters tents were picturesquely dotted among these.

A despatch boat had been waiting on the coast with the mail for the army, and Sherman received despatches from Grant, dated the 3d and 6th of December, in which he directed that an intrenched position be established at any eligible point, and that the bulk of the army should then be shipped by sea, to join the forces before Richmond. Sherman responded to these at some length on the 16th, accepting the rôle assigned him with hearty subordination, but saying that his own expectation had been to reduce Savannah and then march to Columbia. To the officers of Grant's staff, who were the bearers of the despatches, he explained more fully his plans, and very vigorously urged the advantages of the movements he had proposed, so that these might be properly laid before the General-in-Chief. It happened, however, that on the very day when Sherman was thus replying, Grant had himself reached the conclusion to leave his subordinate free to choose his own course, and Halleck was writing to Sherman, by his direction, the authority to act upon his own judgment. The true strategic purpose of the campaign was thus maintained, but as the despatches of the 16th and 18th did not reach Sherman till Savannah was in his possession, the effect was to make him less decisive than he would otherwise have been in putting the left wing of the army into positions on the Carolina side of the river, and in committing himself to siege operations and to a completed investment, from which it

---

[1] My authority for this is Colonel G. W. Nichols, of Sherman's staff, who was present at the conversation.

would not have been easy to withdraw when the expected transports should appear to take away the army. As a middle course, therefore, he determined to rely mainly upon Foster for operations in South Carolina, limiting Slocum to such auxiliary efforts from Argyle Island as might at any time be withdrawn. That such a middle course was a comparatively weak one, no one was better aware than Sherman, but it was that which duty seemed to dictate. He directed his Chief Engineer, Colonel Poe, to lay out an intrenched camp at Fort McAllister, which might be held in the manner indicated by General Grant's first despatches, and ordered the corps commanders to press the siege with the means in hand.

In the hope also that the boldness of the demand might have some moral effect, he sent on the 17th a formal summons to Hardee to surrender, but this was refused. We have already seen that the Confederate commander was determined not to allow himself to be shut up in the city, and the only question with him was how long he could stay without too seriously endangering his escape. Beauregard had reached Augusta, and was in general command, and this officer had accepted and earnestly reiterated the views which Hardee and Taylor had laid before the Confederate Government on this subject. General S. Jones, now in command at Charleston, was ordered to Pocotaligo to keep open the railroad at every hazard, and a bridge of boats was built across the two channels of the river, from Savannah to Hutchinson Island and thence to the Carolina shore.

Meanwhile the waters on the inundated rice-fields were slowly subsiding, Howard and Slocum had their siege batteries in position, some of their divisions had prepared light bridges to be carried by the men and thrown across the ditches, and other preparations were made for an assault which must have been sanguinary, but which they believed could be successfully made. On the 19th Carman's brigade was ferried across from Argyle Island to the Carolina shore, and obtained a strong defensive position at Izard's mill, but the fields were under water there also, and all bridges were burned, so that it was not an easy thing to advance. The movement, however, satisfied Hardee that he could not delay longer, and he began the evacuation, first sending over a strong detachment to resist fiercely the advance of Carman along the dykes. Knowing the danger of Hardee's escape, and believing that a vigorous effort by Foster's troops might still prevent it, Sherman started in person by steamer, on the 18th, to visit Foster, whose physical condition was not such that he could come to the camp. He spent the 20th at Hilton Head, giving directions for a movement of Hatch's division against the Union Causeway, and started to return in the night; but his boat was delayed by high winds and by grounding at low tide, so that he did not get back till toward evening on the 21st, when he found the city already in possession of his troops. Hardee had completed the evacuation in the night of the 20th, and Geary's division of the Twentieth Corps, being the nearest to the town, had marched in at daybreak next morning. Sherman's despatch announcing the possession of the city reached President Lincoln on Christmas eve, and its publication was received by the country as a Christmas gift of priceless value. The moral prestige of the march was greatly heightened by the so quick capture of one of the principal Southern cities and seaports. The escape of Hardee was a disappointment, but as we now know that he had been carefully watching the roads since the first approach of the National army, with the determination to abandon the city before the investment could have been made complete, the only question was whether he should make the evacuation a few days sooner or later.

Hardee had only been able to remove his light artillery with his troops, and the heavy guns, mounted and in store, which were captured, were found to number over two hundred and fifty. Thirty-one thousand bales of cotton also fell into the hands of the National army and were turned over to the officers of the Treasury Department. The retreating Confederate army moved first to Charleston, whence the Georgia militia were sent to Augusta, that they might relieve other Confederate troops there and serve within their own State, in accordance with the terms of their enlistment.

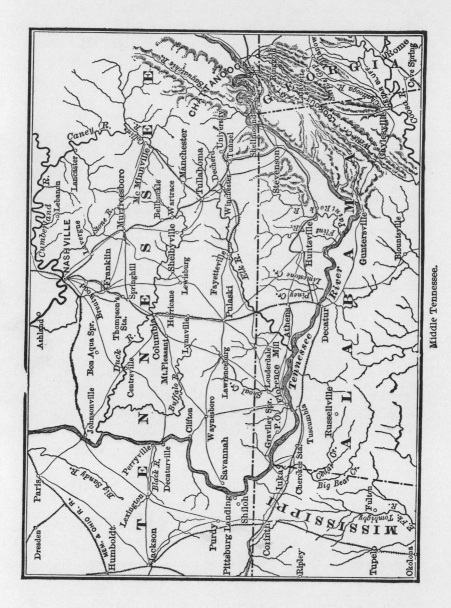

Middle Tennessee.

CHAPTER IV.

MIDDLE TENNESSEE—PULASKI TO SPRING HILL.

WHILE the events described in the last chapters were occurring in Georgia, the struggle in Middle Tennessee had reached a crisis. We have seen that before November 15th Forrest's cavalry had joined Hood, and that a portion of the Confederate infantry occupied Florence, covering the bridge that was laid there in preparation for the advance of the whole of Hood's army. General Thomas had committed to General Schofield the command of the troops immediately opposed to Hood, but it was the universal expectation that a rapid concentration of the National forces would be made in time to prevent the Confederate army from advancing far.[1]

In East Tennessee the enemy, under Breckenridge, made an attack upon General Gillem, who commanded a body of our cavalry there; but this was simply a diversion intended to delay the concentration of our forces, like that made just before by Forrest, and had no further significance. Sherman's march from Atlanta made it necessary for Hood to do promptly whatever he meant to do, and his cavalry began to make demonstrations toward Lawrenceburg and Waynesboro as early as the 15th. The weather, however, had proven a formidable obstacle, delaying the rebuilding of the railroad between Tuscumbia and Cherokee Station, and

---

[1] For organization of the armies of Thomas and Hood, see Appendix B.

delaying still more the wagon trains which were toiling through the mud in the effort to accumulate supplies sufficient to warrant the opening of an active campaign. The storms, of which only the edge reached Sherman near Macon, were continuous and severe in Tennessee, alternating between rains and severe frosts, covering the roads with a frozen crust over deep mire, just strong enough to make the utmost obstruction, without getting the solidity necessary to bear up the wagons and teams.

Beauregard had left Hood on the 17th, after issuing the order which directed the latter to advance with the least possible delay, and on the 20th had reached West Point, Miss., whence he telegraphed to Hood to "push an active offensive immediately." On that day, Lee's corps marched ten miles out from Florence, on a road between those leading to Waynesboro and to Lawrenceburg, and on the 21st the whole of the army was in motion, Hood hoping by a rapid march to get in rear of Schofield's forces before they could reach Duck River. Schofield received word on the 20th from Hatch, who commanded his cavalry, that the advance had begun, and as soon as it was evident that Hood was moving on the Lawrenceburg road, he sent back his surplus stores from Pulaski, and prepared to retreat to Columbia. He had ordered Colonel Strickland, who was at the last-named place, to prepare a defensive line by which he could hold the town, or at least the crossings of Duck River at the railway and pontoon bridges. On the 21st the cavalry reports left no doubt that Hood was near Lawrenceburg, and the next morning Cox's division of the Twenty-third Corps was sent to Lynnville, about half way between Pulaski and Columbia, where it was joined in the evening by Wagner's division of the Fourth Corps. At this point they covered an important cross-road coming in from Lawrenceburg to the railway. Thomas's despatches to Schofield had all contained the strong wish that the troops might retreat as little and as slowly as possible, for on Sunday, the 20th, he had abandoned the expectation of seeing A. J. Smith's troops before the following Friday. He expressed a hope that Pulaski might be held till then, but coincided in Schofield's opinion that, if Hood attempted to get in his rear, it would be necessary to retire to Columbia, covering the railway. The mingled and continuous storms of snow, sleet, and rain were delaying Hood, and he was not yet so far North as to make it sure that he would not seek to reach the railway south of Columbia. On the 23d, Schofield's movement kept pace with Hood's, Cox's division being sent ten miles farther north to Hurricane, the crossing of the railway by the Mount Pleasant and Shelbyville road, and Stanley, with the whole of the Fourth Corps, was moved to Lynnville. But during the night Schofield received word that the cavalry on the Mount Pleasant and Columbia Road were unable to resist the determined advance of Forrest, and before daybreak of the 24th he put his little army in rapid motion for Columbia. Cox's division, having the shorter distance to travel, approached the town first, and hearing the noise of the cavalry combat on the converging road at the west, marched by a cross-road some two miles out of town, and reached that on which the fight was going on in time to interpose the infantry skirmishers, moving at double-quick, between Forrest's cavalry and the brigade of Colonel Capron, which was rapidly retreating into the place. The enemy was quickly checked and a line formed behind Bigby Creek. It was now a little after seven o'clock; in less than three hours Stanley's head of column came up, and a strong position was taken by the whole command, covering the town on the south. Hood did not succeed in getting the whole of

his forces up until the 26th, his utmost exertions having
failed to move his army faster than ten miles a day. Schofield was joined on the march by General Wilson, who took
command of all the cavalry, which was slowly reinforced,
and he was met at Columbia by General Ruger, with one of
the brigades of the Twenty-third Corps, which had been left
at Johnsonville. General Cooper, who had also been at
Johnsonville, was ordered by General Thomas to march
with his brigade from there to Centreville, a crossing of the
Duck River, thirty miles west of Columbia, where it was
thought Forrest's cavalry might try to pass that stream.
Part of Ruger's command was scattered at several points on
the river, within a few miles of Columbia, to protect crossings and fords on Schofield's right flank. Wilson, with the
cavalry, was directed to operate on the left, covering the
country in the direction of Lewisburg and Shelbyville as
well as possible, besides watching the fords and crossings of
the river above Columbia.

Schofield's position was a strong one if the attack were
made upon him in front, but it had the great disadvantage
of a river at his back. No line north of the river could be
occupied without abandoning the railroad bridge to destruction, and this would be needed again as soon as a forward
movement should begin. The river at the town makes a
horse-shoe bend to the south, and the land on the north
bank in the bend is low, and completely commanded by
that on the south. Hood was too wary to make an assault
of the lines, and contented himself with a sharp skirmishing
engagement, while he prepared to turn Schofield's position
by crossing the river some miles above.

Thomas had given orders to General Granger, at Decatur,
prior to the retrograde movement, under which that officer,
on the same day that Schofield abandoned Pulaski, with-

drew his garrisons from Athens, Decatur, and Huntsville, and concentrated his division at Stevenson, a hundred miles east. The relations of this singular divergent movement will be considered later; its immediate effect was to relieve Hood of any embarrassment as to his right flank in operating against Schofield. The garrison at Johnsonville was ordered to remove the public property and retire to Clarksville, fifty miles northwest of Nashville.

On the 24th, a careful examination of the country satisfied Schofield that he must expect Hood to try to turn his position, and he informed Thomas of his purpose to prepare an interior and shorter line, so that when it became necessary he could retire to this and send part of his force north of Duck River. Thomas still urged that the effort be made to cover the railway and pontoon bridges with a bridge-head, so keeping command of a crossing till he should be ready to advance; and Schofield prepared to delay and obstruct Hood to the last moment, urging that the infantry reinforcements be sent to him as fast as possible. The strong efforts which had been made had increased Wilson's cavalry to about seven thousand equipped, five regiments being sent forward from Nashville between the 24th and 27th of the month. These, however, did not reach him at the front till the 30th, and till that time his force remained inferior in strength to Forrest's, even if we deduct from the latter Roddey's division, which seems to have been detached, guarding Northern Alabama.

During the night of the 25th Schofield ordered Cox to move two brigades of his division to the north side of the river, and take a position covering the pontoon bridge which was at the ford. On the 26th, this was strengthened by breastworks on indented lines, where the brigades and regiments were separately intrenched, taking advantage of every

irregularity of the ground and of groves of timber to protect the force from the cross-fire of artillery which the enemy would have from the higher ground on the south of the
stream.   Pits were also made for a line of skirmishers close

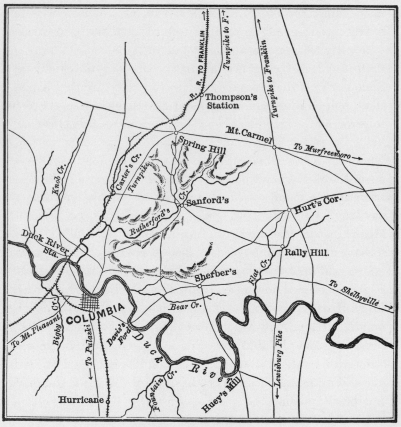

Vicinity of Columbia, Tenn.

to the river bank.   The Fourth Corps troops were brought
into the interior line which had been constructed on the
other side, and the town and bridges were still held.

Hood felt cautiously the new line in front of Columbia

but still did not attack, and the whole of his infantry being up, he began a movement to cross the river above. Forrest assembled most of the Confederate cavalry between Hood's right and the turnpike, and other roads leading from Lewisburg to Franklin eastward of Columbia, trying the different fords. Wilson was actively at work to prevent the crossing, watching the country as far as Shelbyville. The indications of Hood's purpose were now so plain that Schofield felt he could no longer delay, and moved the whole of his command to the north side of the river, in the night of the 27th, partly destroying the railway bridge, so that the enemy could not make use of it. He was also obliged to destroy the pontoon bridge, which was of heavy wooden boats, for which he had no means of transportation. He earnestly assured Thomas that he had held on as long as was at all safe, and he was plainly right, the only doubt being whether, in his zeal to give Thomas all the time possible for the intended concentration, he was not taking too great a risk.

Wilson heard, on the afternoon of the 28th, that Forrest had forced a crossing at Huey's mill, eight miles above Columbia.[1] He tried to unite his forces as rapidly as possible in front of the enemy, but Hurt's cross-roads, between Spring Hill and the Lewisburg road, was the first point at which he was able to make any continued stand. At eight in the evening his information seemed to show that Forrest was moving eastward toward the Lewisburg road, and that none of the enemy had gone toward the Franklin road, in

---

[1] The official reports and memoirs on both sides are full of differences as to the distance from Columbia to the place where Hood's infantry crossed. The Confederate accounts say nothing of Huey's mill, and do not distinctly fix the place of their pontoon bridge. By the courtesy of Capt. R. D. Smith, of Columbia, who was in Hood's army at the time, I am able to say definitely that the bridge was laid at Davis's ford, between five and six miles from Columbia. Some of the cavalry crossed at Huey's mill.

rear of Schofield. At one o'clock, however, he received information that pontoons were laid at Huey's mill, and that
Hood's infantry were crossing. This he immediately despatched to Schofield; but the messenger had to go by
Spring Hill, and the way was long, so that the intelligence
was only received at daylight in the morning. A brigade of
infantry (Post's of Wood's division) was immediately sent
upon a reconnoissance up the river, accompanied by one of
Schofield's staff, with orders to observe and report the movements of the enemy. Stanley was ordered to march at eight
o'clock with two divisions of his corps to Spring Hill, eleven
miles, leaving Wood in support of Post's reconnoissance, and
about a mile in rear of Cox's division, which was ordered to
hold stubbornly the crossing at Columbia and the tongue of
land in the bend of the river. Ruger was ordered to hasten
the blockade of the fords and roads below the town by fell-
ing trees, and then to march also to Spring Hill. Stewart's
brigade of cavalry, which had been watching the lower
fords, had been ordered the preceding evening to proceed
rapidly to join Wilson by way of Spring Hill; and Hammond's brigade, which was coming from Nashville freshly
remounted, was ordered to stop at the same place and move
as Wilson should direct. As another precaution Schofield
had telegraphed Thomas, asking that a pontoon bridge be
sent to Franklin, where the wagon bridge had been carried
away by a freshet.

Soon after daylight the Confederate artillery around the
whole bend of the river opened upon the division entrenched in the lower lands along the north shore, but the
precautions that had been taken by building traverses and
angles in the lines prevented any serious loss. The fire
was returned from our batteries, and the renewal of the
artillery combat at different times through the day, by

showing that Hood's cannon were in position, proved also that his whole army could not have moved.

The truth was that Hood had left two divisions of Lee's corps, and the whole of his artillery, in Columbia, with orders to make strong demonstrations in the morning, and to force the crossing of the river later in the day. The roads by which he was leading Cheatham's and Stewart's corps were not thought practicable for the cannon. Schofield needed time for Ruger to complete his work at the fords below, and to send by rail some artillery which had no horses and other material for which transportation was lacking. He judged also from the strong force of the enemy in Columbia that Hood was not unlikely to move straight down the river upon his flank, when the two parts of the Confederate army could co-operate. He therefore modified his order to Stanley, so as to place Kimball's division near Rutherford Creek crossing, about two miles from Wood, and let Stanley proceed to Spring Hill with Wagner's division alone. Ruger was ready to march early in the day, and leaving one regiment as an outpost on the right, he hastened with the rest of his two brigades over Rutherford Creek, when he halted, by Schofield's orders, a short distance beyond the position of Kimball. The wagon trains of the army had been ordered to Spring Hill, and Stanley reached that place about noon, and just in time to prevent their capture by the enemy's cavalry.

Forrest had, on the 28th, placed Buford's division upon the Lewisburg and Franklin turnpike, Chalmers's division at Holland's Ford, about seven miles east of Columbia, and Jackson's at Huey's mill, between Chalmers and Buford, while he himself, with his escort, and Biffle's demi-brigade attempted Davis's Ford, two miles west of Chalmers.[1] The

---

[1] Jordan and Prior's Campaigns of Forrest, p. 619.

two divisions of the National cavalry were broken into
smaller detachments, part of them well out toward Shelbyville, the nearest to the infantry being part of Capron's
brigade, at Rally Hill, on the Lewisburg road, where a
branch turnpike turns off to Spring Hill. The resistance
made to Buford was so vigorous that he could not get over
the river, but Jackson and Chalmers forced a crossing after
a sharp skirmish, and Forrest himself does not seem to have
found any resistance. He soon struck the Columbia and
Murfreesboro road, and turning Chalmers and Jackson to
the east, drove Wilson's detachment beyond Rally Hill.
The enemy was now between the main body of our cavalry
and the parties watching the fords near the Lewisburg
crossing. These were collected by Major Young (Fifth
Iowa Cavalry) and under his lead they daringly cut their
way through. Wilson now called in his detachments toward Hurt's Corners as rapidly as possible, but his despatch
to Schofield at eight o'clock, giving the information already
referred to, shows that he was misled as to Forrest's purposes. It is true that the latter was moving eastward with
two-thirds of his command, but he was doing so only to
clear the way for Buford, and at Rally Hill he was in possession of the only macadamized road leading directly to
Schofield's rear at Spring Hill. Wilson had been able to
rally his whole command at Hurt's Corners, and checked
the further advance of the enemy in the evening, but Buford
joined Forrest in the night, and early in the morning the
whole of the Confederate cavalry again advanced. Wilson
made a brave and determined resistance, putting Croxton's
brigade of Johnson's division in the rear, to contest every
foot of the way. Capron's brigade of the same division,
which had been badly worsted the evening before, took
the advance on the Franklin road, and Hatch's division was

the middle of the column supporting Croxton. Forrest operated by flank movements, using his heavier force to turn the positions selected by Wilson, and by the middle of the forenoon had gained Mount Carmel, where the Murfreesboro and Spring Hill road crosses the turnpike on which our cavalry was retiring. Here Coon's brigade of Hatch's division occupied a barricade which had been previously made by Capron, and the rest of the command moved through it. The enemy made two determined charges upon it, but were repulsed. Wilson continued, however, to retire slowly on Franklin, and Forrest, who now had possession of the direct road to Spring Hill, covering that by which Hood's infantry was moving, no longer pressed the pursuit; but leaving a detachment in observation, he moved directly upon Spring Hill, where Stanley arrived almost at the same moment with him, as we have seen. It is now plain that Wilson erred in adhering to the line of the Lewisburg and Franklin road after Forrest gained Rally Hill. By doing so he allowed Forrest to cut him off both from Schofield's infantry, and from the two brigades of cavalry which were ordered to Spring Hill to reinforce him, and Schofield was left, during the whole of the critical day and night of the 29th, without the means of learning Hood's movements except from his infantry reconnoissances. The true line of action was manifestly to regain the road from Rally Hill to Spring Hill in the night of the 28th, or, failing that, to have made a rapid march by Mount Carmel to Spring Hill, so as to anticipate Forrest there.

Hood did not cross Duck River with his infantry in the night, as had been expected, but Cleburne's division of Cheatham's corps, which was his head of column, crossed soon after daylight in the morning upon the pontoon bridge at Davis's Ford, followed by Bate and Brown. Stewart's corps came next, the rear being brought up by Johnson's division of Lee's corps, which was temporarily reporting to Stewart. Hood himself accompanied the advance guard, but despite all his efforts it was three o'clock in the afternoon, or later, when Cleburne reached the Rally Hill turnpike where it crosses Rutherford Creek, two and a half miles from Spring Hill. Ordering Cheatham to remain and hurry the crossing of his other divisions, Cleburne was directed to press forward and attack whatever force there might be at Spring Hill, where the noise of Stanley's artillery warned them that Forrest was meeting with opposition. But the distant firing at Columbia could also be heard, and the tenacity with which Schofield hung on to the line of Duck River apparently raised doubts in Hood's mind whether the National commander might not have received reinforcements enough to cut boldly between the now separated wings of his army. Post's reconnoissance had gone far enough to observe the movement, and it is probable that it had in turn been seen by Hood's command, and he would thus know that infantry was approaching his line of march. But whatever the reasons which induced it, Hood ordered Stewart to form his corps in line of battle south of Rutherford Creek, facing west, and this instruction necessarily implies the expectation of the approach of an enemy from that direction, or the purpose of himself making an attack upon the line which Schofield had prepared to receive him by putting Wood's, Kimball's, and Ruger's divisions within supporting distance of each other upon the extension of Cox's left. He may have thought that the resistance at Spring Hill would be slight when Cheatham reached the field, and that this corps sweeping down the turnpike toward Columbia would meet the convergent advance of Stewart in a general attack upon Schofield's flank. The advantages of the defence in a broken and wooded country, and the prudent disposal of his force, by which Schofield had now some miles of line facing the east, would possibly have made such an attack as disastrous as the one at Franklin next day; but Hood did not attack there, and Stewart remained in line till Cheatham had been repulsed at Spring Hill, and was then ordered up when darkness had fallen and it was thought too late for further action that night.

When Stanley had reached Spring Hill he found a part of Forrest's command already in the outskirts of the place. He ordered Wagner to put Opdycke's and Lane's brigades in position to cover the village, and advanced Bradley's brigade to a wooded hill about three-fourths of a mile east of the turnpike, which commanded the approaches from that direction. One battery of artillery had accompanied Wagner, but Captain Bridges, Chief of Artillery of the Fourth Corps, had followed Stanley's march with six batteries, leaving one with Wood's division. This had been done only to get them well forward *en route* to Franklin; but on reaching Spring Hill, Captain Bridges had with wise precaution put his guns in battery on a commanding bench just west of the road, and where a little later they proved of great use and most fortunate in position. The enemy's cavalry made active efforts to reach the trains, which were parked by the roadside, and also to destroy the railway station a short distance west of the turnpike, and the protection of all these kept Opdycke and Lane fully employed. Bradley was engaged at the same time, but the affair was not serious until the arrival of Cleburne's division on the field. This officer formed his command along the Rally Hill road, and, advancing at right angles to it, attempted to reach the Columbia turnpike. He does not seem to have been fully aware of Bradley's position, for his extreme right (Lowry's brigade) alone reached it,

and was received with so rude a shock that Cleburne was
quickly forced to change front nearly at right angles in
order to engage his opponent. Bate's division, which followed Cleburne, had formed in the same manner and took
the same line of direction. It had nearly reached the Columbia road when Bate discovered that Cleburne had
changed direction, and his orders being to form on the left
of that division, much time was consumed in rectifying the
line. Brown's division had followed Bate and had been
sent forward on Cleburne's right. Bradley's position had
been too isolated to be held by a single brigade against so
extended a line of battle, and after his first sharp encounter
with Cleburne he retreated in some disorder, he himself
being severely wounded. The brigade was quickly reformed on the right of Lane, at the southern edge of the
village commanding the Columbia road, and a regiment was
detached from Opdycke to strengthen it. Wagner's line was
now a semicircle, reaching from the Columbia road around
the eastern side of the place to the railway station on the
northwest, Opdycke's brigade being stretched out till it was
only a strong line of skirmishers. A regiment which was
with the trains as a guard was also utilized, and advantage
was taken of the ground to present the strongest front possible. Cleburne and Brown followed up Bradley's retreat,
but were met with so continuous a fire and on so long a defensive line, that they were made to believe they were in the
presence of a superior force. The concentration of artillery
fire upon them was so far beyond what they could expect
from a single division, that it checked them as much, perhaps, by producing the conviction that they had most of
Schofield's army before them, as by the severe losses caused
by the terrible fire of shrapnel and canister. It was now
growing dark, and Hood having reached the conclusion that

he needed Stewart's corps also, ordered this up from Rutherford Creek, with Johnson's division of Lee's corps which
accompanied it. Jackson's division of cavalry occupied
Thompson's Station, three miles north of Spring Hill, and
the rest of Forrest's horsemen were in that direction. When
Stewart arrived it was already night, and he was ordered to
bivouac on the right and rear of Cheatham.

Meanwhile Schofield had issued his orders that Cox's division should continue to hold the bank of the river opposite
Columbia till nightfall, if possible, and then, leaving a skirmish line in position, should march to Spring Hill, followed
in turn by Wood's and Kimball's divisions. The skirmishers
were directed to remain till midnight unless driven off, and
to join the rear guard of the army or follow it. The divisions were all to move by the left flank, so that whenever
they should halt and face they would be in line of battle,
and could use the road fences for barricades if attacked by
Hood. The whole line would thus be shortened from the
right till Kimball only should remain on that flank, when he
also would march to Spring Hill. By this arrangement there
was the least risk of confusion and the greatest readiness
for any contingency which might arise.

On hearing from Stanley that he was attacked by infantry,
Schofield hastened to Ruger's division, which, it will be remembered, was nearest to Spring Hill, and led its two brigades in person by a rapid march to Stanley's support. As
he approached the village he found pickets of the enemy
on the road, but these were driven off and he joined Stanley
at seven o'clock. Whittaker's brigade of Kimball's division had also been ordered up, and followed Ruger closely.
When it arrived it was placed on the right of Wagner's line,
to cover the march of the rest of the column as it should
approach. Learning from Stanley that some force of the

enemy was at Thompson's Station, Schofield immediately
marched with Ruger's division to that point to open the way
to Franklin. At his approach Jackson withdrew his cavalry
and Ruger was placed in position there without a contest.
Schofield now returned to Spring Hill, reaching the village
at midnight, and meeting there the head of Cox's division
which had moved from Duck River in accordance with his
orders.

It is necessary, to a complete understanding of the situation, that we should go back a little and notice the efforts
which Lee made to carry out Hood's orders, and force the
crossing of Duck River in the afternoon. He had kept up,
at intervals, an annoying plunging fire upon Cox's troops in
the bend of the river, but our rifled cannon, by greater range
and better practice, had prevented the enemy's artillery from
maintaining its positions or doing much damage. A line of
skirmishers' pits on the very end of the tongue of land had
been made untenable, but a fringe of wood, a little further
back, afforded a cover which gave complete command of the
open ground to the edge of the river bank. About four
o'clock the efforts of Lee to effect a crossing became more
energetic. Some pontoons were brought to the south bank
of the river, and, under cover of a rapid artillery fire, a few
boats were run down to the water. Some troops were ferried over in these, and so long as they remained under protection of the river bank, they could not be reached by our
fire. As soon, however, as they appeared above its edge,
and attempted to advance against the fringe of woods held
by the Twelfth and Sixteenth Kentucky (part of Reilly's
brigade) they were met by the most determined resistance.
The Sixty-third Indiana and One Hundred and Twelfth Illinois, of Henderson's brigade (temporarily commanded by
Colonel Stiles), were sent forward to support the right of

Reilly's men, and the enemy was driven from the open
ground to the cover of the river bank again, and made no
further effort to cross the river during the evening.

Soon after nightfall the line of pickets near the river was
strengthened, the two Kentucky regiments, under command
of Colonel White, were left as their support, the Division
Inspector-General, Major Dow, being with them, and having
orders to bring them off at midnight. The division then
marched to Spring Hill, where it was directed by General
Schofield to take the advance and proceed at once to Franklin, twelve miles further. The other divisions followed in
the appointed manner and without serious interruption.
The pickets at the river were withdrawn, as directed, and
overtook the rear of Wood's division a little beyond Spring
Hill, and, under orders from that officer, protected the flank
of the trains from the cavalry of the enemy on the remainder
of the march to Franklin.

Wagner's division was kept in position at Spring Hill till
the trains and all the other troops were in movement, and
Opdycke's brigade, which was the rear guard of the whole,
did not march until six o'clock in the morning. About midnight Hood was informed that troops were passing on the
Columbia road, and sent Johnson's division of Lee's corps to
extend Bate's line and stop the movement; but the night
was dark and the country unfamiliar, and nothing came of
it but a slight occasional skirmish, while our columns
marched by in full view of the enemy's camp-fires, which
were burning less than half a mile away.

Here, as at Atlanta, Hood sought to shift the responsibility for his failure upon a subordinate, and Cheatham was now
selected to bear the burden. Hood charged him with tardi-
ness and weakness in the attack upon Stanley, and asked
to have him relieved from his command. This request was

withdrawn after the battle of Franklin, though without re-
tracting the charge. But a commander who is personally
with the head of column in such a movement and upon the
field, has the means of enforcing his orders by direct commands to the divisions. Had his own confidence not wav-
ered, and had he not begun to yield to the belief that much
more than one division was before him, his own energy
would have carried his subordinates with him, and would
have made the assault as desperate, if need be, as it was
next day. But he seems to have lacked the grasp of mind
which enables a general to judge and to act with vigor in
the presence of circumstances which throw doubt upon his
plan, and he proved inferior to his opponent in a strategic
contest, which has been generally regarded as one of the
most critical and instructive conjunctures of the war. The
circumstances, as narrated by the leading Confederate officers who were present, show that Hood had an access of
hesitation at the very moment when the success of his movement demanded that all doubts should be thrown to the
winds and everything risked upon a desperate stroke.[1]

---

[1] A paper read in December, 1881, before a society of Southern officers at Louisville, Ky., by General Cheatham, contains a very full array of the evidence which
sustains the above view.

CHAPTER V.

BATTLE OF FRANKLIN.

THE march of the National army from Spring Hill to Franklin was not seriously interrupted. Forrest's troopers made an occasional dash at the long wagon train, but only in one or two instances did they succeed in reaching it, and very few wagons were lost. After seeing his columns fairly started, Schofield rode forward and overtook General Cox with the advanced division just before the village of Franklin was reached. He had, about noon, urgently renewed his request to Thomas to send a pontoon bridge to the crossing of the Harpeth River, but having received no answer, he spurred forward with his staff to see if it had arrived. It was not yet daybreak, and the division was ordered to mass by the roadside to allow the trains to pass into the town. The division commander and his staff had halted at the house of a Mr. Carter, at the edge of the village (a house soon to become the key-point of a fierce battle) and were trying to catch a few minutes' sleep upon the floor, when General Schofield returned, much disturbed at finding that no pontoons had come.[1] He ordered General Cox to as-

---

[1] In the correspondence on file in the War Records office, no response to the second request for pontoons is found, and General Schofield informs the author that he received none. The same files do not contain any explanation of the destruction of the boats at Columbia, and it would therefore seem that General Thomas must have continued to assume that they were available, notwithstanding the strong implication of Schofield's despatches. See Appendix D.

sume command of both divisions of the Twenty-third Corps, and, as soon as day should dawn, intrench them upon the best line which could be made right and left of the knoll on which the Carter house stood, to cover the crossing of the trains and the rest of the army. He himself, with Major Twining, his Chief Engineer, began immediately to plan such improvements of the river crossings as should enable him to get the trains and the artillery upon the north side of the Harpeth at the earliest possible hour.

The village of Franklin is upon the south side of the river, which partly encloses it in a deep curve to the northeast. The northern bank is here considerably higher than the other, and, upon a hill commanding the railway and wagon-road bridges, an earthwork called Fort Granger had been built more than a year before. The railway approaches the town from the south, parallel to the Columbia turnpike, and about five hundred yards east of it. For a thousand yards it runs close to the bank of the river and on the eastern edge of the village, then crosses without change of direction, for the river here makes a turn to the west, nearly at right angles to its former course. Through a part of the distance last traversed the railway is in a considerable cut, and this as well as the bridges and the reach of the river, is completely under the fire of the fort. The Carter's Creek turnpike runs southwest from the centre of the town.

The line selected for defence was a curve which would be very nearly that struck with a radius of a thousand yards from the junction of the two turnpikes in the village. Its centre was a few rods in front of the Carter house on the Columbia road, and was upon a gentle rise of ground. Its left was at the railway cut close to the river, where was another knoll. Upon this line the Carter's Creek turnpike is about the same distance from the Columbia turnpike as the

railway, and this constituted the proper front facing Columbia and Spring Hill, whence Hood was advancing. The
third division of the Twenty-third Corps (General Reilly in

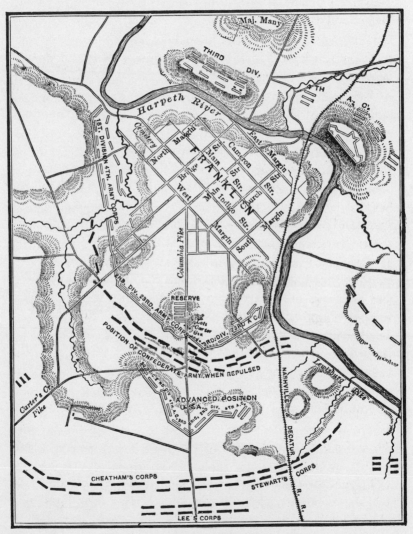

Battle-Field of Franklin.

temporary command) was placed on the left, Reilly's own
brigade resting its flank on the road, with Casement's and
Henderson's brigades (Colonel Stiles in temporary command of the latter) continuing the line to the railway and
river. The front of Reilly's own brigade was shorter than
the others, for the two regiments which were left behind
as pickets at Duck River belonged to it, and these did not
arrive till the line was occupied. They were then placed
in second line, supporting the first and less than a hundred
yards in rear of it. Ruger's division was between the Columbia and Carter's Creek turnpikes, Strickland's brigade on
the left, and Moore's on the right. Along the whole front
the ground sloped very gently from the line, and was only
obstructed by a small grove of locust trees a short distance
in front of Ruger, and by farm buildings, with orchards here
and there in the distance. A range of high hills bounded
this plain on the south, through a gap in which the Columbia
road runs. The Twenty-third Corps immediately began the
building of breastworks, and by noon a strong intrenchment
had been completed, the lack of timber for revetment being
the only thing which prevented it from being equal to those
usually made during the campaign. An old cotton gin in
Reilly's line furnished timber for head-logs, and upon the
knoll near the railway, at the Carter house, and in one or
two other places, where the slope was sufficient, strong
epaulements for artillery were constructed inside of and
somewhat higher than the infantry parapet. At the Columbia turnpike the full width of the road was left open, for it
was all needed to enable the doubled lines of wagons and
artillery to pass, and a retrenchment crossing the road a few
rods in rear was built to command the opening and its approach.

At the river it had been found that by scarping the banks,

the ford, though a very bad one, could be used to some extent. Some wooden buildings were dismantled to furnish planking for the railway bridge, and a wagon approach to this was made. The lower part of the posts of the county bridge were found to be good, and these were sawn off nearly level with the water, crossbeams and planking were laid upon them, and by noon the army was provided with two passable bridges. The artillery of the Twenty-third Corps passed over first of all at the ford, to gain time, and part of it was placed in the fort on the north bank, General Stanley being directed to send several batteries of the Fourth Corps to report to the commandant upon the line when they should arrive. The trench on the left, in front of Stiles, was placed close behind a thick-set hedge of osage orange, which was thinned out so as to make an impassable thorny palisade, and the material was used to make a slight obstruction in front of Reilly's brigades. In front of Ruger the locust grove was cut down for the same use, though the trees were much too small for the purpose. At General Cox's request for troops to cover the right flank, since his force was not sufficient to reach the river on that side, Kimball's division of the Fourth Corps was ordered to report to him as it came in, and was placed there.[1]

Wood's division of the Fourth Corps arrived and crossed to the north bank, Kimball had taken his place in the line, Wilson's cavalry was upon Wood's left, opposing the efforts of Forrest to cross the river in that direction, the town was full of wagons waiting their turn at the bridges, and some of them struggling through the ford. The wearied troops, which had fought and marched since daybreak of the preceding day, dropped to sleep as soon as their breast-

---

[1] See Appendix D.

works were built, and caught such rest as they could preparatory to a more terrible struggle and another night of
marching.

On the Confederate side, Lee had sent forward the artillery from Columbia, as soon as it could be crossed over
Duck River in the morning, and with it went ammunition
for Forrest's men, who were getting short of it. The march
in pursuit does not seem to have been hurried, and the single brigade, which was rear-guard, had no difficulty in holding back the enemy. A more annoying task was to drive
forward the stragglers. A number of new regiments had
joined the army at Columbia, and in these were many inex-
perienced recruits, who were not hardened to their work,
and who had overloaded their knapsacks. It required the
utmost exertion to prevent these men from falling into the
enemy's hands, footsore and dispirited from fatigue as they
were. To keep them up, Colonel Opdycke was obliged to
order their knapsack straps to be cut, and to detail a provost guard to hurry them on.

About noon the rear-guard reached the hills at the border
of the Harpeth Valley, from which the heavy columns of
Hood's army could now be seen advancing rapidly. Opdycke checked them for a time by opening upon them with
artillery, but was then withdrawn and brought within the
lines, where he was placed in reserve upon the west of the
Columbia road, two or three hundred yards from the Carter
house. Wagner placed the rest of his division (Lane's and
Conrad's brigades) astride the Columbia turnpike, about half
a mile in front of the principal line. The commandant
upon the line was notified by General Schofield that Wagner's orders directed him to remain in observation only till
Hood should show a disposition to advance in force, and
then to retire within the lines to Opdycke's position and act

as a general reserve. Wagner, on being shown the note conveying this notice, said that such were his orders.

By three o'clock the trains were nearly all over the river, and Schofield had issued orders that the troops should also pass over at six o'clock if the enemy should not attack before sunset. But the period of depression and recrimination in Hood's army in the morning seems to have been followed by fierce excitement. Cleburne talked with Brown, as they rode along, complaining bitterly that Hood had censured him, and telling of his determination to demand an investigation.[1] Evidently all were keyed to a high moral tension, and were determined that at the next opportunity, their commander should not have it to say that his plans had failed from any lack of energy or courage on their part. Hood, himself, had resolved upon a desperate effort to destroy Schofield's army before any further concentration of Thomas's forces could be made.

About three o'clock word was sent from Wagner's brigades in front that the enemy was forming at the foot of the hills in heavy force, and reiterating to General Wagner the directions already given him, the commandant upon the line went to the knoll in Stiles's brigade, which afforded a better view of the whole field. General Schofield had moved his headquarters to the north side of the river, and was personally at the fort on the hill, which not only commanded a view of the field, but was nearest the bridges by which communication was kept up, and where alone he could see the cavalry demonstrations on the left where Forrest and Wilson were already engaged. The village itself is on a plateau lower than the line intrenched, and from it

---

[1] Statement of General Brown in General Cheatham's paper before referred to. Hood, however, in his Advance and Retreat, p. 294, speaks of a cordial understanding with Cleburne before he entered the battle.

nothing whatever could be seen. General Stanley, who had
been ill during the morning, had also his quarters on the
north of the Harpeth, with Wood's division.

A depression in front of Wagner's brigades and some scattered trees shut out Hood's lines from view at the Carter house,
but from Stiles's position they were plainly seen, formed apparently in double and triple lines of brigades, with artillery
in the intervals between the columns. Hood had placed
Cheatham's corps upon the Columbia turnpike with Cleburne's division on the east of the road, Brown's on the
west of it, and Bate's in échelon on Brown's flank. Stewart's
corps was on the right (east) of Cheatham, the order of his
divisions from Cleburne's flank being French, Walthall, and
Loring. Johnson's division was the only one of S. D. Lee's
corps which had yet come up, and it was kept in reserve.

Very few battlefields of the war were so free from obstruction to the view. Here, along a mile and a half of front, the
imposing array of the Confederate army could be seen advancing at quick step with trailed arms, the artillery in the
intervals galloping forward, unlimbering and firing as soon
as they were within range.[1] A section of artillery with Wagner's brigades first opened on the advancing enemy, but as
they approached it limbered up and deliberately trotted
within the principal line, in accordance with orders sent it
by the Chief of Artillery. It was now four o'clock, and to
the amazement of the thousands who were watching them,
Wagner's infantry opened fire. There was a rattling fusillade
for a few moments, Cleburne and Brown were checked for
an instant, but the Confederate forces passed the flanks of
Lane and Conrad, to right and left, a rush and a yell fol-

---

[1] Hood says he did not use artillery. That he is in error of recollection is
abundantly shown by reports and printed statements on both sides. The writer
speaks from his personal observation.

lowed, and the two hapless brigades came streaming to the rear in a disorganized crowd, running rapidly to reach the parapets behind them. Orders were quickly sent down the line to withhold the fire at the centre till our own men should be in, but to make the utmost use of the artillery and small arms on the flanks. Opdycke was warned to be ready for a rush to the centre if the line should give way there, and the second line along the whole front was similarly prepared. A few moments later, the head of the flying mass was seen swarming over the works at the turnpike, and orders were sent for all reserves to charge. The men in the trenches, confused by the crowd trampling over them, and hearing Wagner's officers calling upon their men to rally at the rear, were carried away by the surging mass, and for the length of a regiment on the left, and more than that on the right, they fell away from the works. Neither Colonel White, commanding Reilly's second line, nor Colonel Opdycke waited for the word to charge, but were in motion before the order could reach them. White was nearest the parapet and reached it soonest, but his line did not reach quite to the turnpike. The Carter house and out-buildings on the right of the road obstructed the movement to the front, and Opdycke made part of his brigade oblique to the left till clear of the obstacles, and they then charged head-long upon the enemy. Part also went forward on the west of the houses, and Strickland's brigade rallying with them, the Confederates were driven back here also ; but that the gap was open longer here than on the left, was proven by the enemy's dead who were found fifty yards within the lines.

Stanley, forgetting his illness, had mounted his horse at the first sound of the cannonade, and the commandants of the two corps met on the turnpike just as Opdycke and his men were rushing to the front. Four guns, which had been placed a few yards to the left of the road, were in the enemy's hands, and were loaded with canister. These were turned upon the flank of Reilly's line, but the frightened horses had run off with the ammunition chests which contained the primers, and while the captors were unsuccessfully trying to fire the pieces, the reserve was upon them. Four other guns on the right of the road were also in the enemy's hands. There was a few minutes' fierce mêlée, but the guns were retaken and all of the men in gray who were inside the parapet were dead or prisoners. Yet the successive lines of assailants charging the works allowed no respite. Colonel White received a severe wound in the face, but refused to leave the line till after nightfall, and Opdycke had joined personally in the thickest of the deadly tussle on the turn-pike. Our men, who had been driven back from the line, rallied by officers of all grades, returned to their posts, min-gling with those who were there, making a wall three or four deep, those in rear loading the muskets for those who were firing. While rallying these men Stanley was wounded, his horse was shot under him, and he was reluctantly per-suaded to return to his quarters for surgical help.

Farther to the right, and in part of what had been Strick-land's brigade line, the Confederates of Brown's division held the outside of our parapet, so that when their com-rades were driven back they were able to prevent our men from reaching it again. These, seizing upon fences and such material as came to hand, made a new barricade within about twenty-five yards of the first, and across the narrow interval the battle raged with most persistent fierceness. It was hard to tell where either brigade line ended, for Op-dycke's men mingled with Reilly's on the one side, and with Strickland's on the other, and the three crowded the space where two had been. Officers and men had been conscious that with the centre broken, nothing but superhuman exertions could keep one wing, at least, of the little army from being driven into the river. They were equal to the occasion and they saved the day.

But though the crisis of the engagement was at the centre, the fight was by no means all there. In other parts the veterans of the Atlanta campaign held their lines without flinching, though the assaults of Stewart's divisions rivalled those of Cheatham in their gallantry, and they made the most daring efforts to reach the bridges which were on that flank. Loring's men came upon the hedge in front of Stiles, and attempted in vain to tear it away, or to pass it. Henderson, who had been for some days ill, rejoined his brigade, and both he and Stiles directed the firing, which, sweeping along the ground, mowed down all before it. The Confederate officers urged their men to the right, hoping to pass through the railway cut, but here they were met by the shrapnel and canister of the guns in the fort north of the river. The batteries in Stiles's line were also admirably handled, and the attack here had never a chance.

On Casement's line, Walthall's and part of Loring's divisions made the assault, and as there was here no obstruction in front of the trench worth naming, the possibility of carrying such a line when properly held was fully tested. General John Adams led his brigade, riding straight at the ditch, leaping it, and mounting the parapet, where his horse was killed astride of it, and he himself pitched headlong among Casement's men, mortally wounded. Scott, commanding another of Loring's brigades, was wounded. In Walthall's division not only had Quarles fallen in leading his brigade to the assault, but the loss of officers was so great that, at the close of the battle, a captain was the rank-

ing officer in that brigade.[1] It was only when the last of
Stewart's reserves had tried all that courage and dash could
accomplish, that they relaxed their efforts.   Some asked
for quarter in the ditch, and came in as prisoners ; some lay
down in front of the hedge, and waited for darkness to
enable them to crawl away undiscovered.   The remainder
fell back to a position near the extension of the line Wagner's brigades had occupied.

Cleburne had led his division forward, on the east of the
central turnpike, with a desperation that was born of the
wounded feelings he had shown in the morning, and he fell
among the first who were at the ditch when the rush of our
reserves restored the line between the cotton-gin and the
road.   His three successive lines pressed forward to avenge
his death, but only to leave a thousand gallant officers and
men beside him.   On the other flank, Bate had moved forward his division at the same time with Brown, deploying as
he went.   His left reached beyond the Carter's Creek road
as he neared the intrenchments, but the shape of our lines,
which there bent back to the river, made him travel on a
large curve, and his assault was considerably later than
Brown's.   It struck the right of Ruger's division, and the
left of Kimball's, but finding the works before him stoutly
held, and that the cavalry which he expected to advance
upon his flank were not doing so, his attack was not pressed
as determinedly as that of Brown.   The success which this
division seemed to have at the first, and the fact that for
some distance they continued to hold the outside of the
works, encouraged them to the most desperate and persistent efforts there.   General Strahl was with his brigade in
the ditch, personally directing the fire of his men who got

---

[1] Walthall's official report.

a foothold in the outside of the slope, and making those in rear supply the front rank with loaded guns. As darkness came on, and it came quickly on that short winter day, the two breastworks, so little apart, were lines of continuous flame, as the men fired at the flash of each other's guns. On other parts of the field, there were, after dark, frequent vollies, as the Confederate generals strove to assist the central attack by strong demonstrations; but here the roar was for a long time incessant and deafening. Others suggested to Strahl to withdraw, or to surrender, but he steadily repeated the command, "keep firing," till he was himself struck down. He called for Colonel Stafford, to turn over the command, and they tried to carry him to the rear, but on the way a second and a third ball struck him, killing him instantly.[1] Colonel Stafford continued the contest with the same determination. Messengers were sent to General Brown to tell him of Strahl's death and ask for orders, but they found that he was already disabled by a wound, and the staff supposed Strahl to be in command of the division. Cheatham had sent in all of Brown's brigades, but Gordon had been captured in the first mêlée, Gist, as well as Strahl, was dead, and Carter was wounded. Hood was called upon for assistance, and he sent forward Johnson's division oi Lee's corps, but this, too, was driven back by that terrible fire, leaving General Manigault wounded on the field.

On the National side the One Hundred and Twelfth Illinois was brought over from Stiles's brigade, and put in to assist Strickland. An effort was made to get this regiment forward over the little interval between the two breastworks, but it was not successful. The oblique fire from our

---

[1] The details of the situation on the Confederate side at this point are chiefly drawn from a pamphlet by S. A. Cunningham, Sergeant-Major, entitled Reminiscences of the Forty-first Tennessee Regiment.

troops, on right and left, when they were not hotly engaged in front, was turned upon Cheatham's men, but it was nine o'clock before they gave up the contest, and those that were left were reformed on the line occupied by Stewart and Lee, though for more than an hour occasional volleys were exchanged. At eleven o'clock, the whole front being quiet, Schofield ordered the withdrawal of our troops to the north side of the river, but an accidental fire broke out in the village, making a bright background on which our lines could be too plainly seen by the enemy, and it was necessary to wait an hour till the fire was extinguished. Kimball's division then marched by the rear to the wagon bridge, Ruger's passed behind the lines to the railroad bridge, Opdycke's brigade was sent to follow Kimball, and Reilly's division crossed behind Ruger, a line of skirmishers, under command of Major Dow, Inspector-General, remaining in the trenches till all the rest were over and the plank taken from the wagon bridge, when these also crossed at the railway. The dead could not be removed, but the well disciplined ambulance corps, under Surgeon Frink, had taken off all the wounded who could endure transportation, except some who had crawled away into buildings and sheds and were not found in the darkness. Reilly's division carried off as trophies twenty-two battle flags of the enemy, and Opdycke's brigade ten.[1]

The battle had been peculiar, partly by reason of the late hour in the day at which it began, which prolonged the hard fighting far into the night, and partly from the character of the weather. A day or two of sunshine had followed the continuous storms of the preceding fortnight,

---

[1] Hood says that thirteen was the number of flags he lost, but the number stated above was officially reported by our division and brigade commanders and verified at the time.

and the air had been still and hazy. The smoke of the battle did not rise or drift away, but settled on the field in a thick cloud, obscuring the vision far more than common. It was said that this had led to the mistake, on Hood's part, of supposing that his first advantage at the centre was much greater than in fact it was, and resulted in greater destruction to the Confederate troops, by repeated assaults after all real chance of success was gone.

The Confederate accounts of the condition of the field next morning are full of tragic interest. Before daybreak it was learned that the National lines were empty, and the plain was covered with torchbearers seeking their comrades and friends. Colonel Stafford was found in the ditch General Strahl and he had so stubbornly held. The dead lay literally in a pile about him. They had fallen about his legs and behind him, till when he at last received a fatal shot, he did not wholly fall, but was found stiffened in death and partly upright, seeming still to command the ghastly line of his comrades lying beneath the parapet. The color-bearer of the Forty-first Tennessee had fallen between the two lines of breast-works, but neither friend nor foe had been able to reach the flag till it was hidden by the night, and in the morning it was found where it dropped.[1]

But even civil war rarely furnishes so sad a story as that which the Carter family have to tell. The house was occupied by an elderly man and his two daughters. Their presence during the day had been respected and had kept their property from unnecessary disturbance, and the day was so far gone that they thought there was no need to leave their home. The battle, when it came, broke upon them so suddenly that they did not dare to leave, and they took

---

[1] Sergeant-Major Cunningham's pamphlet.

refuge in the cellar. The house was in the focus of the storm which raged about it for hours. They said that while the horrid din lasted, it seemed that they must die of terror if it did not cease; but when there was a lull, the suspense of fearful expectation seemed worse than the din, and it was almost a relief when the combat was renewed. The long night ended at last, and with the first light the young women found relief in ministering to the wounded who had crept into the house and outbuildings, and in carrying water to those on the field. But, as they climbed the parapet at the rear of the house, among the first they found was a young staff officer, their own brother, mortally wounded, lying, as he had fallen at sunset, almost at the door of his home.

The withdrawal of Schofield's forces in the night left no opportunity to reckon the Confederate losses. Hood says that his casualties, computed ten days after the battle by means of the returns of "effective strength," were found to be 7,547 since the opening of this campaign, and including the losses about Columbia and Spring Hill. This, however, excludes all the slightly wounded who had returned to duty, and all officers, and makes no account of the accessions he had by the return of absentees and the joining of recruits. It still acknowledges a loss of 6,300 in this battle, of which 700 were prisoners in our hands. It is very certain that the whole Confederacy was deeply impressed with the frightful carnage of their troops, and their writers, with common accord, spoke of the desperate fighting as remarkable even in this war of desperate combats. The partial returns accessible seem to show clearly that no one of the divisions engaged (except Bate's), lost less than eight hundred, and that Brown's and Cleburne's, at the centre, and Loring's, on our left, lost much more heavily. The long list of general officers killed and wounded gives terrible significance to the recriminations which the affair at Spring Hill had excited. We have seen that Brown and all four of his brigadiers were disabled or killed. In Cleburne's division, Granberry besides himself fell. In Loring's division they lost Generals John Adams and Scott. In French's, Cockrell; in Walthall's, Quarles; and in Johnson's, Manigault; twelve generals in all, besides Stafford, and a long list of colonels and field officers who succeeded to brigade commands.

On the National side the losses were 2,326, of which more than one thousand were in the two brigades of Wagner, which were so unnecessarily compromised at the front. Near the centre, where the line was temporarily broken, the losses were naturally much heavier than on the flanks, where our men stoutly held the breastworks and fought under good cover. The result well illustrates the fearful odds at which the bravest troops assault a line of earthworks over open ground, even when a grave fault of a subordinate has given them an exceptional and unlooked-for advantage. General Wagner's place of duty was with the two brigades of his division which were exposed in front, and the order to bring them in without fighting had been sent through the Fourth Corps' head-quarters, and had been received by him. He was at the Carter house when the message came from the front that Hood was forming in line of battle, and, in a moment of excitement, forgetting himself and his orders, he sent back a command to fight.[1] The overwhelming of the two brigades and the peril to the whole line were the necessary consequence. He rallied the disorganized brigades at the river, but they were not again carried into action.

During the battle and in preparation for any contingency

---

[1] This is stated to the writer by two officers who were present and heard it.

which might arise, General Schofield directed General
Wood to put the three brigades of his division in position to
cover the flanks of the troops in front of the town, and to
protect the bridges in case of need. Wood accordingly
placed Post's brigade opposite Kimball's flank, below the
town, Streight's near the bridges, and Beatty's above Fort
Granger, all on the high ground of the north bank of the
Harpeth; and these brigades maintained their position in
the night till the rest of the infantry had passed through
their lines and marched to Brentwood. General Wilson,
with the cavalry, had, during the afternoon, a warm skirmish
with Forrest, who tried in vain to cross the Harpeth beyond
the left of Schofield's forces. Thomas sent a warm con-
gratulatory despatch when the result of the engagement was
announced to him ; but, as he thought three days would still
be needed to prepare his concentrated army for aggressive
operations, and as this was a longer time than Schofield
could engage to hold the line of the Harpeth without reinforcements, he directed the latter to retire upon Brentwood,
and thence to Nashville.[1] Despatches had been sent to
General Cooper, who, it will be remembered, had been
stationed at Centreville, on Duck River, with a brigade of the
Twenty-third Corps, directing him to fall back on Franklin.
But unavoidable delays occurred, and when he approached
Franklin, the enemy was in possession. He was similarly
anticipated at Brentwood, but by coolness and good conduct
brought in his command safely to Nashville.

---

[1] For correspondence between these officers on November 29th and 30th, see
Appendix D.

CHAPTER VI.

BATTLE OF NASHVILLE.

SCHOFIELD's little army reached Nashville in the morning of December 1st, and was merged in the forces which General Thomas was assembling there. General A. J. Smith, after many unforeseen delays, had arrived with his detachments from the Army of the Tennessee, consisting of three divisions, aggregating nearly twelve thousand men. Of these, something over nine thousand men reached Nashville early in the morning of November 30th, and the rest on the next day. The first intention of General Thomas had been to meet Schofield at Brentwood, ten miles in front of Nashville, with these troops, while Schofield marched the ten miles from Franklin to the same point; but he concluded later to make the union at Nashville. When he received from Schofield and from Wilson the reports of Hood's movement of the 28th and 29th, by which the cavalry had been separated from Schofield, and Forrest was reported pushing eastward, he ordered Steedman to leave a garrison in Chattanooga and take his other available forces to Cowan, a station near Elk River, on the Nashville and Chattanooga Railway. Steedman reached there on the morning of the 30th and put his troops in position; but in the evening, Thomas, having learned of Hood's attack in force upon Schofield at Franklin, ordered Steedman to hasten to Nashville. The troops were accordingly put upon the railway trains again, and most of them reached their destination safely on the evening of December 1st. One train, being delayed by an accident, did not arrive till the 2d, and was attacked by Forrest five miles south of Nashville, but the troops made their way through without serious loss, though the train was captured and destroyed. Of the 8,000 men who had been at Chattanooga on the 30th, Steedman brought with him 5,200, consisting of two brigades of colored troops, and a provisional division made up of soldiers belonging to the army with Sherman, but who had arrived at the front too late to rejoin their own regiments.

Most of the troops under General R. S. Granger, in North Alabama, and of those under General Milroy, at Tullahoma, were ordered to Murfreesboro, where the whole, amounting to about eight thousand men, were placed under command of General Rousseau, and remained until after Hood's defeat on December 15th and 16th. The block-house garrison, at the important railroad bridge on the Elk River, was the only considerable detachment left along the line of the Chattanooga Road, between Murfreesboro and Stevenson.

In Nashville, on November 30th, besides Smith's forces, Thomas had about six thousand infantry and artillery, and three thousand cavalry, mostly dismounted.[1] The Chief Quartermaster, General Donaldson, had also armed and organized into a division the employés of his and the commissary department, and these were prepared to serve as an addition to the garrison when needed. The new regiments which arrived were gradually assigned to the old divisions,

---

[1] By the table in Appendix A, it will be seen that the cavalry "present for duty" were 10,884, of which 2,272 were not "equipped," i e., were dismounted. I have not been able to procure the exact figures showing how many were with Wilson in the field, and what other small detachments there might be. The infantry would be the difference between 14,000 and the number at Murfreesboro. See Appendix A.

and the additions to the list of Sherman's convalescents and returning men were united to those who had come with Steedman, making, by December 14th, a division of over five thousand men, under command of General Cruft.

Accepting Hood's statements of his losses thus far in the campaign, the army which he led against Nashville consisted of about forty-four thousand men of all arms.[1] His means of information were such that he had pretty full knowledge of the concentration Thomas was now effecting, and the motives which induced a march to Nashville are matters of interesting inquiry. Beauregard, in his preliminary report to the Confederate War Department, said : "It is clear to my mind that after the great loss of life at Franklin, the army was no longer in a condition to make a successful attack on Nashville." Hood's own statement, which would be entitled to the greatest weight if his subsequent writings were not so full of evidence that they are labored apologies for his misfortunes, is that he expected reinforcements from Texas, and that he hoped by intrenching near Nashville he could maintain himself in a defensive attitude till these should arrive ; or that he might even take advantage of a reverse to Thomas, if the latter should be beaten in an attack upon his fortified line. The hope of aid from Texas was a forlorn one, for no organized body of Confederates had for a long time succeeded in passing the Mississippi River. From other sources, however, we learn that the show of confidence and of success was relied upon to induce recruiting in Tennessee, and that the pretended Governor, Harris, was with Hood, endeavoring to enforce the conscription in that State. This, and the collection of supplies, give an intelligible reason for occupying as much territory as possible,

---

[1] See Appendix A.

and for an appearance of bravado which could hardly be justified on military grounds. Doubtless, too, Hood believed that while his veterans might be forced to retreat, they could not be routed; and he underestimated the discouragement that began to pervade them when they were taught, by the terrible lesson of Franklin, how hopeless was that dream of conquest with which their leaders had tried to inspire them when they crossed the Tennessee. Hood also says he learned that Schofield retreated in alarm; but never was a greater mistake. Schofield's officers on the line had reported their perfect confidence in their ability to hold it, and the withdrawal from the Harpeth had been based solely on the probability of the position being turned before reinforcements could be sure to arrive.

In truth, Hood's situation was a very difficult one, and to go forward or to go back was almost equally unpromising. He followed his natural bent, therefore, which always favored the appearance, at least, of aggression, and he marched after Schofield to Nashville. On approaching the town, he put Lee's corps in the centre, across the Franklin turnpike, for it had suffered least in the campaign, and was now his strongest corps. Cheatham took the right, and Stewart the left of the line, while Forrest, with the cavalry, occupied the country between Stewart and the river below Nashville. Attempts were made to repair the railway from Corinth to Decatur, and thence by Pulaski to Hood's rear. Hood tells us that he gained possession of two locomotives and several cars (perhaps at Spring Hill), and that these were used to help transport supplies.

Thomas put his troops in position upon the heights surrounding Nashville, General Smith's divisions on the right, the Fourth Corps (General Wood temporarily commanding) in the centre, and Schofield's Twenty-third Corps on the left. Steedman, who arrived later, was first put on the Nolensville road, about a mile in front of Schofield's left, but was placed on the extension of Schofield's line a day or two later, when Wilson, with the cavalry, were sent over the river to Edgefield, on the north bank.

On December 2d, Hood sent Bate's division of Cheatham's corps to destroy the railroad between Nashville and Murfreesboro. Bate reached Overall's Creek, ten miles from Murfreesboro, and attacked the block-house protecting the railway bridge there; but the little garrison held out against a severe cannonade till General Milroy arrived with reinforcements from Murfreesboro, and drove the enemy off. Bate now took the road toward Nashville, and at Stewart's Creek and two other places in that neighborhood, found the block-houses evacuated, and burned them with the bridges they were built to protect. He also reported that he had torn up several miles of track. Forrest, meanwhile, who had been directed to co-operate with Bate, had sent Buford's division against the block-houses nearest Nashville, and succeeded in reducing three of them near Mill Creek, beginning with one five miles from the city. On the 5th he united Jackson's division with Buford's, and moving toward Lavergne took two more block-houses. He now met Bate, who was moving in the opposite direction, and turned the united forces upon Murfreesboro. Here, on the evening of the 6th, he was further reinforced by Sears's brigade of French's division, and Palmer's brigade of Stevenson's, and on next morning approached the town, reconnoitring the fortifications in person. Rousseau now sent Milroy against the enemy, with seven regiments, and these attacked vigorously the left flank of Forrest's infantry, while they were moving by his orders in the same direction for the purpose of taking ground farther to the left.

Milroy's attack fell obliquely upon the extremity of Bate's line, which was quickly rolled up and put to rout, losing two pieces of artillery.   Bate admits 213 casualties in the infantry, but those of the cavalry are not given.   Milroy took 207 prisoners, and his own losses in the affair were 30 killed, and 175 wounded.   Meanwhile, Buford's division attempted to enter the town by another road, but was also defeated and driven off.

Bate's division was now recalled to Nashville, and replaced by a brigade under Colonel Olmstead (formerly Mercer's) so that Forrest retained three brigades of infantry as a support for his cavalry.   He continued till the 15th to operate on the east of Nashville, and along the south bank of the Cumberland, part of his duty being to " drain the country of persons liable to military service, animals suitable for army purposes, and subsistence supplies." [1]   On the 15th Jackson's division captured a railway train of supplies going from Stevenson to Murfreesboro, for the garrison there, who, it would seem, must have been in danger of running short of rations, since the breaking of their communications with Nashville.

At Thomas's request, Lieutenant-Commander Fitch patrolled the Cumberland with gunboats above and below Nashville, to prevent the crossing of that stream by the enemy, and Wilson sent Hammond's brigade of cavalry to Gallatin to watch the north bank of the river as far as Carthage.

From the time of Hood's arrival in front of Nashville, the President and Secretary of War became very urgent in their desire that Thomas should at once assume the aggressive.

---

[1] Campaigns of Forrest, p. 634.   Thomas's report puts the affair at Murfreesboro on the 8th, but both Bate's report and Forrest's biographers say it was the 7th.

At their suggestion, General Grant telegraphed on December 2, advising Thomas to leave the defences of Nashville to General Donaldson's organized employés, and attack Hood at once. Grant's language was scarcely less imperative than an order, but Thomas was so desirous of increasing his force of mounted men that he determined to wait a few days. On the 8th, the weather, which had been good for more than a week, suddenly changed. A freezing storm of snow and sleet covered the ground, and for two or three days the alternations of rain and frost made the hills about Nashville slopes of slippery ice, on which movement was impracticable. As Hood's positions could only be reached by deployed lines advancing over these hills and hollows, everybody in Thomas's army felt the absolute necessity of now waiting a little longer, till the ice should thaw. This was not fully appreciated by the authorities at Washington, who connected it too closely with Thomas's previous wish for more time, and a rapid correspondence by telegraph took place, in which Thomas was ordered to attack at once or to turn over his command to General Schofield. He assembled his corps commanders and asked their advice, saying that he was ordered to give Hood battle immediately or surrender his command. To whom the army would be transferred was not stated, but it was matter of inference, and he declined to submit the despatch itself to the council of war, though one of the junior officers intimated a wish to know its terms. By the custom of such councils the opinion of officers is given in the inverse order of their grade; but General Schofield, feeling the delicacy of his position as senior subordinate, volunteered his own opinion first, that till the ice should melt it was not now practicable to move.[1]

[1] In the account of this meeting, the author follows a written statement of General Schofield.

All concurred in this, and Thomas telegraphed Grant that he felt compelled to wait till the storm should break, but would submit without a murmur if it was thought necessary to relieve him. On the 13th, General Logan, who, it will be remembered, was temporarily absent from the Fifteenth Corps, was ordered to Nashville for the purpose of superseding Thomas in command of the Department and Army of the Cumberland, and Grant himself was on the way there also, when the result of the first day of the battle of Nashville (December 15th) stopped further action in that direction.

As early as December 6th, the troops had been ordered to be ready to move against the enemy, and the plan of battle afterward adopted had been in substance determined. From day to day Hood appeared to be taking ground to the east, so as to bring himself more closely into support of Forrest's operations. This led to a suggestion to Thomas from his corps commanders to modify his plan which had looked to the use of the Twenty-third Corps to demonstrate on the left, and give more weight to an attack by the right. From the 8th to the 14th, it was definitely understood in camp that an attack would be made the moment the ice melted, and on the date last mentioned a warm rain made it certain the ground would be bare next day. The position of Hood had not materially changed for a week. Chalmers was operating with a division of cavalry along the Cumberland, for some miles below Nashville, as Buford was above; but, while ordinary steamboat transportation was thus interrupted, the navy patrolled the river and prevented the enemy from crossing. Hood had sent a detachment of cavalry also, supported by Cockrell's brigade of infantry to the mouth of Duck River, on the Tennessee, to blockade that stream also, if possible. In his anxiety to cover so large a territory, the

Confederate general was too much extended, and in front of Thomas's right his flank was only covered by Chalmers's division of horse. To make some connection with the river on this side, he had built a number of detached works, but these were not completed, though he had put artillery in them, supported by detachments of infantry from Walthall's division. Reports brought in by deserters indicated that he was intending to withdraw from his advanced lines since the 10th, but the same causes which prevented Thomas from moving, affected him also, and a change of quarters, to his ill-clad and poorly shod troops, would have been the cause of much suffering, if it were made during the severe weather of that week.

On the morning of the 15th a heavy fog obscured the dawn and hid the early movements of Thomas's army. The ice had given place to mud, and the manœuvres, like those of all winter campaigns, were slow. The modified order of the day directed a strong demonstration by Steedman on the extreme left, with two brigades; one commanded by Colonel Grosvenor, Eighteenth Ohio, and the other (colored troops) commanded by Colonel Morgan, Fourteenth United States Colored. General Wood, with the Fourth Corps, and General Smith, with the Sixteenth Corps, were ordered to form upon a position nearly continuous with the eastern line of the city defences, extending from a salient on the Acklen place across the Hillsborough turnpike toward the Hardin turnpike in a southwest direction. Advancing toward the southeast these corps would make the principal attack obliquely upon the left of Hood's line. General Wilson, with three divisions of cavalry, was ordered to clear the Hardin and Charlotte turnpikes of the enemy (still farther to the west) and move forward on the right of Smith's corps. General Schofield, with the Twenty-third Corps, constituted the reserve, and was placed in rear of Wood, to strengthen and extend the attack on the right. As Smith had occupied the fortifications on the right of the line about the city, these orders would be executed by wheeling the whole of both corps forward to the left, upon the salient at the Acklen place as a pivot, after Wood had taken ground to the right by the distance of say half a mile, so as to bring his left flank at the point named. Schofield, who had been in the fortifications still to the left of Wood, marched from his lines at daybreak, and passing through the works at the Hillsborough road moved to the east into the position assigned him, as soon as the wheel of the right wing made room for him. The interior lines at the city were held by General Donaldson's men, while General Cruft, with his division, occupied those from which Schofield and Steedman moved.

Standing in the salient in Wood's line, which has been mentioned, the topography of the country about Nashville is clearly seen. On the left, toward the east, is a valley in which Brown's Creek flows north into the Cumberland. It rises in the high Brentwood Hills, which shut out the view toward the south a little more than four miles away, and its course is nearly parallel to the eastern line of Thomas's intrenchments. On the right, but a little farther off, is Richland Creek, flowing northwest into the Cumberland. It rises also in the Brentwood Hills, not more than a mile west of Brown's Creek, and runs nearly parallel with it toward the city for some distance, when the two curve away to right and left, encircling the place, and marking its strong and natural line of defence. On the high ridge between the creeks is the Granny White turnpike. A mile eastward is the Franklin turnpike, diverging about thirty degrees. At nearly equal distances, on that side, the Nolensville and

Murfreesboro turnpikes leave the city successively. Turning toward the west from our station, the Hillsboro, the Hardin, and the Charlotte turnpikes successively go out at

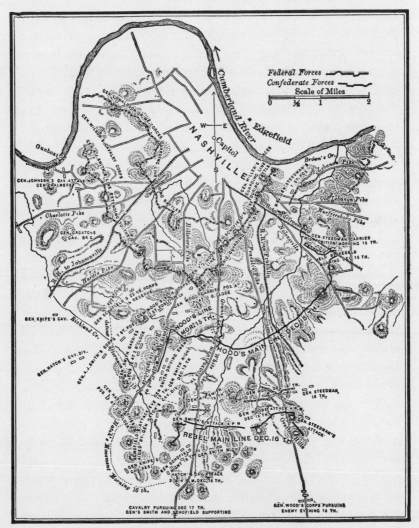

Map of Battle-Field of Nashville.

similar angles, all radiating from the centre of the town.
The ground is hilly, rising into knobs and eminences two or
three hundred feet above the Cumberland, but mostly open,
with groves of timber here and there.

Hood's line was over Brown's Creek, on the high ground
from the Nolensville turnpike and the Chattanooga railway
to the Franklin turnpike, then crossing the creek and
mounting a high hill west of it, it extended to the Hillsboro
road, where it turned back along a stone wall on the side of
the turnpike. The detached works, of which mention has
been made, were still to the southwest of this, and across
Richland Creek. The relative places of his several corps
were the same as when he first came before the town. His
main line at his left, where it reached the Hillsboro pike, was
about a mile in front of Wood, but he also occupied an advanced line with skirmishers, only half that distance away,
and terminating in a strong outpost on Montgomery Hill, at
the Hillsboro road.

Before six o'clock in the morning Steedman was moving
forward under cover of the fog by the Murfreesboro road, on
the extreme left, and about eight he attacked Hood's right
between the turnpike and the railway. The vigor of the assault made it something more than a demonstration, and the
rapid fire of both artillery and small arms attracted the attention of the enemy in that direction. The distance Smith's
right wing had to move was found to be greater than had
been reckoned on, and it was ten o'clock before McArthur's
division had moved sufficiently to the left to open the way
for Wilson's cavalry to advance upon the Hardin road.
Johnson's division moved forward on the Charlotte turnpike, looking also after the enemy's battery at Bell's Landing, on the Cumberland; Croxton's brigade took the interval
to the Hardin turnpike, Hatch's division continued the line

to the flank of Smith's infantry, and Knipe's division was in reserve. Smith formed the Sixteenth Corps with Garrard's division on his left, connecting with the Fourth Corps, and McArthur's division on the right. The division of Moore was in reserve. On the other side Chalmers did what he could to oppose them, supported by Coleman's (formerly Ector's) brigade of infantry,[1] but the odds was too great, and they were driven steadily back. Half a mile southeast of the Hardin road the first of Hood's detached works, containing four guns, was found. The batteries of McArthur and Hatch were brought to bear upon it from all sides, and, after a severe cannonade, McMillan's and Hubbard's brigades of infantry and Coon's of cavalry (dismounted) attacked and carried the redoubt.[2] Stewart now recalled Coleman and directed him to report to Walthall, whose division occupied the stone wall bordering the Hillsboro turnpike. Walthall placed him on the extension of his line southward, upon some high points covering the Granny White road. This left the other redoubts to their fate, as Chalmers was far too much over-matched to make much resistance with his cavalry. He had been driven back so fast that his train, with his headquarters baggage and papers, had been captured. The next redoubt, about four hundred yards to the right, was carried by the same troops, and two guns in it were taken. Another four-gun battery, intrenched on a detached hill, was stormed and captured by the cavalry, and a two-gun battery by Hill's brigade of McArthur's division, though with the loss of Colonel Hill, who fell in the

---

[1] This was of French's division, but French seems to have been absent, and his brigades were separately used as occasion required. Sears's had been recalled from Forrest, and was temporarily reporting to Walthall.

[2] Smith and Wilson each claim for their men the honors in the attack of all these works, but in such a combined movement it is vain to discriminate minutely as to the exact credit due each brigade.

moment of success. Smith's corps now bore somewhat to
the left, striking the extreme flank of the stone wall held by
Walthall's division, driving Reynolds's brigade from it in confusion. At the same time, Schofield, who had followed the
movement closely with the Twenty-third Corps, in accordance with Thomas's order, pushed Couch's division (formerly
Cooper's) past Smith's flank, and beyond the last redoubt
which had been captured. Now advancing on the line from
the Hillsboro road, eastward, across an open valley half a
mile wide, Couch assaulted and carried the left of a series
of hills parallel to the Granny White turnpike. The assault was made by Cooper's brigade, and the rest of the
division was quickly brought up in support, while Cox's
division marched still farther to the right and occupied the
continuation of the line of hills along Richland Creek with
two brigades, keeping the third (Stiles's) on the heights west
of the creek to cover the flank.

These last movements had occurred just as darkness was
falling, and completed the day's work on the extreme right.
It is now necesaary to go back and trace the progress of the
Fourth Corps. General Wood had formed the corps with
Elliott's division (formerly Wagner's) on the right, connecting with Smith's corps, while Kimball's and Beatty's extended the line to the left. The time occupied in the deployed
movement of the right of the army made it one o'clock before it was time for the extreme left to move. Wood then
ordered forward Post's brigade of Beatty's division to attack
Montgomery Hill, the high point half a mile in front of the
salient of our line, on which was Hood's advanced guard.
The assault was preceded by rapid artillery fire and was
gallantly executed. The general advance of the line was
now progressing, and Schofield's corps was ordered away by
General Thomas to support the movement of the right flank.

Wood met with a strong skirmishing resistance, but the lines went forward steadily, keeping pace with the troops on the right, till Smith's attack upon the south end of the stone wall along the Hillsboro road, which was held by Walthall. Kimball's division was opposite the angle in Hood's line where Walthall joined upon Loring, having Sears's brigade of French's division between them. Kimball pushed straight at the angle, and the right of the stone wall having already been carried, Walthall's brigades, under Johnson (formerly Quarles's) and Shelley, successively gave way. Elliott's division of Wood's corps lapped upon Garrard's of the Sixteenth, and the whole went forward with enthusiasm, capturing several guns and many prisoners.

Hood's left was now hopelessly broken, and he made haste to draw back his shattered divisions upon a new line. Schofield's advance had separated Coleman's brigade from Walthall, but it occupied a commanding hill (afterward known as Shy's Hill),[1] and held on with tenacity till Walthall, helped by the gathering darkness, could form along its right across the Granny White road. At the first news of the loss of the redoubts, Hood ordered Cheatham's corps (except Smith's, formerly Cleburne's division) from the right to the left, and his divisions, hurrying by the Franklin pike toward Overton's Hill, passed great numbers of stragglers streaming to the rear. Bate was ordered to relieve part of Walthall's division, so as to make a stronger line between Shy's Hill and the Granny White road, and Walthall closed to the right upon Loring. South of Shy's Hill, Lowry's (formerly Brown's) division extended the Confederate left in front of Schofield, and the whole worked diligently to intrench themselves. Lee's corps was drawn back till his right en-

---

[1] This name is given the hill by General Bate, whose troops held it, in honor of Colonel Shy who fell there. It seems to have had no special name before.

circled Overton's Hill, on which Clayton's division was placed, supported by Brantley's brigade, while Stevenson's and Johnson's divisions extended the line to the west till it united with Loring's division of Stewart's corps.

On our left Steedman had kept his men active. He had attacked and carried an earthwork near the Raines house early in the day, and had followed up the progressive movement of the army, harassing the enemy's right as it drew back.

About nightfall there was a strong appearance of a precipitate retreat of the enemy, and Thomas ordered Wood to move his corps farther to the left, reaching the Franklin turnpike, if possible, and to push southward upon it. This direction was a wise one if the enemy continued his retreat, for it prevented the crowding of the army upon a single road ; but had Thomas been sure that Hood would reform upon the new line, he would, no doubt, have continued the general movement of the day by extending his forces to the right. The darkness stopped Wood before he had reached the Franklin road, and he bivouacked where night overtook him, ready to continue the march in the morning. His right was near Smith's left, and his own left was diagonally toward the rear, in the works which Lee's corps had abandoned on the hither side of Brown's Creek.

For the results obtained, the losses had been astonishingly light. Wood reports only three hundred and fifty casualties in his corps, Smith's were about the same, and Schofield's not over one hundred and fifty. Those of Steedman and of Wilson were proportionately small, though the exact figures cannot be given, as the losses of the first and second days are not discriminated in any report but Wood's. Sixteen pieces of artillery and twelve hundred prisoners had been taken, and Hood's whole line had been driven back fully two miles. The work was not completed, but should the enemy maintain his position, the promise for the morrow was good.

Hood now realized the mistake his over-confidence had led him into, by inducing him not only to extend his lines beyond what was prudent, but, worst of all, to allow Forrest to become so far detached that he could not be recalled in time for the battle. Sears's brigade had been brought back to the lines before the 15th, but two others were still with Forrest, and Cockrell's was at Duck River. The Confederate commander set to work in earnest, however, to repair his mistake. The cavalry was too far away to join him in twenty-four hours, but orders were despatched recalling Forrest, and preparations were made to hold the new line another day. As his left still seemed his weak point, Hood ordered the whole of Cheatham's corps to that flank. Shy's Hill, which was held by Coleman's brigade, made the angle in the line, from which the sharply refused flank continued southward, Lowry's division and Smith's (formerly Cleburne's) extending it to the Brentwood Hills. Bate's division was placed, as we have already seen, between Shy's Hill and the flank of Stewart's corps, facing north. Chalmers's division of cavalry was close upon the left of the infantry, bending the line back, somewhat, toward the Granny White road.

The Confederate line now rested upon high hills, Overton's and Shy's, between which the ground was lower, though rolling, and was broken by the upper branches of Brown's Creek, which ran in nearly straight courses northward, crossing Hood's position at right angles. Overton's hill was a broad, rounded elevation, and the works, in curving southward around its summit, did not present any sharp angle to weaken their strength. Shy's Hill, however, though

high, was of less extent, and the lines of Bate and Lowry
made a right angle there.   Bate complained of the position,
but Hood's engineers had established it, and Cheatham did
not feel at liberty to change it.   Indeed, it could not have
been changed much, unless the whole Confederate army
were to retreat.   Coleman had been driven to Shy's Hill by
Schofield's advance at dusk, and had all he could do to hold
on to it at all.   The extension of the Twenty-third Corps
along the east side of Richland Creek left only the hills
directly south of Shy's unoccupied, and it was there alone
that the advance of Thomas's right wing could be checked.
The National skirmish lines were so close that the digging had
to be done on the inside of the parapet chiefly, getting cover
for the men as soon as possible.   The hill on our side, held
by Couch's division, was only three hundred yards from
Shy's, and the work on the latter, built under fire, was weak.
Farther south, the confronting hills, held by the rest of
Cheatham's corps on the one side, and Schofield's on the
other, were farther apart, and that in the Confederate line
was considerably higher and well wooded on the top.   A
strong work was made upon it, revetted with timber, with
embrasures for cannon, and a parapet high enough to defi-
lade the interior; but the fire of our sharpshooters prevented
any abatis being made.

General Thomas held a council with his corps commanders
in the evening, but no new orders seem to have been issued,
except some directions as to movements in the event of a
retreat of Hood during the night.   If he remained in position, the movements progressing at the close of the day
would be continued.   During the night the lines on the
National side also were adjusted.   In Schofield's corps,
Couch's division, in making connection with Smith, opened
a gap between it and Cox's division, which, after extending

the two brigades, which were over Richland Creek, in single line, without reserves, was still unable to join Couch's left by as much as three hundred yards. The disadvantage of drawing in and contracting the extension of the right flank was so manifest, that, upon the report of the fact, Schofield applied to Smith for some of his reserves to complete the line, and at six o'clock in the morning, Colonel Moore reported with five regiments and a battery, and was placed there.[1] Three of the regiments were put in the trenches already there, and two in support of the artillery in rear.

At the same hour, Wood resumed the movement of the Fourth Corps, which had been interrupted in the evening, and Steedman advanced upon the Nolensville road to the abandoned line of the Confederate works, where he half wheeled to the right and came up on Wood's left. The latter first formed his corps with Beatty's division on the left of the Franklin road, and Kimball's on the right, with Elliott in reserve ; but finding a large space vacant between himself and the centre of the army, he moved Elliott's division forward into line continuous with Smith's corps. The left of the Fourth Corps, where it now connected with Steedman, remained across the Franklin road, and opposite Overton's Hill, where Hood's line bent back to the south. The National line, therefore, instead of being oblique to the enemy, and far outreaching it on the right, as on the previous day, was parallel and exterior to it from flank to flank, nowhere reaching beyond it, except where Wilson's cavalry was operating beyond Schofield on the Hillsboro road.

About noon, Steedman's troops formed a connection with Wood's, and the latter, by order of General Thomas, took direction of both. Along the whole line the skirmishers

---

[1] In Smith's report this is spoken of by mistake as Moore's division, but it was, in fact, only part of his division.

were advanced close to the enemy's works, and various
points were reconnoitred to determine the feasibility of an
assault. Thomas did not order an attack upon the intrenchments, but left the corps commanders to their own discretion in this respect. Wood concentrated his artillery fire
upon Overton's Hill, Smith and Schofield maintained a severe cross-fire upon the angle at Shy's Hill, and at other
points on the line the opposing batteries were warmly engaged.

Finding that the enemy was strongly intrenched in
Wood's front, General Thomas rode to Smith, and learned
the results of the reconnoissance there, and, after examining
for himself the position, continued on to Schofield's lines
on the right. Schofield had ordered Stiles's brigade of
Cox's division to leave its position in rear of the extreme
right and march farther south, then, turning to the east,
to push forward upon a wooded hill on the extension of
the line of the division. Thence he was to keep pace with
the advance of Wilson's dismounted cavalry, and attack with
the rest of the line when it should go forward. The termination of the Confederate continuous works in Cheatham's
line, was the embrasured earthwork already referred to,
with a recurved flank facing the south. A four-gun battery,
of smooth twelve-pound guns, was in this fort, with four
more in the curtain connecting it with Shy's Hill. The
rifled guns of Cockerell's battery, on the west side of Richland Creek, were able to reach the embrasures of the work in
front, while the shells of the smooth guns fell short in the
efforts at reply, and the superiority of the National artillery
was such that the Confederate gunners were forced to reload their pieces, by drawing them aside with the *prolonge*,
to the protection of the parapet.

On learning the nature of the works in front of Schofield,

and the extent of the enemy's line, Thomas ordered Smith to send one of his divisions to extend that flank, but on representations as to the condition of affairs in Smith's front, the order was withdrawn.

Wilson, however, was making good progress with his cavalry, which must now be traced. Johnson's division had not felt strong enough to attack the position of Chalmers, near Bell's Landing, on the 15th, and Wilson's movements had been made with the rest of the corps. The concentration of Chalmers's division in the night, enabled Wilson to bring Johnson up in the morning, and he now had all three of his divisions in hand. Hammond's had pickets toward the Granny White turnpike, in rear of Hood's left, Hatch's division was ordered to move from his bivouac on the Hillsboro road, on the left of Hammond, and upon the enemy's rear. Johnson was moving across the country from near Bell's Landing. By noon, or shortly after, Wilson's skirmishers formed a continuous curved line from Schofield's right around the enemy's flank across the Granny White road. It was at this time that Schofield ordered the movement of Stiles's brigade, which has been mentioned, and had suggested the desirability of sending a full division of infantry beyond Hood's flank, if one could be spared from the line. He did not think it wise to assault the heavy work in front of Cox's division, except in connection with a general advance.

The situation at the angle on Shy's Hill, however, was opening the prospect of a successful attack there. The advance of Wilson's dismounted cavalry from one wooded hill to another on the south, was making Hood uneasy, and his vehement exhortation to Chalmers, to hold his own, not being enough to overcome the odds against that officer, he was forced to withdraw Govan's brigade from Cheatham's

line, and send it to Chalmers's support. Bate was ordered
to extend his left, and occupy Shy's Hill, while Coleman,
who had been there, was sent to fill Govan's place. Bate's
line was now a good deal stretched, and he found also that
the earthworks built in the night were too far back from
the brow of the hill, so that they did not command its slope.
The fire upon it was too hot to change it, he could get no
reinforcements, and he could only hold on to the last.
Bate's own words best describe his situation in the afternoon :
" The enemy, he says, opened a most terrific fire of artillery,
and kept it up during the day. In the afternoon, he planted
a battery in the woods, in the rear of Mrs. Bradford's house
(this was in McArthur's line), fired directly across both lines
composing the angle, and threw shells directly in the back
of my left brigade ; also placed a battery on a hill diagonally to my left, which took my first brigade in reverse.
(This was in Cox's line.) The batteries on the hill, in its
front, not more than three hundred yards distant (in Couch's
line) had borne the concentrated fire of my Whitworth
rifles all day, and must have suffered heavily, but were not
silenced. These rifled guns of the enemy being so close,
razed the works on the left of the angle for fifty or sixty
yards." [1]

General McArthur, from his position, was able to see
something of the mischief done to Bate's line, and reported
that an assault upon the angle was practicable. He proposed to move McMillan's brigade to the right, in front of
the hill held by Couch, and to charge under the cover of
Couch's guns, where the hillside gave most protection to an
advance. Thomas approved the plan, and Smith sent to
Schofield for directions to Couch to co-operate. Schofield

---

[1] General Bate's official report.

acceded to this, and directed Cox also to attack the hill in his front simultaneously, while Stiles should advance beyond the flank with the cavalry. It was now near four o'clock, and Thomas was in person at Schofield's position, from which Shy's Hill, and the whole range south, to the Brentwood Hills, were in full view.

The whole connection of events will be best understood if we now return to the left flank, where Wood had been making anxious examination of the enemy's position on Overton's Hill, and upon the report of a reconnoissance by Colonel Post, had determined to try the chances of an attack there. The assault from the Fourth Corps' position was assigned to Post's brigade of Beatty's division, supported by Streight's. Thompson's colored brigade, of Steedman's command, supported by Grosvenor's brigade, were to attack at the same time from the east. A concentrated artillery fire upon the hill preceded the assault, and at three o'clock the order to advance was given. A cloud of skirmishers ran forward to draw the enemy's fire and to annoy the artillerists in the works, and the brigades in line followed them. Nearing the intrenchments, they rushed forward, some of the men gaining the parapet, but they were received with so hot a fire, that they could not endure it, and after a short, sharp struggle they recoiled. Their retreat was covered by the rest of Beatty's division and Steedman's reserves, and by the artillery. These were so handled that the enemy did not venture from his works, and our wounded were brought safely off; but the casualties were probably half of all that occurred in the battle, adding another to the many proofs of the terrible disadvantage at which a direct assault of a well intrenched line is usually made. Colonel Post was wounded, and the loss in officers was heavy, for they exposed themselves fearlessly in leading their men.

At the angle in the Confederate works held by Bate, at Shy's Hill, the circumstances were different. His lines, as we have seen, were enfiladed and taken in reverse; his parapet was levelled for some distance; the closeness of Couch's batteries, the near approach of our skirmishers, the attenuation of Bate's troops, the cover for the approach of the assailing force under the hill-slope, all combined to neutralize the advantage of modern weapons, and to give the assault the preponderance of chances which justify it. While the fire upon the angle was kept up with increasing severity, McArthur ordered Colonel McMillan to form his brigade in the hollow before Couch's works, and when they should be half-way up the hill, the brigades to the left were to advance in *échelon*, attacking the lower line before them.

Wilson's dismounted cavalry had been advancing from the south, gaining position after position, and increasing their ardor as they advanced. Their numbers enabled them to outflank Govan's brigade, which Hood had sent to assist Chalmers in holding them back, and as they approached Schofield's position Stiles's brigade of infantry came in close support.[1] The balls from this attacking force were now falling in rear of Bate and Lowry, and the men of Cleburne's old division were vainly trying to form a line long or strong enough to match that which was coming from the south. Wilson had gone in person to Thomas, at Schofield's position, to report what his men were doing, and reached him just as McMillan's brigade was seen to rush forward upon the slope of Shy's Hill. At a sign from Schofield, Cox's division started also on the run, Doolittle's brigade in

---

[1] In his report General Schofield expressed some disappointment that this brigade had not been able to get forward faster; but Colonel Stiles's account of the matter and of the nature of the ground show that he accomplished all that could be expected of so small a force moving over rough, detached hills.

advance. Wilson turned to gallop back to his command, but before he could get half-way there, the whole Confederate left was crushed in like an egg-shell.

McMillan swept unchecked over Bate's ruined line at Shy's Hill. The gallant Colonel of the Twentieth Tennessee did all that man could do to hold it, and dying at his post, gave to the height the name it bears. The arch was broken; there were no reserves to restore it, and from right and left the Confederate troops peeled away from the works in wild confusion. From the heavy earthwork in front of Doolittle one volley of cannon and small arms was fired, but in the excitement it was aimed so high as to do no mischief, and Cox's whole division was over the works before they could reload. At the same time Hatch and Knipe, with their divisions of dismounted men, rushed in from the right, and, abandoning their artillery, the Confederates west of the Granny White road crowded eastward, running for life. Some were killed, many were captured, and Smith's and Schofield's men met upon the turnpike at right angles, and were halted to prevent their organizations from being confused together.

Hubbard's brigade, of McArthur's division, which followed McMillan's movement, met with more resistance, and suffered more severely; but though some of the Confederate regiments held tenaciously to their works, and surrendered in form, most of the troops broke their organizations entirely when the advance was taken up from centre to wings, and Wood's divisions now charged, with hardly a show of opposition, over Overton's Hill, from which they had been driven back an hour before.

CHAPTER VII.

THE PURSUIT AFTER THE BATTLE—RESULTS OF THE CAMPAIGN.

NIGHT was falling when the victory was complete, and a drenching rain had set in to add to the darkness and confusion. Thomas ordered Wood to pursue by the Franklin road, and the cavalry by the Granny White road, to the intersection with that to Franklin, when Wilson was to take the advance. Smith and Schofield were ordered to follow Wilson on the next day. But few, if any, of the Confederates fled by the Granny White turnpike, for it was commanded by Wilson's cavalry, and the masses streamed through the Brentwood Hills, making the best of their way to the Franklin road. There was hardly the semblance of organization among them till they passed the Harpeth River. Forrest was ordered to retreat on Shelbyville and Pulaski, but he hurried Armstrong's brigade of cavalry across country to get in rear of Hood's routed forces and cover their retreat. Reynolds's and Coleman's brigades had been taken from the line, at the last moment, to cover the passes through the Brentwood Hills from the Granny White road, and had pre served their organization. By delaying the advance of Wilson's horsemen toward the Franklin turnpike, these brigades had saved the larger part of Hood's army from capture. The hospitals at Franklin were abandoned, containing over two thousand wounded. Wilson, with his cavalry, had come up with the rear guard four miles north of Franklin, at Hollow Tree Gap, and Knipe's division, charging it in front and flank, carried the position, capturing over four hundred prisoners and their colors. At the Harpeth, Johnson's division crossed some distance below, and compelled Hood to abandon the defence of the river at Franklin. At Rutherford Creek, on the 18th, the water was up, the stream was a torrent, and some delay in getting a pontoon train forward gave the enemy a little respite. At Columbia, Forrest rejoined Hood, and his cavalry, with an infantry rear guard under command of Walthall, covered the retreat to the Tennessee. General Walthall's force was made up of the two brigades which had been detached with Forrest, and of three others besides his own division.[1] This force was able to present so strong a front that, aided by the condition of the roads and streams, which retarded pursuit, our advance guard was not able to break through again, and Hood reached the Tennessee, at Bainbridge, by way of Pulaski, on the 26th. Here he was favored by a gleam of good fortune in the arrival of pontoons, which had been floated down from Decatur, where, by some blunder, they had been left by our forces when General Granger had evacuated that post in November.[2] Their own pontoon train was delayed by the condition of the roads, and part of the defeated army passed the Tennessee before it arrived; but when it came it was laid, and Hood had his shattered forces on the southern bank by the evening of the 27th. A Confederate account

[1] Featherston's brigade of Loring's division, Heiskell's and Field's of Lowry's division, were the three others. Coleman's was now part of Walthall's own division. See Appendix B, II.

[2] The author learns from officers who were at Decatur that the pontoon bridge had been cut loose, with the expectation that it would be taken in tow by gunboats; but he is unable to trace the responsibility for the failure either to take it up or to destroy it.

states that soon after the first bridge was down, two National gunboats appeared in the direction of Florence and steamed toward it; but General Stewart opened upon them with a battery of smooth field guns, which was all he then had, and the boats desisted from the attempt to break through the pontoons.[1]

From Franklin, on the 17th, Thomas had ordered Steedman to march to Murfreesboro, and thence to proceed by rail to Decatur, occupying the posts in Northern Alabama which had been abandoned earlier in the campaign. At the close of the month Steedman was at Decatur, Wood was near Lexington, in North Alabama, thirty miles southwest of Pulaski, Smith was at Pulaski, and Schofield at Columbia. Thomas issued his orders announcing the close of the campaign, assigning winter quarters to the various corps; but directions were received from Washington to continue operations. The expected march of Sherman northward, from Savannah, made it important that no rest or time for concentration should be given the enemy in the Gulf States, and Thomas prepared for a new campaign.

Among the results of the two days' battle at Nashville had been the capture of about four thousand five hundred prisoners, and fifty-three pieces of artillery, besides small arms in great number. Among the prisoners were Generals Johnson, Smith, Jackson, and Rucker, and a number of regimental officers commanding brigades. The losses in killed and wounded on both sides were small, compared with the material results, though the demoralization of Hood's army, followed so soon by the close of the war, leaves us without the full returns which are necessary to

---

[1] Sergeant-Major Cunningham's pamphlet. The author has found the statements of Mr. Cunningham so accurate when he has the means of verifying them, that he does not feel at liberty to ignore them in this case.

determine the casualties on the Confederate side. Hood assembled the remnant of his army at Tupelo, Mississippi, and then gave furloughs to part of his men (particularly the Tennesseeans), and asked to be relieved from the command of the army. He does not admit a loss from all causes, from December 15th to 30th, as great as the number of prisoners taken by Thomas's army on the 15th and 16th, and claims that he reassembled at Tupelo an army of 18,500 effective muskets. These figures are nearly worthless for any historical purpose. General Thomas's return of prisoners captured, and deserters received during November and December, show the number to be over thirteen thousand; besides these he reports the capture of 72 cannon and 3,000 muskets. We shall meet with some of the veterans of Hood's army again in the Carolinas, maintaining their old corps organization; but, for the time, they were scattered and demoralized, and seemed almost to lose the character of a disciplined army.

Thomas's losses in the battle of Nashville were 3,057, of which less than four hundred were killed. The analysis of these figures shows that the Fourth Corps suffered a little less than a thousand casualties, of which two-thirds were in the unsuccessful attack upon Overton's Hill. Steedman's losses were over eight hundred, and nearly all of them seem to have occurred in the same assault, those of his second colored brigade (Colonel Thompson's) being fifty per cent. heavier than in any other on the field. The Sixteenth Corps lost 750, which appear to have been pretty evenly divided between the two days. It is noteworthy that the attack upon the angle at Shy's Hill was not a costly one, for the preceding preparation by the enfilading artillery fire, and the shape of the ground, which enabled McMillan to approach closely before exposing his men, show that

success in such cases (when success is possible), follows the
use of proper means. The total number of casualties in
McMillan's brigade was 118, of which not more than two-
thirds occurred in the final assault, and they were less than
half of those which occurred in Hubbard's brigade, which
went forward on its left against the works in the lower
ground, and where Bate's centre and right, holding on with
better cover, were able to inflict considerable loss before
the crushing of the whole of Hood's left made their position untenable. The Twenty-third Corps was in reserve
nearly all of the first day, and its only losses worth men-
tioning were in Couch's division, when carrying the hill
close to Shy's in the evening. The position was of inestimable importance for one so cheaply gained, for the casualties
were only 150. Those of the other division in the final
assault were less than twenty. As nearly always happens in
a panic, the break of the enemy's line was so sudden and
complete that the loss was almost wholly on one side. The
loss in the cavalry corps was 329, and when distributed
among the three divisions, it must also be regarded as
trifling, and the larger part, even of this, undoubtedly occurred in carrying the redoubts on the 15th.

These considerations show that the success was due chiefly
to the tactical combination of a superior force, and that
moral causes, growing out of the preceding part of the
campaign, must have had a great effect in producing discouragement among Hood's men, and predisposing them to
panic when the break in the line occurred. Hood was evidently in fault, as a tactician, on the 15th, when he allowed
Thomas to array his whole force diagonally beyond his left
flank, and awaited an attack in such a position. His only
hope was to have drawn back to the Brentwood Hills at
once, without allowing his troops to become engaged. He

would thus have saved them from the demoralizing effect of
being driven from position after position on the first day,
and from the conviction (which. was partly the cause of its
own fulfilment), that they were wholly unable to cope with
the National army. On the morning of the 16th he issued
orders to his subordinates to prepare for a retreat in the
evening; but he could not withdraw under fire, and the decision was reached too late to be of successful accomplish-
ment. The evening found his routed army a disorganized
crowd flying from the lost battle-field.

Hood's retreat from Nashville to the Tennessee and
Thomas's pursuit were almost equally laborious for their
armies, though very different in their effect upon the spirits
of the troops. The roads were in horrible condition, even
those which had been macadamized being almost impassable. The ordinary country roads were much worse, and,
after passing Pulaski, till the Tennessee was reached, the
wrecks of wagons and the carcasses of animals filled the
way. Hood had been forced to destroy ammunition to get
teams to take forward his pontoons, and Wilson and Wood
in pursuit had been obliged to leave most of their cannon,
and double the teams of the rest. On getting orders from
Washington to resume the campaign, Thomas ordered Wood
to assemble the Fourth Corps at Huntsville, Ala., Schofield,
Smith, and Wilson to concentrate at Eastport, Mississippi.
Schofield marched the Twenty-third Corps to Clifton on the
Tennessee, preparatory to taking boats up the river, but
other orders met him there, transferring him to a distant
field upon the sea-coast.

The completeness of the victory at Nashville caused a joy-
ful revulsion of feeling throughout the Northern States.
The impatience of the President and of General Grant had
only been the expression of a feeling which all the country

had shared. The conviction was general that Hood ought to have been met much nearer the Tennessee River, and the fear that he would be allowed to march to the Ohio was all but universal. Now, however, all vied in giving honor to the successful general, and not a few were ready to blame the authorities at Washington for having doubted, even for a day, the wisdom of Thomas's management of the early campaign. The President, the Secretary of War, and General Grant were not slow or stinting in their congratulations, and between the chief actors in the scene a cordial good understanding was at once established. On the one hand, it was ungrudgingly conceded that the final battle had been skilfully delivered and crowned with the most satisfactory results; on the other, it was felt that the anxiety of the early December days was reasonable, and that the demand for prompt action was such a stimulus to great exertion as the responsible authorities of a government may apply to its most trusted officers in such a crisis, without giving cause for lasting chagrin. In such a time, the reward for success and the responsibility for ill-fortune may neither of them be quite justly proportioned to real desert, and both are apt to be exaggerated. In war, more than in anything else, the proverb "all's well that ends well" is the popular one, and the popular sympathy was evidently with the hero of the great victory.

Few men have the qualities which deserve public confidence in greater measure than General Thomas. He was a patriot whose love of his country was greater than his attachment to a province; a Virginian who refused to follow the example of Lee in taking arms against the National Government which Washington had founded. He was a man of large mould in body and mind, of a quiet, modest dignity, who hated pretence, and avoided notoriety. He was transparently true to his superiors, and kindly considerate to his subordinates. He had the personal courage which would be ashamed of its own display as much as of a cowardice, but which seemed simply oblivious of danger when duty required a risk to be taken. These qualities made him always a trusted lieutenant to his chief, and were the basis of an affectionate and respectful attachment in his own army which was peculiar. His real and unaffected aversion to taking the chief responsibility of command had kept him in secondary positions when his rank in both the regular and volunteer armies would have made him the head of a separate army in the field. In this respect he was not unlike Hardee, in the Confederate Army, who also steadily refused a supreme command. The duties of the soldier, and the exhibition of courage and skill in making the details of a campaign successful, were easy to him ; but to become the theme of discussion in Congress and in the newspapers, to be the butt of ten thousand public critics, and to carry the burden of plans whose failure might be ruin to the country—this he hated so heartily and shrunk from so naturally, that, after all his long experience, we have seen him protesting that the position assigned him in this last campaign was "the one thing he did not want." That these qualities in some degree unfitted him for an independent command cannot be questioned. The very anxiety to be right, if it is excessive, produces hesitation in action and timidity in plan. Under such conditions the stimulus from without, coming in the form of urgency from the Government and command from the General-in-Chief, may not have been wholly unwelcome, and unquestionably added vigor to the final movements.

It is, however, in the earlier part of the campaign that the steps taken were most open to question, though very few of the officers and men who served there had any exact knowledge of the means which were at General Thomas's disposal, or of the manner in which they were used. The magnitude of the final success was so splendid, that it seemed to prove each step toward it the best possible.; and it is only when we examine the official evidence of the number and position of the troops in Tennessee that we are able to apply to the events which followed the tests afforded by the rules of military art.[1]

General Thomas tells us in his official report that, had Hood delayed his advance from Florence ten days longer, he would have met him at Columbia, or some other point south of the Duck River. An early concentration in front of the enemy is thus indicated as the controlling purpose, and Hood's march on Nashville is recognized as the result only of the unforeseen delays in the arrival of General Smith with his divisions. The military student of the campaign is therefore led to inquire whether a concentration of the means at hand would not have opposed to Hood a force which would have kept him at least south of Duck River till Smith could have arrived.

Communication with Sherman was broken on November 12th, and Hood began his advance from Florence on the 20th, though it was not till the 26th that his infantry was all assembled in front of Columbia, Schofield having abandoned Pulaski on the 22d. A fortnight was thus unexpectedly given for concentration, and the resources of the railways were at Thomas's disposal. His tri-monthly return of November 20th shows a force in Tennessee of 59,534 officers and men "present for duty equipped." To determine the deductions necessary for smaller garrisons and bridge

---

[1] The author has been led by this examination to conclusions quite different from his own predilections. He had assumed, in common with most of his comrades in that campaign, that the Fourth and Twenty-third Corps were the only forces available to oppose Hood until the arrival of Major-General A. J. Smith with the Sixteenth Corps.

guards, no better method can be used than to make them
the same as was actually done when the battle of Nashville
was imminent. Add to these a garrison of 2,500 for Nashville and Chattanooga each, and we shall find still remaining a force of 47,000 infantry and artillery, and about six
thousand cavalry, which there could have been no difficulty
in assembling at Columbia before Hood reached there.
After Sherman started from Rome, it was known that
Wheeler's cavalry had hastened after him. The raid of
Breckenridge into East Tennessee was a feeble diversion
which the troops in that part of Schofield's department were
quite able to meet. Roddey's division of cavalry was the
only Confederate force in North Alabama, and gave no trouble during the campaign. Everything combined, therefore,
to point to an immediate concentration in front of Hood, as
the true policy on our side. General R. S. Granger was at
Decatur on November 1st with over five thousand men.
Steedman could have joined him there with the five thousand which he subsequently took to Nashville. The bridge
and trestle between Pulaski and Athens could have been rebuilt, and if demonstrations on the south of the Tennessee
did not keep Hood from committing himself to a campaign
north of the river, the divisions of Steedman and Granger
could have joined Schofield at Pulaski. If Thomas had
joined them there or at Columbia with the remainder of his
available force, he would have been superior to Hood in
everything but cavalry from the beginning, and would have
been able himself to dictate whether a battle should be
fought before the arrival of Smith's corps.[1] From the
knowledge of the facts we now have, it would seem that
Thomas gave undue importance to the necessity of having

---

[1] See tables in Appendix A.

the Sixteenth Corps present before decisive operations against Hood. When the battle of Nashville was fought, Rousseau's eight thousand or more at Murfreesboro were as wholly out of the account as if they had been north of the Ohio, and nearly five thousand of Cruft's division, besides the post garrison, were kept in the works at the city with General Donaldson's employés, and were not brought into the action. The battle was fought, therefore, with a force numerically less than it would have been if Smith's corps had been entirely absent, and Rousseau and Cruft had been in line instead. It is true that a good many new regiments had taken the place of old ones; but these were not what is commonly meant by raw recruits. They were always officered by men of experience, and many veterans were in the ranks. Four thousand of them swelled the old divisions of the Fourth Corps, and there was no complaint that they did not fight well. As to the provisional organization of convalescents and furloughed men of the different corps with Sherman, their conduct in Grosvenor's brigade in this action, and subsequently on the North Carolina coast, proved they were scarcely distinguishable from veteran troops under their accustomed flags. But if the troops had not been of the best quality, there would be no less need of handling them according to the principles which military experience has established, and a rapid concentration would still be proper.

When Hood began the campaign in earnest, the first movements of our forces were the reverse of concentric. Granger, instead of joining Schofield, was sent a hundred miles to the east, and the garrison at Johnsonville was taken to the rear of Nashville. This would seem to have been with the idea that it was necessary to protect the railways against expected raids. If so, it was an error, for had

Hood been unwise enough to have detached Forrest for such a purpose, he would have been at the same disadvantage he subsequently was at Nashville, where the absence of the hostile cavalry made the opportunity which resulted so gloriously for our arms. No raid of Forrest's could have done more damage to the Chattanooga Railroad than the forced retreat from Pulaski did to an equally important line, to say nothing of the damage actually done to the former while Hood lay in front of Nashville.

The delay in concentration was also fraught with the very gravest perils to the portion of the army under Schofield. It was Hood's policy to force the fighting with this, in the hope of destroying or capturing it before it could be aided, yet nothing was farther from Thomas's wish than that it should make a precipitate retreat. Had it reached Nashville a single day sooner, Thomas would have been wholly unprepared to meet his adversary, and Steedman's reinforcements would have been cut off. To save time, Schofield took the gravest risks ; but as he well said, the slightest mistake on his part, or the failure of a subordinate, might have proved disastrous. The misconduct of Wagner at Franklin would certainly have proved so, but for the heroism of Opdycke and White and the brave men of their commands.

A consideration of all the facts, therefore, seems to show that Thomas should have concentrated every available man in front of Hood before the latter moved ; and that the great success of the closing part of the campaign was in spite of this error in its beginning, and by no means because of it. The difficulties had certainly been very great, and to an ordinary man they would have been overwhelming. There was a great scarcity of animals for the cavalry, for the artillery, for the pontoons, and for the wagon trains, while the season was such as to use up the animals with double rapidity. The army was new to its organization, and though it did all that an army could do, Thomas could hardly have full faith in it till it had been proven. But through all these difficulties a triumph was achieved which has been rarely equalled, and without which even Sherman's position in the heart of the Confederacy and on the communications of its only remaining great army must have lost half its significance.

CHAPTER VIII.

FORT FISHER.

THE subsidiary operations which were intended to co-operate with Sherman's march northward from Savannah were two. First, the capture of Fort Fisher at the mouth of Cape Fear River in North Carolina, and second, the transfer of Schofield from Middle Tennessee to the Carolina coast, where, with the Tenth Corps under Major-General A. H. Terry and the Twenty-third under Major-General Cox, he was to reduce Wilmington and advance upon two lines from that city and from Newbern to Goldsboro, at which place it was expected a junction with Sherman would be made. The attack upon Fort Fisher was practically simultaneous with Sherman's departure from Savannah and with Schofield's from Clifton on the Tennessee River; and the result of all, accomplished two months later, was the reunion at Goldsboro of the army which Sherman had led at Atlanta, except that the Tenth Corps was substituted for the Fourth, which still remained at the West.

The city of Wilmington, which had been one of the principal ports of the Confederacy, is on the left bank of Cape Fear River, about thirty miles from the ocean. The river, near its mouth, runs parallel to the sea-coast, the sandy tongue between, called Federal Point, being hardly more than a mile wide for the last five or six miles of its length.

Fort Fisher was upon the southern point of this, and consisted of sand parapets sodded with marsh grass on the slope,
and revetted with the same. The land face extended across
the tongue, from the sea beach to the river, something over
a mile from the point, and the parapet was about five hundred yards in length. The sea-face was thirteen hundred
yards long from the bastion where it joined the land front
to a work known as the mound battery at its southern end.
On the extreme point was a smaller detached work known
as Fort Buchanan, mounting four heavy guns. Smith Island
lies opposite the mouth of the river, giving two channels
from the sea into the harbor. Fort Fisher with Fort Buchanan commanded the northern entrance, called New Inlet,
and on the main land south of the entrance, two other forts,
Caswell and Johnson, protected the principal channel. A
village of pilots and fishermen, called Smithville, lay under
the guns of Fort Johnson, a quaint little place embowered
in live-oaks, where the daring men lived who chose the
stormiest nights and the foggiest days for piloting in the
blockade runners upon which the South was dependent for
its commerce.

Fort Fisher not only commanded New Inlet where the
turns of the channel brought every entering vessel under
its guns, but the narrowness of Federal Point gave it control of the river also ; and when it should once be in our
possession the port would be closed. It had been constructed in accordance with its situation and use, with the
two long faces described, but open at the back upon the
river and having only a light rifle trench extending from the
mound battery to the river, facing Fort Buchanan. As any
military force intending to attack the place would necessarily land out of cannon range to the northward, the land
face of the fort was the most elaborately built. Starting

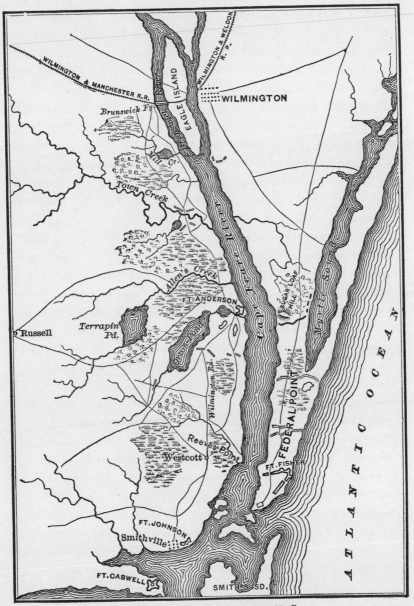

Fort Fisher and Wilmington, N. C.

from a half bastion on the river, a curtain ran to the bastion
at the angle on the sea. The parapet was about twenty
feet high, with a shallow ditch, most of the sand for the
work being taken from the interior. Midway the curtain
was a small outwork covering an entrance to the fort. Two
field-pieces in this gave a flanking fire upon the ditch and
assisted the guns in the bastions in sweeping the front. A
heavy loopholed palisade was before the ditch and about
fifty feet from the foot of the slope. This front was armed
with twenty-one heavy guns and three mortars. A formidable system of torpedoes had been planted beyond the palisade, to be discharged by electricity from within the fort.
To protect the guns from an enfilading naval fire, very heavy
traverses had been built, about a dozen in number, at right
angles to the parapet, from twenty-five to forty feet long,
and rising ten feet above the gunners' heads. These were
strongly built, as hollow bomb-proofs, and served both as
magazines and as shelter for the garrison when driven from
the guns by a cannonade from the fleet. A large interior
magazine and some stores and quarters were similarly constructed. The sea-front was built in the same way, but was
not so continuously heavy as the other, the guns being
grouped in batteries connected by a lighter parapet for infantry. Twenty-four guns were on this face, and among
them an Armstrong rifled gun of 150 lbs. calibre, mounted
upon a solid mahogany carriage, a gift from English friends
of the Confederate cause. The armament was mostly of
eight- and ten-inch columbiads, interspersed with heavy
rifled cannon. The garrison numbered about twenty-five
hundred men under Colonel Lamb, though Major-General
Whiting was present in the fort when it surrendered.[1]

General Terry reports his prisoners at 2,083, but does not state the casualties
among the Confederates.

An attempt to take the fort in December had been fruit-less, but the strong opinion of Rear-Admiral Porter and of some of the army officers that it could be taken, led to the speedy renewal of the effort. General Terry was put in command of Ames's division and Abbott's brigade of the Twenty-fourth Corps, and Paine's division of the Twenty-fifth Corps, with two light batteries. A fleet of transports conveyed them and a siege-train to the rendezvous on the North Carolina coast, where they met Admiral Porter's fleet. Storms delayed the landing, which was effected January 13th, upon the beach about five miles north of the fort and under cover of the fire of the fleet. The shore there is a mere key of sand a few hundred yards wide, and separated from the mainland by Myrtle Sound, a long and shallow bay of which the outlet is at Masonboro Inlet, a few miles further north. Nearly two hundred small boats from the navy, besides steam-tugs were employed in taking the troops from the transports to the shore, and the whole was done between eight in the morning and four o'clock in the afternoon, though a heavy surf beat continuously upon the open coast.

After several reconnoissances, it was determined to establish a line of contravallation across the point about two miles from the fort, which should protect Terry's camp from any attack in rear during his operations. This line was established and occupied by Paine's division and Abbott's brigade. The interior of Federal Point and the part of the peninsula along the river is a shallow fresh-water swamp, overgrown with pines, and with a thicket of smaller trees and shrubs. The first efforts were aimed at establishing the line farther away from the fort, with its flanks resting upon the swamps ; but these were found to be so shallow as to make no protection, and the trench was therefore put where it could reach from river to the sea. Under cover of the fire of the fleet, Curtis's brigade of Ames's division was moved down along the river toward the fort, and reached a small unfinished outwork in front of the west end of the land face, while Terry, with General Curtis and Colonel Comstock of General Grant's staff (who accompanied the expedition as chief engineer), made a reconnoissance within six hundred yards of the works. Curtis had approached the fort at this place on the former expedition, and the result of the reconnoissance confirmed his opinion that it was the proper point for an assault, which it was determined to make the next day. Admiral Porter was requested to maintain a steady fire of the fleet upon the works, and to destroy the palisade in front of the ditch, so as to prevent delay when the attacking force should move forward. After consultation, the hour of 3 P.M. of the 15th was fixed for the assault, which General Ames was ordered to make with his division, and the Admiral ordered a party of sailors and marines, under Commander Breese, to land and attack the bastion at the sea-angle at the same time with Ames's assault upon the other end of the land front.

Admiral Porter had maintained an occasional fire on the fort during the night, and at an early hour in the morning of the 15th, sixty men-of-war and gunboats, arranged in a great curve off the shore, opened a steady and systematic cannonade upon it. The method adopted was to fire slowly and with great care to get the range accurately, taking the traverses in regular order, and endeavoring to dismount the guns between them. A designated section of the fleet directed their fire upon the palisade. A steady rain of great projectiles was thus kept up upon the fort, many of them eleven and thirteen inch shells, driving the infantry of the garrison to their bomb-proofs. The Confederate artillerists vainly tried to match the persistent cannonade of the ships.

One by one their guns were silenced, many were dismounted and broken, till, by the time fixed for the assault, hardly any of the larger cannon were in condition to be used.

Ames had kept Curtis's brigade in the advanced work it had occupied the evening before, with Pennypacker's and Bell's in supporting distance. At two o'clock a line of sharpshooters, provided with shovels, ran forward and established themselves in pits a hundred and seventy-five yards from the fort. The infantry of the garrison now began to man the parapet, and opened with their muskets upon Curtis's line, which advanced to a point about four hundred yards in rear of the sharpshooters, when they also quickly covered themselves with a shallow trench in the sand. Again Curtis was moved forward to the cover of a little ridge in the sands much nearer the enemy, while Pennypacker's brigade occupied the trench he had left, and Bell's brigade came to the advanced work, which had been Curtis's first position. The signal was now given to the fleet to change the direction of its fire, and Curtis's brigade rushed at the end of the half-bastion next the river. The ground along the river bank was marshy, and the palisades were standing in some places ; but a party of axemen with the head of the column quickly cleared the way of obstructions, and there was no halt till the men swarmed over the parapet, and took it in reverse as far as the first traverse. At the same time Commander Breese's storming party from the ships charged upon the bastion at the sea-angle, but the enemy ran forward a light gun or two in the bastion, and another in the outwork at the middle of the curtain opened on them, while they were met with a steady musketry fire from the parapet. Their position had none of the advantages of Ames's, and they were soon driven back with considerable loss.

At the river side Pennypacker's brigade went forward to

Curtis's support, and carried the palisade reaching from the end of the earthwork to the water, taking a number of prisoners. A hand-to-hand conflict began, in which the garrison were slowly driven back from one traverse to another. In carrying the third traverse, Colonel Pennypacker fell badly wounded; Bell's brigade was ordered up and formed along the river within the fort, but the interior was full of trenches from which sand for the parapet had been dug, and the magazines and the ruins of barracks and storehouses made tenable defences for the garrison, so that the progress was slow. By six o'clock nine traverses had been carried, and Terry now ordered to Ames's assistance Abbott's brigade and the Twenty-seventh colored regiment from Paine's division. Abbott was able to complete the occupation of the land front, and Ames directed a general advance upon the reverse of the sea front, which cleared the works and took full possession of the fort. In the final effort Curtis had been wounded in the head by a canister-ball, and Colonel Bell received a fatal shot while leading forward his brigade.

The garrison retreated precipitately to the shelter of Fort Buchanan, where, upon the advance of Abbott's brigade against them, they were surrendered late in the evening by General Whiting and Colonel Lamb, their commanders. While the attack upon the fort was going on, General Hoke had made some demonstrations of attack upon the line of General Paine, and Commander Breese's sailors and marines were sent, after their repulse, to strengthen that line; but a slight skirmish was all that followed, and Hoke retired, leaving the garrison to its fate. The fighting along the parapet had been obstinate, and the losses were severe in proportion to the numbers engaged, especially in officers, of whom fifty were killed and wounded. The casualties in the rank and file were about six hundred.

From the time the assault began the ships could give no
further assistance, and the advantages for defence which the
traverses and the obstructions within the fort gave, were
such as to make the work of Ames and his brigade commanders hardly less difficult than the assault of a well-
manned field fortification. The assault of the detachment
from the ships, though unsuccessful, was of assistance as a
diversion, and enabled the infantry to get forward faster than
they could otherwise have done. The cannonade from the
ships appears to have destroyed the connection between
the torpedoes which had been placed in the ground along the
front which was assailed and the electric battery within the
fort, for no explosions took place and the attacking parties
did not suffer from this cause.

The victory was in itself an important one, and it was all
the more grateful to the country because of the chagrin at
the so recent failure of Butler's expedition against the same
fortress. The other forts near Smithville were immediately
abandoned by the enemy, and their armament also was captured, making in all one hundred and sixty-nine cannon, besides small arms and stores, and over two thousand prisoners.
The harbor was now in our possession and blockade running was nearly ended. General Hoke, the Confederate
commander of the District, intrenched himself with his own
and the remainder of Whiting's divisions, on a line reaching
from Myrtle Sound to Cape Fear River, a mile or two above
the southern end of the Sound. Nearly opposite this line,
upon a projecting point of the right bank of the river, was
Fort Anderson, a heavy earthwork, either built or enlarged
and strengthened at this time. From this point also, the
channel was planted with torpedoes, and full use was made
of all the means for obstructing the passage of the fleet
which the ingenuity of the Confederates had devised.

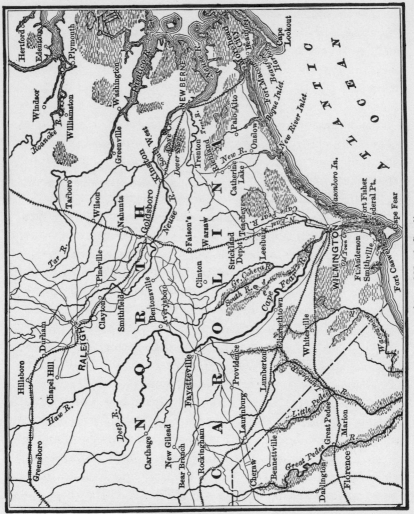

Map of North Carolina.

CHAPTER IX.

CAPTURE OF WILMINGTON—BATTLE OF KINSTON.

THE orders which had been sent General Schofield to move the Twenty-third Corps eastward reached him on January 14th. River transports took the troops down the Tennessee and up the Ohio to points where railway transportation could be got, and the transfer to Washington and Alexandria was then completed by rail. The distance travelled was fourteen hundred miles, and the corps was ready to take ship before February 1st; but the unusual severity of the winter weather had frozen the Potomac River, and it was not till the 4th that the first detachments of the troops sailed. Meanwhile Schofield had joined General Grant at Fortress Monroe and had accompanied him to the mouth of Cape Fear River to hold a consultation with General Terry and Admiral Porter with regard to future operations in the Department of North Carolina, as the new command was designated. The result was the decision to make Wilmington the first objective point of the campaign, so that a new base might be secured for Sherman if circumstances should oblige him to concentrate his army south of Goldsboro. The first step accomplished, Schofield's task would be to open the route from Newberne to Goldsboro, rebuilding the railway, and uniting both his corps there in time to meet Sherman for the final operations of the general campaign when the concentration of the grand army should be complete.

Returning to Washington, Schofield embarked with Cox's division on February 4th, leaving the rest of the corps to fol-

low as fast as ships could be procured. A gale off Cape
Hatteras delayed the transports for a day or two, but the division landed safely at Fort Fisher on the 9th. The fort
still bore evidence of the extraordinary bombardment it
had undergone, and its broad sandy interior was thickly
strewn with great shells rusted red in the weather, and re-
sembling nothing so much as a farmer's field strewn with
pumpkins. On the 11th Terry's line was advanced close
enough to that of the enemy to compel him to hold it in
force. The next night the attempt was made to convey
pontoons up the coast by the navy, while Cox's and Ames's
divisions marched along the beach to receive the boats, haul
them over the sands and lay a bridge across Myrtle Sound in
a narrow place in rear of Hoke. The weather became so
stormy, however, that the boats could not be brought to
the rendezvous and the infantry marched back to their
camps before morning. The night was dark but intensely
cold, and the gale from the ocean seemed to find every
button-hole in the men's clothing, and to chill them to the
marrow. A severe northeaster swept the coast for several
days, but on the night of the 14th a new attempt was made
to move the pontoons to the selected place. This time
the boats were put on their wagons and all the scanty supply
of horses and mules was used to haul them forward along
the beach. The high tide and surf proved too great a
hindrance; the sand, where not washed by the water, was
too deep and soft for the teams, and where the waves broke,
the sea was too much for them; so this also had to be given
up. Before they reached the appointed position the moon
rose, revealing the naval squadron in the offing, and revealing also the marching troops to the enemy, who were put
upon the alert to defeat the effort to cross the Sound.

Schofield now determined to try the right bank of the

river, where there was at least room for manœuvre, although the country was very swampy and filled with ponds and lakes. Cox's and Ames's divisions were ferried to Smithville, where they were joined by Moore's brigade of Couch's division, just landed, and the whole, under command of General Cox, was directed to advance upon Fort Anderson and attempt to turn it. The vessels of the fleet had from time to time engaged the fort at long range, and Admiral Porter ordered a section of them to renew the fire when the land forces should advance. General Schofield made his headquarters temporarily upon a steamer, passing from one bank to the other as circumstances required.

The 16th was used in getting the troops over the bay with a few field pieces and a small train of wagons. Cox's division marched on the morning of the 17th, meeting the enemy's cavalry within two or three miles of the village, and pressing them back by a continuous skirmish till within two miles of the fort, established a line with the right flank resting on the river, and opened communication with the fleet, having marched ten miles during the day. Next morning the advance was resumed and the enemy driven within the fortifications. A reconnoissance showed that besides the principal fort upon the river, a line of infantry trench ran at right angles from the bank to the foot of Orton Pond, a lake several miles long, giving it a front which could not be turned except by a long detour. The line was protected by abatis, and epaulements for field artillery were seen in places along it, from which a rapid fire with shrapnel was opened as the National forces came within range. In accordance with his orders, Cox intrenched two brigades to invest the fort on this side, and with two others marched for the head of Orton Pond, sending directions to Ames's division to join him there. The detour required a march of about fifteen miles, and it was almost night when the cause-way through the marsh at the head of the pond was reached. The enemy made a sharp resistance with cavalry, but by sending detachments on the flanks to pass the swamps by wading, the crossing was forced and high ground beyond was occupied. During the day the fleet had continued a cannonade of the fort, and demonstrations had been kept up by the two brigades in position. In the night the enemy abandoned the place, and the troops hastening forward by the west side of Orton Pond to complete their work, were met by the news that the fort was in our possession, with ten pieces of heavy ordnance which made its armament.

On the right bank of the river the enemy retreated to Town Creek, destroying bridges and obstructing the road. On the other side of the river he fell back to a strong position opposite the mouth of Town Creek, covered by swamps on the east. General Terry followed Hoke's retreat up the left bank, and it appearing that the greater part of Hoke's force was in his front, Ames's division was taken back to that side on the 19th, while Cox continued his advance to Town Creek, eight miles above the fort, driving a rear guard before him. Town Creek is a deep, unfordable stream, with marshy banks, which, near the river, had been dyked and cultivated as rice-fields. A strong line of earthworks had been built on the north bank of the stream before the evacuation of Fort Anderson, and in them were a Whitworth rifled cannon and two smooth twelve-pounder field pieces. Hagood's brigade, of Hoke's division, strengthened by another Confederate regiment, held the works, and had removed the planking from the bridge. The artillery swept the long causeway through the marsh by which the bridge must be approached.

Henderson's brigade was advanced to the edge of the low

ground, and a strong line of skirmishers worked their way through the marsh to the edge of the stream. Careful reconnoissance was made above and below, and during the night a small flat-boat, of the kind used for collecting the rice crop, was found a mile or two down the creek, and was secured and guarded. The north bank, occupied by Hagood, was a bluff near the bridge, rising twenty or thirty feet from the water. Farther below the ground falls off into marsh and rice fields, bordered by forest, which hid them from view. The situation was reported to General Schofield, with Cox's purpose to cross part of his force at the place below the bridge, by means of the flat-boat, in the morning. The vessels of the navy had ascended the river, keeping pace with the troops on the shore, removing torpedoes and obstructions as they advanced, and prepared to assist the army by shelling any of the enemy's positions they could reach. The Confederates were careful, however, to select their points of defence out of range from the river after the evacuation of Fort Anderson.

Early in the morning of the 20th Henderson's brigade renewed active demonstrations on Hagood's front, while the slow work of ferrying the other brigades went on. The boat would carry only fifty men, and the marshes and dykes were impassable for animals, so that the mounted officers left their horses behind. Casement's and Sterl's brigades were all the morning getting over. Henderson's sharpshooters had succeeded in getting cover so close to the creek as to prevent any of the enemy from showing themselves above the parapet. The Whitworth gun had also been disabled by our artillery fire. Moore was now ordered to cross his brigade, and about the middle of the afternoon Cox assembled the three brigades on the north edge of the swamp, which they had succeeded in wading. The impracticability

of the country had been so relied upon by the enemy that
no pickets were found posted, and the division was marched
rapidly to the west till it crossed the road leading to Wilmington, about two miles in rear of the Confederate position.
Moore was ordered to march still farther westward to reach
a parallel road, and prevent escape in that direction. Casement and Sterl were formed facing toward the creek, and
marching rapidly forward, made the attack. The brigade,
commanded by Colonel Simonton in Hagood's absence,
made a brave resistance, but was broken by a charge. Simonton had begun a line of breastworks facing to the rear,
upon hearing of the presence of the National troops, and
leaving a small force to hold the dismantled bridge, he had
formed here ; but the charge swept everything away, and he
himself, with three hundred and seventy-five of his men and
both his cannon, were captured.   The rest of the brigade fled
by the " old public road " toward which Moore had been sent ;
but the latter did not reach it in time to intercept them.

The bridge was repaired during the night, and Cox resumed his march in the morning. Hoke held stubbornly to
his position in front of Terry, and the column on the right
bank of the river was therefore directed by Schofield to proceed cautiously toward Wilmington, to ascertain the condition of the Wilmington and Manchester Railway, and take
advantage of any opportunity to get possession of the crossing of Brunswick River, which is the name given to the west
channel of Cape Fear River, where it passes around Eagle
Island, in front of the city. About noon Mill Creek was
reached, six miles from the last camp, and the bridge was
found to be burned. This caused a couple of hour's delay
till it could be repaired so that the artillery could pass.
The negroes of a large plantation there made the most ex-
travagant jubilation over the advent of the National troops.

The forage and provisions were, as usual, applied to military use, but the recent slaves assumed ownership of the household goods in the deserted plantation homestead, and comical disputes were witnessed among the women, as they claimed title to a bed or a table because they had long since mentally appropriated it, and inwardly determined to make it theirs when this eagerly expected day should come. This novel administration upon an estate was conducted as if the world could never have another dark day for them; but it was followed, within twenty-four hours, by a serious revulsion of feeling, when they learned that, in a country eaten up by an army, it became a troublesome question to tell how even they could live.

By the time the bridge was rebuilt the troops had eaten their noon meal and marched more rapidly to Brunswick ferry. The ruins of the railway bridge were still smoking, for it had been burned only that morning. A pontoon bridge had been at the ferry, and in the hasty retreat the order to scuttle and destroy the boats had been so incompletely carried out that more than half of them were uninjured, and many of the rest could be quickly repaired. This work was immediately begun, while some of the boats were used to ferry a detachment over to the island, which was about a mile wide, but an almost unbroken marsh. A causeway led to the city ferry, but an epaulement had been made across this near the further end, and a cannon or two swept the narrow road. The advanced guard was ordered to deploy skirmishers in the swamp and drive off the gunners if possible. A field battery of rifled guns was put in position, on a rise of ground on the west bank, to cover the detachment on the island, and the explosion of some of its shells in the city helped to hasten matters by showing that the town was within range. Meanwhile the work of repairing the pontoons was hurried, and reconnoissances made in the vicinity. Some railway employés came into camp and from them was learned the falsity of a rumor that General Hardee had brought his Charleston troops to Wilmington. Great columns of smoke soon began to ascend in the city, telling of the destruction of naval stores, and of preparation to evacuate the town.

Late in the afternoon a despatch was received from General Schofield, stating that Terry had been unable to make progress, and had evidence, which seemed reliable, that Hoke had been largely reinforced. Cox was therefore ordered to return down the river, and be ferried over to the left bank. Sure that the evidence before him made the immediate evacuation of the city certain, he put only one brigade in motion, and reported fully the circumstances. The great difficulty couriers found in reaching the points on the swamp-lined river, where they could communicate with the fleet and get a boat to put them over, made it midnight before a mutual understanding could be reached and different directions from Schofield could be received; but the latter warmly approved his subordinate's exercise of discretion, in remaining with the greater part of the division in apparent disobedience of reiterated orders. Hoke's appearance of resuming the aggressive proved to have been a demonstration to cover his retreat during the night, and the city was entered without opposition at daybreak next morning, thus celebrating Washington's birthday by the completion of another important step in the campaign.

Several things combined to make Newberne a more useful base of supply for Sherman than Wilmington. The harbor at Morehead City and Fort Macon was a better one than that at the mouth of Cape Fear River, and would admit vessels of deeper draught. The railway, between the harbor

and Newberne, some forty miles long, was in operation, with
some locomotives and cars already there, while nothing of
the kind was at Wilmington, the enemy having carefully removed all railway rolling stock on that line. From Newberne, much of the way to Kinston through the Dover
Swamp, the iron was not so injured that it might not be
used again, and the reconstruction of the railway by that
route would be both easier and more economical. As,
therefore, a safe base for Sherman was assured at Wilmington in case of need, Schofield turned his attention to the
work of preparing a still better line of communication from
Newbern to Goldsboro.

Several thousand convalescents returning to Sherman's
army had been sent from Washington to Newbern, and a
division of new troops, under General Ruger, assigned to the
Twenty-third Corps, had also been ordered to proceed to
that place. The old garrisons of the district would furnish
another division. On February 26th General Cox was detached from his command at Wilmington, and ordered by
sea to Newbern to carry out the purposes described. Colonel Wright, Sherman's Chief Engineer of Railways, was
ordered to the same point to take charge of the railway
rebuilding. Reaching Newbern on the last day of February, the organization of forces was immediately made. The
convalescents were formed into temporary battalions, with
as much reference to their former associations as practicable, and these were distributed among the brigades of the
properly organized troops. In this way two divisions were
formed, and Generals I. N. Palmer and S. P. Carter were,
respectively, assigned to their command. Ruger's division
arrived a little later. On March 1st Classen's brigade, of
Palmer's division, was sent to Core Creek, sixteen miles, to
be followed next day by Carter's division, so that the me-

chanical work might begin at once. At that time only one Confederate brigade (Whitford's) was known to be in the vicinity; but the almost total lack of wagons made it necessary to limit operations to the covering of the railway work. The whole number of wagon-teams in the district was fifty, and the utmost these could do was to supply the divisions at points near the end of the completed railway.

About three miles below Kinston a considerable stream, known as Southwest Creek, crosses the railway and wagon-roads leading to Newbern. The upper course of this stream is nearly parallel to the Neuse River, and almost the whole country between the Neuse and Trent Rivers, thirty miles long, is a great marsh, called the Dover Swamp in the lower part, and Gum Swamp in the upper. It was important to get control of the position along Southwest Creek as soon as possible, for the slight ridge on the hither side of that stream was the only dry land in the vicinity, and upon it were the principal roads of the Neuse Valley. Information had been received that Hoke had reached Kinston with a large division, and rumors of still further reinforcements to the enemy were rife. It was also known that a Confederate iron-clad steamer was at Kinston, and it was desirable to get positions on the Neuse where batteries could be placed. At the risk, therefore, of being short of rations, Cox advanced two divisions on the March 7th to the upper margin of the swamp at Wise's Forks, Palmer's on the right, covering the railroad, and Carter's on the left, covering the Dover Road, with an interval of nearly a mile between them. The Twelfth New York Cavalry, the only mounted men in the command, were used to patrol the roads to the left, and watch the crossings of Southwest Creek for five or six miles above, the stream being unfordable at this season. An old road, known as the British Road, ran parallel to the creek a mile in front of the position, and Colonel Upham, of Carter's division, was placed with two regiments at its inter-

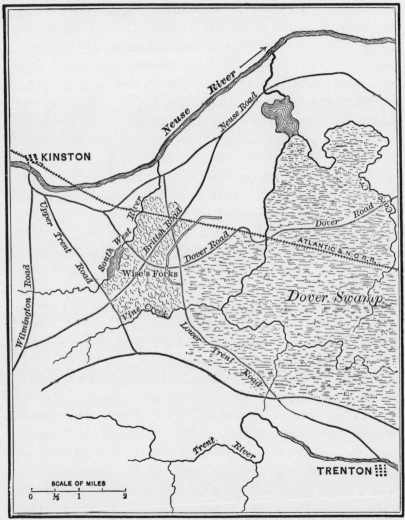

Map of Battle of Kinston.

section with the Dover Road, to cover approaches from the left. Some artillery fire had been drawn from the enemy

on the other side of Southwest Creek in taking these positions, both at the railway crossing and at the Dover Road;
but a chain of pickets was established along the stream, and
the cavalry reported that they had dismantled all the
bridges within the prescribed distance above, and had out-
posts at the crossings. Ruger's division was marched to
Gum Swamp, the end of the next section of railroad to be
rebuilt, where it was about three miles from the lines of
Carter and Palmer, and could support either in case of need.

General Schofield arrived at Newbern the same day,
coming by sea from Wilmington, and was in consultation
with his subordinate at the end of the railway, on the morning of the 8th, when a rapid artillery fire was heard at the
left front. Ruger was ordered to march quickly to Carter's
support, and, hastening in that direction in advance, Cox
found that the enemy had suddenly appeared on the flank
of Upham, and attacked him without warning. The cavalry
had failed to give notice of the advance, and Upham's men,
being most of them new recruits, had been unable to rally
after the surprise. He succeeded in bringing off about
one-fourth of his whole brigade in tolerable order, but
the rest was almost wholly captured. Carter's line was
partially protected by a light intrenchment, and the division met, without flinching, the assault which quickly followed the rout of the advanced post. Palmer was ordered
to send one brigade rapidly to the left, to support Carter,
and with the rest of his division to make a vigorous demonstration of crossing the creek in his front. Some prisoners
taken were found to belong to both Stewart's and Lee's
corps of the Army of Tennessee, and it was learned that
General Bragg was commanding the Confederate forces in
person, with the troops of the North Carolina district under
Hoke, strengthened by that part of Hood's Army of Tennes-

see which had reached North Carolina, under Clayton and
D. H. Hill.

The fact was that as Sherman was rapidly approaching
from the South, Johnston, who had just been assigned to
the command of all the forces opposing him, had authorized
Bragg to take the troops the latter had assembled at Goldsboro, with the available part of Hood's army, which had
reached Smithfield, and with these strike fiercely at the National column coming from Newbern, in the hope of routing
and driving it back in time to make a new concentration of
the whole in front of Sherman before he should reach the
Cape Fear River. The success, however, was limited to the
surprise of Upham's little command. Carter's division, at
Wise's Forks, aided by the brigade sent from Palmer, maintained the fight till Ruger arrived, when his division filled
the space between the two wings, and speedily making a
barricade with fallen timber and other material at hand, a
connected line of breastworks soon covered the whole front.
The country was of tangled wood and swamp, which im-
peded movement and prevented either side from seeing far.
The success of Bragg's first onset led him to think he had
the whole of Cox's command broken, though the principal
line had not been reached and was never shaken. Learning
the mistake, the Confederate General adjusted his lines
anew and advanced again, but was easily repulsed.

As the information received from prisoners showed at
least three divisions of the enemy engaged, Schofield directed Cox to maintain a watchful defensive till the arrival
of the remainder of the Twenty-third Corps, which was
marching across the country from Wilmington, and might
be expected in a day or two. He himself returned to Newberne to get into more immediate communication with
other portions of the Department. During the 9th lively

skirmishing continued : Bragg rebuilt the bridges over the creek behind him, and endeavored to push detachments beyond Palmer's right flank, between it and the river. This was prevented without much difficulty, though it kept Palmer harassed. On the morning of the 10th a serious attack was made upon Carter's front and left flank. Anticipating this, Carter's line of breastworks had been extended a long distance on the left, recurving to the rear, and these had been occupied by a skirmish line. As soon as the attack came (which proved to be by Hoke's division) McQuiston's brigade, of Ruger's division, which had been placed in reserve, was ordered at double quick step to Carter's left. Hoke was met by a severe fire of canister and shrapnel from the artillery, as well as by a steadily sustained infantry fire, and after a vain but strenuous effort to carry the line he was forced to withdraw. McQuiston was ordered to charge after him from the flank and did so, capturing several hundred prisoners. But the advance of the enemy upon Ruger now came, and McQuiston was not allowed to follow Hoke far, but was quickly recalled to support the centre, where the line was very thin. Palmer was also called upon for several battalions from the right, and Ruger was made strong enough to repulse Hill's and Clayton's men in their turn. During the progress of this latter attack, General Schofield arrived again from Newbern, and learning the persistent character of Bragg's effort, sent urgent messages to Couch to hasten the marching of his command. Bragg, however, had become convinced that he could make no farther impression on the line before him, and retreated in the night to Kinston, where a small detachment was left, and the rest of his forces were moved rapidly through Goldsboro, to join in the concentration which Johnston was making in front of Sherman.

The question of numbers, whether of those engaged or of the casualties, in this, as in all the later engagements of the war, is not easy to solve. The best Confederate authorities speak of the forces under Bragg, which properly belonged to the North Carolina district, as about eight or ten thousand men.[1] The number of the Army of Tennessee, who were reported as being with Bragg at Smithfield a week later, was 3,950. It is probable that these were the same who had been in the engagement at Kinston, diminished by their losses in that action ; and as the well-known method of the Confederate officers, in reporting their " effective" force, always reduced it ten or fifteen *per cent.* and often much more below our "present for duty," the figures given represent a total force of thirteen to fifteen thousand. Certainly Bragg thought they were enough to " enable him to win a victory," as he wrote Johnston, over the three divisions advancing from Newbern, and the recent experience of the enemy in attacking Schofield's troops, either at the west or east, had not warranted him in hoping much from an assault with inferior force, even if he had been aware of the irregular nature of the organizations which made up the provisional command.

The losses on the National side were 1,257, of which 935 were captured from Colonel Upham's advanced post. The remaining 322 were killed and wounded in defending our breastworks from the assaults of Bragg's troops. No part of the principal line was for a moment in his possession, and the character of the engagement was the oft-repeated one of a destructive repulse from a stoutly held intrenchment. The prisoners taken by the sally from our left were 266, and the overwhelming presumption is that Bragg's total

[1] Johnston's narrative, p. 378, says they were "supposed to amount to six or eight thousand men." Beauregard put them at ten thousand, and the Army of Tennessee at six thousand. See Appendix E, II.

loss must have equalled or exceeded that of Schofield's
troops, including what resulted from the surprise of the
advanced guard, and which was primarily occasioned by the
inadequate performance of outpost duty by the cavalry.

After Bragg's retreat, Schofield steadily pressed the woi k
of rebuilding the railway. Kinston was occupied on March
14th, and a large force was set at work to build a wagon-
bridge over the Neuse River there, as well as in assisting
Colonel Wright in renewing the railway bridge and complet-
ing the railroad to that point. The iron-clad steamer which
had been at Kinston was burned and sunk when Bragg retreated, and its remains were among the last traces of the
navy which at one time had swarmed in the Southern bays
and rivers.

On reaching Kinston, Schofield had ordered Terry to
advance from Wilmington along the line of the railroad
toward Goldsboro. This was done, reaching Faison's Station, twenty miles south of the Neuse, on the 20th, and
Terry now came within communicating distance of Sherman, by whose directions he marched upon Cox's bridge on
the 22d, and secured for the army that crossing of the river.
The obstructions in the Neuse River below Kinston were
removed, and steamboats reached Schofield's camp on the
18th. A day or two was spent in the accumulation of supplies, and, during the 19th, the dull pounding of a distant
cannonade was heard, which proved to be the Battle of
Bentonville, nearly fifty miles away. On the 20th, Schofield marched toward Goldsboro, which he entered with
little opposition on the 21st, and there, in a couple of days
more, was reassembled the grand army under Sherman,
whose march from Savannah had been quite as remarkable
as the former one from Atlanta to the sea, and the outline
of which we have now to trace.

CHAPTER X.

SAVANNAH TO COLUMBIA.

THE occupation of Savannah brought with it many questions of administration of a semi-political character, which
Sherman was glad to turn over to the civil officers of the
Government as quickly as possible. Secretary Stanton visited the city as soon as its capture was known, and authori-
tatively announced the action of the President in regard to
the captured cotton and other stores, the abandoned lands,
and the refugee negroes. In his consultations with Sherman, the latter learned what was then the purpose of the
Government regarding terms of peace if symptoms of a desire to submit to the National Constitution should be shown
by any of the States in rebellion. The General, however,
as far as he could, avoided all affairs that were not strictly
military, and devoted himself to preparations for an early
renewal of the campaign. The men were clothed and shod,
the artillery and wagon-trains were overhauled and repaired,
and supplies were collected and distributed. The experience of the march through Georgia was turned to the best
account in determining what stores should be taken with
the columns, and what could probably be obtained from the
country.

Sherman's plan of campaign was fixed early in January,
and preliminary movements were immediately begun. General Howard concentrated most of the right wing at Beau-

fort, S. C., by means of transport vessels, part of one corps being ordered to march from Savannah by the Union Causeway in the same direction. The left wing, under General Slocum, was directed to move up both banks of the Savannah about forty miles, then to unite at Robertsville in South Carolina, while Howard should advance from Beaufort to Pocotaligo, driving Hardee's forces over the Combahee River, and occupying the country between that stream and the Coosawhatchie. Howard's movement to Beaufort would thus seem to threaten Charleston, while Slocum's looked toward Augusta; and the enemy would be left in doubt as to Sherman's purpose, though the positions of his troops would be the best possible for the advance upon Columbia, which was the objective for the first stage of the campaign. At Pocotaligo, Howard would be fifty miles on his way, yet he would still be near a water base for supplies until the moment of beginning the long march into the interior. The same would be true of Slocum, for Robertsville was near Sister's Ferry, on the Savannah, and the wagons of all the columns could therefore be full when communication with Savannah should be broken. An interior line of defences about the city was prepared by Colonel Poe, Chief Engineer, and a garrison was assigned from General Foster's department, so that the army in the field might not be diminished. A few changes were made in the organization of the corps. Logan returned and resumed the command of the Fifteenth; in the divisions and brigades a few officers were relieved and went north by sea, while others, who had been wounded or ill, rejoined the army.

Sherman's purpose was to feint on both Augusta and Charleston, but to march directly upon Columbia and thence to Goldsboro, where he hoped to open communication with Newbern and Beaufort, N. C. The capture of

Fort Fisher just before he began the campaign, and the transfer of General Schofield with the Twenty-third Corps to the Department of North Carolina were steps determined upon by General Grant to facilitate his work, and gave him greater assurance of success. His plans had been settled, however, before he knew of either of these auxiliary movements. He felt sure that no sufficient force could be brought by the Confederate Government to oppose him till he should reach the Cape Fear River. There, the contingency to be provided for was that Lee might break away from Richmond, and throw himself upon his army before Grant could overtake him with the Army of the Potomac. To guard against this, Grant redoubled his efforts to extend his left to the westward of Petersburg, so that no direct Southern route could be open to Lee; but the latter, forced to move westward before turning south, might be no nearer to Sherman than himself. If this should not prove true, Sherman would still be abundantly strong to make a dilatory defensive contest with the combined Confederate forces in the East till Grant could reach him. The controlling policy of this campaign, therefore, was activity in marching, with great caution in fighting any considerable bodies of the enemy until a new base were established and rapid communication opened with the General-in-Chief.

The route for the march was practically determined by the topography of the country, which, like all the Southern seaboard, is low and sandy, with numerous extensive swamps and deep rivers widely swamp-bordered, only approachable by long causeways on which the narrow head of a column may be easily and long resisted by a small force. The rivers of South Carolina are nearly parallel to the Savannah, and, to avoid frequent and difficult crossings, it would be necessary to march into the interior upon the ridges be-

tween two or more streams, till the upper and narrower
waters were reached, and then cross to the watersheds
which lay most nearly in the proper direction. Another
important object was to cut the railway system of South
Carolina in a way similar to the work done in Georgia, so
as to cripple the transportation resources of the country
and prevent the easy concentration of Confederate troops.
An examination of the map will quickly show that Sherman's easiest way to accomplish his purpose was to march
northwestward between the Combahee (or Salkehatchie, as
its upper course is called) and the Savannah, as if going to
Augusta, till more than half that distance is made, then passing the Salkehatchies, Big and Little, strike the Charleston and Augusta Railway near its crossing of the Edisto
River. After destroying a section of this road, the south
fork of the Edisto could be crossed, and no other deep river
would be met till the Saluda is reached at the capital of the
State. This was the route Sherman adopted, making only
the deviation by which he reached the Columbia branch of
the railway at Orangeburg, and destroyed a portion of it for
twenty miles north of that place.

The report which Generals Taylor and Hardee made to the
Confederate Government at the beginning of December has
already been mentioned, and shows that the principal mili-
tary officers in the theatre of operations made a good fore-
cast of Sherman's purposes and of the probable results.
Upon the news of the great disaster to Hood at Nashville,
Beauregard asked to be relieved of the care of South
Carolina and Southern Georgia, so that he might give his
exclusive attention to the Army of Tennessee and the Gulf
States. He suggested that Augusta naturally belonged to
Hardee's command, and, in a letter of final instructions to
the latter, written on December 31st, he indicated the prob-

able necessity, at an early day, of evacuating Charleston, and uniting all the available troops in Hardee's department to oppose Sherman's advance. He directed all the cotton to be removed, and if any remained in the city at the time of evacuation, it should be burned. This was in accordance with the general policy of the Confederates in regard to the great Southern staple; that of the National armies, in like manner, was to save for the public treasury all that was captured in seaports or in territory likely to remain under our control, but to destroy that which, by the passage of our armies, could fall again into the enemy's hands. It often happened, therefore, that both armies were co-operating in the destruction of cotton when both were in doubt whether their opponents might not gain something by its preservation. In this way Wheeler had offered to spare the cotton in the Georgia march if Sherman would give assurances as to other property; but Sherman had answered: "If you don't burn it, I will."

The evacuation of Charleston was so grave a question of public policy for the Confederate Government that it could not be determined as a purely military problem. Beauregard had said, in the letter just referred to, "The fall of Charleston would necessarily be a terrible blow to the Confederacy, but its fall, with the loss of its brave garrison, would be still more fatal to our cause."[1] Knowing the opinions of all the Confederate generals, as we now do, we must conclude that the Richmond authorities delayed the abandonment of the city until it was too late to concentrate in Sherman's front. It is true, however, that the National commander surprised all of his opponents by the speed at which he forced his way northward, and that Hardee had

---

[1] Jones's Chatham Artillery, p. 210.

reported the Salkehatchie swamps to be entirely impassable at the time Sherman's army was marching through them at the regular pace of ten or twelve miles daily, making cor-duroy road for his trains nearly every mile of the way.[1]

Sherman had hoped that he might rely upon fair weather after the middle of January, and had planned his march to begin at that time. The season disappointed him, for it proved to be a winter of almost continuous rains. The Savannah rose so that, at Sister's Ferry, forty miles up the river, where Slocum laid his bridge, the stream was three miles wide, and long trestle bridges had to be made to con-nect the ends of the pontoon bridge with the shores. It was also almost impossible to protect the structure against the force of the current and of the drift-wood brought down by the freshet. The Union Causeway, on which one or two divisions attempted to march from Savannah to join General Howard at Pocotaligo, was under water, and the whole re-gion was more like a great lake than a habitable land. On the last day of January, Howard had concentrated at Poco-taligo the right wing, except Corse's division of Logan's corps, which had been forced by the high water to join Slo-cum and cross the Savannah at his bridge, awaiting an op-portunity to rejoin the corps some days later. This concen-tration had been effected with but little fighting, for Hardee had evidently determined to take up the line of the Comba-hee and Salkehatchie, and to make no serious defence west of it. Force's division, of Blair's corps, was sent to make a demonstration as if to cross the Combahee ten miles below the railroad bridge, and so to create the impression that

---

[1] At the time of paroling the Confederate Army at Greensboro, N. C., speaking of this part of Sherman's march, and of the combination of physical labor with military hardihood, General Johnston said, in the hearing of the author, that, when he heard of it, "he made up his mind that there had been no such army since the days of Julius Cæsar."

Charleston was aimed at. This done, the order was given
to march northward on the route already described, in the
expectation that Slocum and Kilpatrick's cavalry would be
over Sister's Ferry, and ready to join the movement by the
time Howard should be opposite that crossing.

It happened that simultaneously with the beginning of
the new campaign by Sherman, a conference of Confederate
officers was held near Augusta to arrange the details of their
own plans. Beauregard, Hardee, D. H. Hill, and G. W.
Smith were all there, and a careful estimate was made of
the effective force they hoped to combine against Sherman.
Of 18,000 men under Hardee's command in South Carolina,
they reckoned 14,500 as available for concentration, while
the heavy artillery and some other troops would garrison
Charleston and other points along the coast. Beauregard
promised 11,000 infantry and artillery from Hood's army,
though only half of these were then present. Wheeler's
cavalry was 6,700 strong, besides Butler's division which
has been counted among Hardee's men. The Georgia militia and reserves were 1,450. A total of 33,450 was the force
they agreed they could concentrate by February 4th or
5th, though about three thousand from the Army of Tennessee were not expected to reach Augusta till the 10th or
11th.[1] It was not expected that the State Militia would
serve far outside their own States, nor does there seem to
have been any hope that new recruits could be added to
their army. The conscription had exhausted itself, and the
population not already in the ranks was paralyzed rather
than stimulated to exertion by the presence of the National
army. As Hardee afterward expressed it, they knew that it
was now only a question of the time it would take to use up

---

[1] See Appendix E, II.

the military force already organized, for the politicians could not face the thought of surrender.[1]

The outlook was surely far from encouraging, but Beauregard, as the superior officer present, though sick in body and in mind, was forced to assume command, and make such dispositions as he could to obstruct Sherman's march. But while their somewhat tardy consultation was going on, the opportunity for an effectual concentration, even of the little force at their disposal, had passed, for Sherman was in motion. On February 7th, General Howard was upon the line of the Charleston and Augusta Railway at Midway, and on the 12th he had crossed both forks of the Edisto and had broken the Columbia branch of the road at Orangeburg. Butler's division of cavalry, a light battery or two, and some small detachments of infantry were all of Hardee's that succeeded in getting in front of Sherman. These joined Wheeler, and did what they could to burn bridges and hold the long causeways through the swamps; but the leading division of a column was usually strong enough to outflank them and drive them off with little loss, so that the laying of the corduroy road never ceased, and Sherman's twenty-five hundred wagons rolled on unchecked. Leaving the Georgia militia to garrison Augusta, where they were useless, Beauregard could only lead the remnants of the Army of Tennessee by the country roads and by a long detour through Newberry and Chester to Charlotte in North Carolina, while Hardee at Charleston was awaiting the inevitable day when he must abandon Sumter and the cradle of the rebellion, to make haste by his only remaining railway through Florence to Cheraw, that the concentration talked of at Augusta might be finally made near the capital

---

[1] This was said by Hardee to the author after the close of hostilities.

of North Carolina. General Wade Hampton had been sent from Virginia to command the cavalry in South Carolina, in the hope that his great personal influence would rouse the people from their despair, and do what proclamations and levies-in-mass had so signally failed to do in Georgia; but the only result was to lay the foundation of a somewhat bitter dispute whether he or the National soldiery caused the burning of Columbia, the beautiful city of his home.

An itinerary of the march through South Carolina would furnish interesting daily illustrations of the expedients by which an army of expert woodsmen can overcome difficulties in logistics commonly thought insurmountable. In a country where many of the rivers are known by the name of swamps, continuous rains so raised the waters that scarce a stream was passed without deploying the advanced guard through water waist deep, and sometimes it reached even to their armpits, forcing them to carry the cartridge-box at the neck and the musket on the head. The fitness of the name swamp for even the rivers will be felt when it is remembered that at the crossing of the Salkehatchie at Beaufort's Bridge the stream had fifteen separate channels, each of which had to be bridged before Logan's corps could get over. Whoever will consider the effect of dragging the artillery and hundreds of loaded army wagons over mud roads in such a country, and of the infinite labor required to pave these roads with logs, levelling the surface with smaller poles in the hollows between, adding to the structure as the mass sinks in the ooze, and continuing this till the miles of train have pulled through, will get a constantly growing idea of the work, and a steadily increasing wonder that it was done at all. Certainly he will not wonder that the Confederate generals believed they could count upon Sherman's remaining at his base till the rains ceased

and the waters subsided. If the march through Georgia remained pictured in the soldiers' memories as a bright, frol-
icsome raid, that through South Carolina was even more
indelibly printed as a stubborn wrestle with the elements,
in which the murky and dripping skies were so mingled
with the earth and water below as to make the whole a fit
type of "chaos come again;" but where, also, the indomitable
will of sixty thousand men, concentrated to do the inflexible
purpose of one, bridged this chaos for hundreds of miles,
and, out-laboring Hercules, won a physical triumph that
must always remain a marvel. And mile by mile as they
advanced, the General and his men were equally clear in the
conviction he had expressed to Grant before starting, that
every step they took was "as much a direct attack upon
Lee's army as though I were operating within the sound of
his artillery."

Sixteen days' marching, working, and skirmishing brought
the army to the Saluda River, just above Columbia. The
Augusta Railway had been destroyed from the Edisto nearly
to Aiken, some fifty miles, The Columbia branch had been
ruined from a point five or six miles south of Orangeburg
to the Congaree River, about thirty miles. These great
gaps in the interior lines of communication effectually separated the Confederate forces, and were by far too great to be
repaired during the campaign. A few hours were enough
to secure the crossings of the Saluda and Broad Rivers,
which unite just above Columbia to form the Congaree.
This was easier than to cross the latter stream, for it is bordered by the wide Caw-caw swamp, and the approaches
were very difficult.

On the approach of the National troops, the Confederate
cavalry burned the bridges, sprinkling them first with resin
and tar, so as to make a quick fire: indeed, it was so quick

that some of the rear guard could not pass, and had to gallop off by a long circuit to escape capture. In Columbia they burned the two railway stations and depôt buildings, one at the south and the other at the north of the place. Long, narrow piles of cotton bales were made along the middle of the streets, and these were cut open and fired. Some of Wheeler's cavalry, acting upon the rule they had often avowed, that it was not worth while to leave what they wanted for an enemy to take, broke open the shops and pillaged them.[1]

Before entering the city, Sherman issued orders that private dwellings and property, colleges, libraries, charitable institutions, and the like, should be respected, but that the arsenals, foundries, machine-shops, and public workshops should be destroyed. The order was in substance the same as he had issued at Savannah, and was appropriate both because Columbia was the first city of any considerable size the army occupied after leaving the coast, and because the long continuance of a march in which the troops were living on the country had gradually increased the number of stragglers, and relaxed the bands of discipline in portions of the command. General C. R. Woods's division of Logan's corps entered the city, Stone's brigade being the advanced guard. The other troops passed on and encamped beyond. A strong wind from the northwest was blowing, scattering the loose cotton about, and Colonel Stone directed his men to assist the citizens, who, with a wretched hand-engine and buckets, were trying to quench the fire in the cotton, which the wind was making dangerous. Sherman himself entered the town soon after the advanced guard, with Howard and Logan. The mayor presented himself, and was informed of the orders for the protection of private property. Some

---

[1] Testimony before Mixed Commission on American and British Claims. See also Appendix C.

foolish persons, thinking to please the soldiers, brought out whiskey by pailfuls, and before the superior officers were aware of it, a good many men of Stone's brigade were intoxicated. Woods immediately ordered the brigade relieved, and that of W. B. Woods [1] was substituted as provost guard. All the whiskey that could be found was emptied on the ground, and the intoxicated men were put in arrest. The wind continued to rise, and before night was blowing a gale. The cotton bales, tenacious of fire, were smoldering. It would seem that a flake from one of these set fire to a shed or building near by, and the flames soon spread. Sherman himself gave prompt orders to do all that could be done to conquer the fire, and the whole division was put at work to quench or to girdle it. The houses of the city were built of pine wood, and, from the place of starting, the southeastern part of the town was soon a roaring, leaping mass of flame, utterly beyond control. But there were not wanting intoxicated men among the soldiers, and others equally excited by the tales of horror which the escaped military prisoners had to tell of their cruel sufferings in a prison pen near the city, where they had been exposed to the weather and forced to burrow in the ground for their only shelter. These seized upon the idea that the destruction of the capital of South Carolina was a fit retribution upon the State for its leadership in the great rebellion, and carried the fire to windward of its starting-place to make the destruction more complete. Drunken soldiers, camp followers, and escaped convicts from the penitentiary, made a dangerous mob, and the fire which began by accident was becoming the occasion of mischiefs of other kinds. Noticing this, Howard ordered a brigade from Hazen's division to be deployed as skirmish-

---

[1] Now Justice of the U. S. Supreme Court.

ers, to sweep through the town, arresting all disorderly persons, citizens and soldiers, white and black, and to hold them under guard. After midnight the gale subsided and the progress of the fire was stopped, but the greater part of the city was in ashes.

Sherman was sincerely grieved at the misfortune of Columbia, and did what he could to lighten the trouble of the citizens. He gave them a large herd of cattle and other provisions to supply their immediate wants, and directed the issue of these to be made by the city authorities to the destitute. No one was more unbending than he in the destruction of whatever could be of military assistance to the enemy; but no one drew more clearly the line between the destruction which was useful to a cause and that which would merely make private suffering and irritation. The Confederate authorities made haste to proclaim the burning of Columbia as a deliberately planned and ordered piece of incendiarism; but no event was ever more fully investigated, and no conclusion can well be more solidly established by testimony than that which is given in the foregoing narrative of the occurrence. Orangeburg had been partly burned by fire, set by an exasperated resident trader in revenge for the destruction of his cotton by the Confederate cavalry, and this too was loudly charged to the National army. An even-handed justice will, however, admit that the stragglers from the army were increasing in number and in familiarity with pillage, through the natural education of such a war, and that there were some officers among the infantry who were not unwilling to compete with Kilpatrick in his effort to leave the route marked by "chimney-stacks without houses, and the country desolate."[1] Some careless expressions of

---

[1] In the "Ninety-second Illinois," commonly attributed to General Atkins who was one of Kilpatrick's brigade commanders (p. 211), it is said that on the evening

Sherman, in a letter to General Halleck, have been seized upon as evidence of his approval of lawless pillaging; but the consistent character of his commands to his subordinates from the beginning of the campaign, and the treatment of all the cities on the line of his march from Atlanta to Savannah, and from Savannah to Raleigh, show that his policy was one of mildness to the individual citizen and of destruction only to the public resources of the country. The city of Atlanta is to-day proof, to him who cares to see, that the far-echoed assertions that it was destroyed are consistent with the continued existence of its original buildings, except the depots, machine-shops, and military factories, with a very few houses that were immediately contiguous to them. War cannot be other than a fearful scourge, but the assertion that the late civil war surpassed others of modern times in wanton destruction or cruelty is the reverse of true.

In Columbia there were factories of powder and fixed ammunition, an arsenal, armory and machine-shops, and an establishment for the engraving and manufacture of Confederate paper money. All these were destroyed on the 18th and 19th of February, for their detached positions about the town had saved them from the general conflagration. On the 20th the army resumed its march, leaving behind it a community overwhelmed with its losses, almost stupefied by the terrible change a few days had wrought, and only saved from starvation by the store of food which the National com mander took from his army supplies to give them.

---

of January 27th, near Savannah, " General Kilpatrick gave a party to the officers of his command, and in his speech said, ' In after years, when travellers passing through South Carolina shall see chimney-stacks without houses, and the country desolate, and shall ask, Who did this? some Yankee will answer, Kilpatrick's cavalry.'" The same narrative, pp. 212, 215, seems to claim for the cavalry the burning of the villages of Barnwell, Lexington, and Monticello, beside the destruction of plantation houses.

CHAPTER XI.

AVERASBORO AND BENTONVILLE.—REUNION OF THE GRAND ARMY.

THE military operations in the first part of the campaign had not cost many lives, though the skirmishing had been incessant. Occasionally a determined stand would be made, as at Rivers' Bridge on the Salkehatchie, where, in a cannonade upon our advanced guard, Colonel Wager Swayne, an esteemed and valuable officer, lost a leg. More commonly, the trees and thickets made safe cover for the troops, and detachments sent a mile or two above or below would gain the farther bank of the stream by ferrying men over in pontoons, and the enemy would retreat as soon as this was done. After passing Columbia the face of the country changed. It became more rolling, the streams were narrower and less difficult, the plantations were more numerous and richer, and the foragers collected more abundant supplies. The Fifteenth Corps (Logan's) returned upon the line of the Charleston Railway to Cedar Creek, destroying about twenty miles of the road on the left bank of the Congaree, in addition to the injury already done it on the other side of the river. Howard then turned this column northward to overtake Blair's (Seventeenth) Corps, which had marched along the railroad toward Charlotte, and had torn it up almost to Winnsboro, forty miles from Columbia. The only other railway running out of Columbia was a branch road going

westward to Abbeville, and this was committed to General
Slocum with the left wing and the cavalry, who ruined it for
a distance about equal to that destroyed by Blair on the
Charlotte road. This part of the army then turned toward
Winnsboro, where they supplemented Blair's work by tearing up ten or fifteen miles more of the Northern line. While
Sherman's chief purpose in making this strong demonstration northward was to make thorough work of the interruption of the railway communications between Beauregard's
and Hardee's forces, it also had the effect of creating the impression that he would continue his march on Charlotte, and
delayed any concentration of the enemy toward Raleigh.
The National columns were now turned sharply to the east,
crossing the Catawba River and making for the Great Pedee
at Cheraw, while the cavalry kept well out on the left flank.
The extreme right visited Camden, and while moving between the two rivers, the flanks of the army were often forty
miles apart. There was scarcely any cessation of rain, and
the marching was hardly less laborious than before, though
the swamps were not so continuous.

As soon as Hardee knew of Sherman's occupation of Columbia, he evacuated Charleston, moving his troops by rail
to Cheraw, where great quantities of stores, both public and
private, had been sent. The cotton, which was stored in
the city in large quantities, he burned in the warehouses, and
the fire, spreading, did a good deal of mischief to the city.
A great store of powder and ammunition blew up, killing
two hundred of the citizens who were crowding about the
conflagration.[1] Admiral Dahlgren and General Foster had
kept up active demonstrations along the coast, and occupied
the city on February 18th, the day after its evacuation.

---

[1] Pollard's Southern Hist. of the War, Vol. IV., pp. 150, 151.

Hardee had constructed strong works at the Pedee, behind Cheraw, but they met the usual fate of fortifications made by a very inferior force. The advance of Slocum with the left wing turned the position, and the right wing, under Howard entered Cheraw on March 3d, capturing 28 pieces of artillery, 3,000 stands of small arms, and an immense quantity of ammunition and stores.[1] Hampton, with the Confederate cavalry, at first moved off toward Charlotte, but making a wide circuit, he joined Hardee again before the latter crossed the Cape Fear River at Fayetteville, on the 11th, retreating before Slocum, who entered that place with the Fourteenth (Davis's) Corps on that day. Hampton appears to have been deceived regarding Sherman's intended line of march, and to have thought he was aiming at Charlotte, where Hood's Army of Tennessee was assembling; and in the effort to return to his place in front of the National army, he unexpectedly ran into Kilpatrick's cavalry, in the night of the 9th, not far from a hamlet called Solemn Grove. Kilpatrick had assigned to his three brigades halting places at the corners of a triangle, where they would hold different cross-roads and mutually protect each other, but Atkins and his brigade were anticipated by the Confederates at his intended position, and notwithstanding the most industrious efforts to reach Spencer's brigade by a circuit in the night, he was unable to do so in time to warn it of an attack by Hampton from the side supposed to be covered. Kilpatrick was with Spencer, and Hampton having, as he thought, made dispositions of his force to assure success, charged, with Butler's division, upon the camp a little before daybreak. It was a complete surprise. A house in which Kilpatrick and Spencer were sleeping was surrounded; a battery near headquarters was in the

---

[1] Howard's official report.

enemy's hands, and the brigade was routed, and fled into the swamp. Kilpatrick himself managed to escape from the house in the darkness, half-dressed and unarmed ; but the hardy troopers were used to rough-and-tumble fighting, and began to rally as soon as they reached the protection of the cypress trees. Kilpatrick was soon among them, and, after a little organizing under cover of the train guard and of volunteer skirmishers, they charged back upon Hampton, whose men were too eager for plunder, retook the cannon, with which they fired upon their adversaries, and turned the rout into a victory. Spencer and the staff officers had taken refuge in the upper part of the house, where they had barri-caded themselves, and were released by the unexpected success of their friends. Atkins, guided by the sound of the combat, came up as the affair ended, and Jordan's brigade arrived soon after, as did also a brigade of infantry sent from Slocum's column at the noise of the fight. With all their cool courage, the routed camp would hardly have been able to reform but for the fact that four hundred dismounted men had been armed with rifled muskets and bayonets at Savannah, and these, commanded by Lieutenant-Colonel Stough, of the Ninth Ohio Cavalry, were with the train, a little way from the general camp. At the noise of the attack they formed, making a line to which the rest rallied, and advanced. When the gleaming bayonets were seen in the gray light, the cry was raised that the infantry were upon them, and the disconcerted Confederates were thrown into confusion. Then came the general rally of Kilpatrick's men, and the tables were completely turned. The affair had no special importance, but is a fair type of the cavalry combats which enlivened the laborious march. Hampton released a number of prisoners, and claimed to have captured five hundred, though Kilpatrick only reported two hundred missing. The Confederates suffered severely, "especially in officers," Johnston says, but the exact number of casualties is not given. Over a hundred killed, and many wounded, were left upon the field, arguing a loss probably greater than that which was inflicted upon Kilpatrick.[1]

At Fayetteville Sherman destroyed the Arsenal, originally built by the National Government, but which had been greatly enlarged by the Confederates and filled with machinery for the manufacture of weapons, brought from Harper's Ferry at the beginning of the war. Here, also, he heard the whistle of a steamboat which opened communication by the Cape Fear River with Wilmington, and got news of the progress Schofield was making on both his lines. He had thought of the possibility that he might have to move down the right bank of the river to make his intended junction, and establish a new base; but the retreat of Hardee northward, and the certainty that Kinston was soon to be in our possession, now removed the last doubt of a successful concentration at Goldsboro. He did not know of Bragg's effort to overwhelm the corps operating from Newbern, but he believed that his own advance must now bring all the detachments of the enemy together to resist his progress. He determined, therefore, to march the left wing up the river by the east bank for some distance, as if aiming at Raleigh, and then to move rapidly to the right and meet Schofield at Goldsboro.

The news of the assignment of General Johnston to the command of all the Confederate forces in the Carolinas reached Sherman at Cheraw on March 3d, though the appointment had been made on February 23d, when the news of the presence of the National army at Winnsboro had pro-

---

[1] General Atkins in Ninety-second Illinois, p. 228.

duced in Richmond the belief that Sherman meant to follow
the line of the railway through Charlotte.   Every effort had
been made by the Confederate Government to accumulate
army supplies along that, its only remaining available line,
and nearly four months' food and clothing for Lee's army
was collected in its dépôts.   The Confederate Congress had,
in the emergency, made Lee General-in-Chief of all their
armies, and he had called Johnston from the retirement in
which he had lived since the preceding July to assume the
direction of the forces which were trying to prevent Sherman from closing in upon the rear of Richmond.   Mr.
Davis, the President of the Confederacy, had openly declared
that he would never give Johnston a military command
again, but the responsibility was now with Lee, and Mr.
Davis could only acquiesce.

It is not overstating the truth to say that the news of
Johnston's assignment was received throughout Sherman's
army as a note of warning to be prepared for more stubborn
and well-planned resistance to their progress.   Officers and
men were agreed in the opinion that the Richmond Government had at last taken a wise step, though they were quite
sure it was too late for even Johnston to save the campaign.
Sherman's estimate of the forces Johnston might concentrate
to meet him was about forty-five thousand men of all arms ;
and reckoning those under Bragg in North Carolina at ten
thousand, his figures will be found to be almost exactly those
which the Confederate generals had set down in their conference near Augusta at the beginning of the campaign.[1]
But Hardee's eighteen thousand had dwindled rapidly since
the evacuation of Charleston, the militia of South Carolina
and Georgia had gone home, the cavalry had suffered con-

---

[1] See Appendix E, II.

siderable losses, the remnants of Hood's army had grown
less as they travelled northward, and when Beauregard submitted his estimates to Johnston at Charlotte in the beginning of March, about twenty-six thousand infantry and artillery, and about six thousand cavalry, was the extent of the
army on which they could depend.

Johnston soon satisfied himself that Sherman's course lay
toward Fayetteville, and leaving Beauregard with some
force at Charlotte to protect the railway to Danville, went
in person to Fayetteville to meet Hardee and Hampton, giving orders for the concentration of other troops near Smithfield.   It was at this time that he authorized Bragg to take
the troops of Stewart's and Lee's corps to unite with Hoke's
and make the movement against Schofield near Kinston,
calculating that there would still be time to reassemble in
front of Sherman before he could reach the Neuse River.
It would be difficult to better his plan, but his numbers
were not enough to make either part of it successful, though
he did everything that courage and activity could do.

Sherman had waited at Fayetteville a day or two, in the
hope of receiving from Wilmington some shoes and clothing
of which his men were almost destitute, but no supply of
these could yet be got, and he pushed forward.   Slocum's
columns with the cavalry crowded Hardee closely on the
15th of March, capturing Colonel Rhett, the commander
of the brigade acting as rear guard.   They approached
Averasboro on the 16th, where Hardee had intrenched on a
narrow ridge between the river and swamp, and Slocum
ordered Jackson's and Ward's divisions of the Twentieth
(Williams') Corps to be deployed, Kilpatrick's cavalry being
on the right flank.   Sherman, being present, directed a
brigade of infantry to be sent well to the left to attack the
line in flank.   This was vigorously done by Case's brigade,

and Taliaferro's division was routed, falling back in haste
upon a line about a third of a mile in rear, where Hardee
had intrenched McLaws' division. The chief weight of the
stroke fell upon Rhett's brigade, which had lost its commander the day before, and it fled with a loss of over a hun
dred left dead upon the field, and more than two hundred captured. A battery of three field guns was also among the
trophies of this brilliant affair. Williams's divisions pressed
on, found Hardee's lines again intrenched, and a warm engagement began; but darkness put an end to the day's
operations. Hardee retreated during the night, and Sherman's movements were resumed in the morning.[1] The National loss in the affair at Averasboro had been seventy-seven
killed and nearly five hundred wounded. Hardee admitted
a loss of about the same number. Seriously encumbered
with his own injured men, Sherman directed the Confederate
wounded, who numbered about seventy, to be left in a field
hospital in charge of an officer and some of their own men,
after proper surgical attention had been given them.

The two or three days that followed are remembered by
the officers and men of that army as among the most weari-
some of the campaign. Incessant rain, deep mud, roads
always wretched but now nearly impassable, seemed to cap
the climax of tedious, laborious marching. Sherman had
changed his order of movement at Fayetteville, directing
four divisions of each wing to march light, and the remainder to accompany the trains and assist them forward. By
this arrangement he reckoned upon having a force ready for
battle on either flank, large enough to hold at bay the
whole of Johnston's army if the Confederate commander

---

[1] Rhett's brigade, which suffered so severely, was an organization of heavy artillery at Charleston, and had been the garrison of Sumter. It took the field as
infantry when Charleston was evacuated.

should suddenly assail one wing. In spite of every exertion, however, the columns were a good deal drawn out, and long intervals separated the divisions. On the morning of the 19th, two divisions of Davis's corps (Fourteenth) were about eight miles from Bentonville, a hamlet on the southeast side of Mill Creek, a small tributary of Neuse River, where the north and south road from Smithfield to Clinton crosses one leading from Averasboro to Goldsboro. Two divisions of Williams's (Twentieth) corps were eight miles farther at the rear. Kilpatrick with his cavalry had followed the retreat of Hardee to the north, and was at the left and rear of Williams, making his way back to the principal column. Howard with the four light divisions of the right wing was upon parallel roads to the southward, if they can be called parallel when they were sometimes six miles apart and sometimes ten or twelve. The trains with their guards were toiling along, somewhat farther back, taking intermediate roads when they could.

Sherman reasoned that Hardee's affair at Averasboro had been made to delay his approach to Raleigh till Johnston could unite his forces in front of the State capital, and the fact that battle was given with only Hardee's command seemed to prove that his adversary would be in no condition to venture south of the Neuse River before his own concentration at Goldsboro could be made. He did not know, however, that Johnston had just struck fiercely at the column advancing from Newbern, and that Hardee's stand at Averasboro had been made to give time to get Bragg's forces back and deliver him a blow before his junction with Schofield could be made. The Confederate commander, from his central position, was in telegraphic communication with his subordinates, and knew better than Sherman on the morning of the 19th what progress

Schofield's two columns were making. He could therefore make his combinations knowingly, while the National commander was still left to conjecture. If Johnston meant to do anything more than make a purely defensive retreat, it was essential to him to gather his forces and strike quick ; twenty-four hours later would have been too late, for Slocum and Howard would have been together at Cox's bridge, and Terry would have joined with the two fresh divisions. Johnston was now giving good proof that if he could not be made to fight unless he chose, he could assume the most active offensive when it was necessary. He knew on the 17th that Sherman had turned off from Averasboro toward Goldsboro, and that Hardee was resting at Elevation about two-thirds of the way on the road from his late battle-ground to Smithfield. Bragg had reached the last-named place, and the information from Hampton was that Slocum's two corps were nearly a day's march apart, and as far from Howard's. They must pass by the flank three miles in front of Bentonville, the little village whose position has already been described. He saw that this was the only opportunity likely to occur for fighting Sherman's several corps in detail, and gave orders to concentrate everything at Bentonville on the 18th.

Sherman had been loth to widen the lines of his march, but to do so was the condition of feeding his men on the country as he still had to do, and for the same reason he must keep moving till he should get upon a railway line of communication with the base Schofield was establishing. But he frankly tells us, also, that the evidence before him induced a confident belief that Johnston would hold to the north line of the Neuse and dispute its passage. This belief induced him to leave Slocum's line early in the morning of the 19th, and make his way across to Howard's

In accordance with his habit, he had remained with the exposed flank till he thought the point of danger passed, and now went to the right wing because he would thus get quickest into communication with Schofield, and be nearer to the point where he meant to cross the Neuse and reach Goldsboro. His reasoning was strictly in accord with sound principles, but as constantly happens in war, the facts which he did not know were essential to a right conclusion. It would, however, have been more prudent to have delayed Slocum's advance with the two divisions of Davis's corps till Williams with the Twentieth should have come nearer, and a little carelessness in this respect must be attributed to over-confidence in the belief that Johnston would not now take the aggressive.

But Johnston also found his calculations fail in some respects. He intended to have his troops ready to attack the head of Slocum's column early in the morning, but the maps were wrong, as they uniformly were, and Hardee's road to Bentonville proved to be too long to be marched by daylight after his orders were received. Consequently Hampton was directed to obstruct Slocum's advance, and prevent his reaching the cross-roads before Hardee. The Confederate cavalry under Wheeler was therefore close in front of Davis's corps when his march began on the 19th, and had made breastworks at some points, behind which they offered an unusually stubborn resistance.[1] Carlin's division had the lead, and as his men went forward the foragers were found on right and left of the road, having been unable to drive off

---

[1] The first prisoners captured were from Dibrell's division. Johnston says (Narrative, p. 392) that Butler's division was in front of Howard, yet he also says that Wheeler's command was not engaged on the 19th. There must be error in this, unless the organization of Wheeler's corps had recently been changed. Slocum was certainly fighting *some* mounted force, which resisted stubbornly all day.

the enemy or get out beyond his flanks. This was an omin
ous sign, for where these enterprising skirmishers could not
go, the opposition must be stronger than a cavalry rear guard
usually was. As Carlin pushed on, however, Hampton gave
way slowly, and it was seen that the opposition came from
horsemen only. On this report, Sherman started on his ride
to the right wing. About noon, he was overtaken by a messenger from Slocum, who still announced that they were
resisted by nothing but cavalry; but the firing of artillery
now began to be more rapid, and to indicate more serious
work.

As one goes southward from Bentonville, a country road
forks to the right from the Clinton road, about half a mile before the crossing of the Goldsboro road is reached. This turns
toward Averasboro, and a triangle of roads is thus made having sides of half a mile. Hoke's division of the Confederate
forces was first on the ground, and was ordered to take this
route, cross the Averasboro road and continue seven or eight
hundred yards farther. Here he halted and intrenched, his
line slightly recurved, but still at an acute angle to the road
on which Davis was advancing. Stewart with the troops of
his own and Lee's corps of Hood's army, came next and intrenched the line of the road they had travelled, showing a
front of four or five hundred yards. From this point the
right was swung forward along the margin of woods looking
into the open farm-lands of Cole's farm. Hardee, when
he came up, found General Bate with two divisions of
Cheatham's corps (his own and Smith's, formerly Cleburne's)
placed on the extreme right, and put Talliaferro's division in
reserve in support of Bate: his other division (McLaws') was
ordered by Johnston to the left wing. The centre of Johnston's position, therefore, was not on the Averasboro road,
but at the corner of Cole's fields, a quarter of a mile north.

The two wings went forward from this point, the left crossing diagonally the road on which Davis's corps was advancing, and the right, hidden in the thicket, reached forward
ready to envelop any force that might attempt to pass to the
west of the Cole farm. The country, except at the farm
mentioned, was covered with a dense thicket and wood, with
marshes from which small streams ran in all directions.

It was nearly noon when General Davis, with Carlin's division slowly driving Hampton's cavalry back, came upon
the breastworks crossing the road. Hobart's brigade had
been deployed some time before, and was in line across the
road, on which was moving a four-gun battery. To the right
of the road but little could be seen; but on the left the
enemy's line could be traced, apparently bending back along
the farther side of Cole's field. Still thinking he had before
him only the cavalry which he had slowly followed for five
miles, Davis ordered Buell's brigade to make a detour to the
left around the open farm lots and take the enemy in flank.
But Hobart's skirmishers were developing a line of fire
farther to the right, reaching toward our flank, and Hambright's brigade (Colonel Miles in command) was deployed
on Hobart's right. Carlin now advanced with his two brigades to charge the works before him, but soon recoiled
before a fire which had another sound than that of the cavalry carbines. A few prisoners had been taken, among them
one who had been a national soldier and had been induced
to enlist to escape from a Confederate prison. From him
the fact that Johnston was present in person with his whole
army was learned. Slocum had come up, and after consultation with Davis, Morgan's division was ordered to deploy
forward on the right of Carlin, with Mitchell's and Vandever's brigades in front and Fearing's in second line. Heavy
lines of skirmishers engaged the enemy, while the troops of

the deployed lines hastened to cover themselves with a
breastwork.

It was now about two o'clock, and Slocum wrote a dispatch
to Sherman telling of the situation, and sent Colonel Mc-

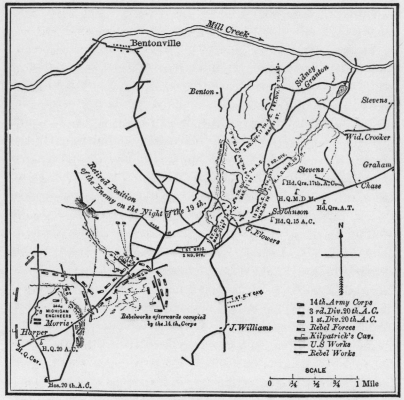

Battle of Bentonville.

Clurg, of Davis's staff, to hasten up the divisions of Williams's
corps.   Buell's brigade was making its way slowly through
the marsh and thicket on the left, when the crash of musketry there gave warning of an assault.   Hardee had sent
Talliaferro's division still beyond Bate's right upon the flank

of Buell's brigade, and Bate, now attacking in both front and flank, that single brigade was overwhelmed, and driven to the rear in confusion. The attack was taken up in turn by Stewart's divisions, sweeping across the Cole farm diagonally upon Davis's left, taking Carlin's brigades successively in flank and rear, and pushing them back. But this took time, for there was no panic, and our men were not used to be beaten. The enemy suffered terribly as he crossed the fields, played upon by the battery in the road near Cole's house, and cut down by Hobart's infantry fire. Step by step they advanced, each regiment of Hobart's, as it found itself attacked in rear, retreating and fighting, forming a new line of its own, and again making a stand, till all of this brigade also had thus been pushed off in detachments, and the left was curved a full mile to the rear. Now a rush upon the road captured the battery. Miles's brigade was also driven from its line, and all connection between Carlin and Morgan was broken. Davis, whose soldierly qualities came out brilliantly in the trial, now rode rapidly to Morgan and ordered Fearing to move his brigade toward the left, deploying parallel to the road as he went, and to charge headlong upon the flank of the enemy, who was following Carlin. The work could not have been put into better hands than those of the unfearing descendant of Israel Putnam. He changed front upon the run, swept everything before him at the point of the bayonet till the road was reached, and forming there, his destructive volleys drove the Confederate centre in confusion upon its right and into the swamp.

At the sound of fighting, Williams had hurried forward the troops of his corps. Robinson's brigade, of his own division, was the first to arrive, and it formed across the road in front of the Morris farmhouse, about a mile from Cole's house. The ground here was a little higher, and the Twen-

tieth Corps artillery was put in position as it came up.
Robinson connected with Fearing's left, and Carlin's brigades
were rallied upon this line, still farther to the left. A
country road ran along this point, and Bate attacked the line
again and again, now advancing, now driven back, until
Hardee withdrew him some distance in consequence of the
rout of the troops in the centre.

The rest of Morgan's division had not been idle while
Fearing's brigade had been so sharply engaged. Their first
assault upon Hoke's division had been a vigorous one, and
Bragg, who commanded that wing, had called for reinforcements. Hardee was just coming on the field, and Johnston
ordered McLaws' division to the support of Hoke, while
Talliaferro took the position in rear of Bate already indicated.[1] Morgan had not been able to break through the
enemy's left, and had resumed his own line and strengthened it during the lull which followed the severe check
given to Stewart's advance in the centre.

Coggswell's brigade, of Williams's corps, came up about
four o'clock, and formed on Fearing's right, though the line
was still too short to reach to Mitchell, whose left was a little refused, so as not to present an uncovered flank. Soon
after five a general attack on our lines was again made, and
was persistently kept up till night. Hoke's division charged
upon Morgan's works, but was again repulsed, and Vandever's brigade made a return charge, capturing the colors of
the Fortieth North Carolina Regiment. But the Confederates had found the gap between Morgan and the rest of the
line, and pushed fiercely upon Coggswell, who stoutly held
his ground; but some of them, passing through the interval,

---

[1] Johnston says that he yielded "very injudiciously" to Bragg's call for help.
The effect of strengthen ng Hardee's right by another division might well have
been fatal to Slocum's defence under the circumstances.

tried to take Morgan in reverse. Colonel McClurg, chief of staff, who was taking a warning of this to Morgan, narrowly escaped capture by them. Mitchell and Vandever now faced to the rear and quickly routed these, the Fourteenth Michigan Regiment, the same which had taken the colors in the preceding charge, now capturing those of the Fifty-fourth Virginia in the charge to the rear. The Confederate troops had exhausted their power upon Davis's corps, and Johnston, knowing well that by this time heavy reinforcements were approaching, directed Hardee and Bragg to recall their men as soon as the wounded could be carried from the field. Even after dark a detachment, seeking its way back, came again in rear of Mitchell's brigade, but was received with a volley which made them drop their arms and fly precipitately. Hardee's wing reoccupied the line along the north of the Cole farm, but early next morning Bragg was drawn back till the angle at the centre was salient instead of re-entrant, and the left flank rested near Mill Creek facing toward the East, whence Sherman was to be looked for with Howard's troops.

Slocum's dispatch of two o'clock, which seems to have reached his commander about five, was written before the battle was fairly opened; and Sherman, while determining to concentrate upon Johnston next day unless he retreated, made no immediate change in his dispositions, except to direct Kilpatrick's cavalry to remain with Slocum instead of passing to the right flank, as had been intended. At two in the morning of the 20th, however, Sherman was roused by a message from Slocum, dated at eight o'clock, telling of the hard fighting of the latter part of the day. A courier was at once sent to Hazen's division (which was with Howard's trains, and nearest Slocum) to hasten instantly to his assistance. The other divisions of Logan's corps were at

Falling Creek Church, where the roads the two wings were
upon crossed, about three miles from Cox's bridge. These
were directed to march at break of day, and Blair's corps,
which had gone further on the Wilmington road, was recalled.

Hazen reached Slocum at dawn, and found that the whole
of the left wing was up, and a good defensive line had been
made to connect the position so stubbornly held by Morgan
with that which Carlin reformed upon before night. By
noon Sherman himself had come with the head of Logan's
column, and the rest of the day was fully occupied with de-
ployments in the woods and swamps, and a sharp skirmishing fight, while communication was made with Slocum and
the lines adjusted. Hazen had been placed by Slocum on
the right of Morgan, so that he was in line with his own
corps when Logan approached. The whole of Johnston's
left flank was covered by a brook running through a very
difficult swamp, and, under his skilful direction, his men
had built intrenchments covered by abatis of the formidable sort with which he had made us familiar in Georgia.
His position was in the nature of a bridge-head covering
Bentonville and the bridge over Mill Creek, which he only
intended to hold till he could carry off his wounded and
prepare a safe retreat to Smithfield.

Sherman found that Slocum's wounded men were numerous enough to fill his ambulance train, and that Johnston's
line was one to manœuvre against rather than to attack in
front. He contented himself, therefore, with pushing his
lines close to his adversary's, especially on the right, where
Blair's corps extended Logan's deployment. Orders were
sent by courier to Schofield to march at once from Kinston
upon Goldsboro. Terry was directed to move from Faison's
Depot to Cox's bridge, and make a strong effort to secure a

crossing of the Neuse River there. Shortly after noon on
the 21st, General Mower, who had the extreme right of the
line, managed to thread the swamp before him, and finding
but a weak force opposing, advanced rapidly with two brigades till he was within musket range of the bridges behind
Johnston. The movement was made without concert with
the rest of the corps, and was not known to Howard till the
rapid firing, as Mower was met by Johnston's reserves, told
of his position. It was one of peril for the division as well
as of possibilities of great results had Mower's movement
been made by understanding with his superior officers.
Johnston first threw Wheeler's cavalry against this division,
following it with Lowry's (formerly Cheatham's) division of
the Army of Tennessee, which had just arrived. Howard
ordered General Blair to support Mower, and directed an
advance of Logan's line by way of a strong demonstration.
A line of rifle-pits for skirmishers was taken and Logan's
men intrenched within fifty yards of Bragg's front. The
topography, however, was so blind and unknown that full
advantage could not be taken of Mower's partial success.
He was recalled by Sherman's order, the National commander
preferring to rest for the present upon the certainty that
Johnston must retreat, and that he himself could unite his
whole army in the open country north of the Neuse, rather
than rush blindly into a general engagement in the thickets
and swamps about him.

He afterward blamed himself for not following up Mower's
movement, and with more knowledge of the ground he
would no doubt have done so; but with his lack of information of the topography as well as of the force before him, his
prudence was wiser than impetuosity. His game was a perfectly sure one with patience, and unless Johnston's rout had
been complete, the sacrifice of life in a general and des-

perate charge upon the intrenchments would have been frightful and unjustifiable. The Confederate army had pre-served the organization of the troops which had come from Hood, and down to the time of the surrender, a month later, Cheatham's, Stewart's, and Lee's corps kept their complete roster of divisions and brigades, notwithstanding the very great reduction of their numbers. The common method of judging of the enemy's force by the number of brigades rep-resented by captured prisoners, is one of the most trust-worthy ; but in this instance it was misleading, as it was no doubt intended to be. Sherman, therefore, from this and other causes which have already been mentioned, somewhat overestimated Johnston's army, and was the more inclined to leave nothing to hazard, but to hasten the concentration which would give him an overwhelming force, and which in fact enabled him to close the campaign and the war without another sanguinary engagement.

Johnston retreated in the night, and Sherman resumed his march on the 22d. Schofield had entered Goldsboro on the preceding day, placing Cox's corps on the north of the town, covering the Smithfield road. Terry's corps reached the Neuse at Cox's bridge at the same time, and laid a pontoon bridge there, so that, on the 23d, Sherman rode with the head of his column into the place, bringing together his whole army, now nearly ninety thousand strong. The casu-alty lists were heavy for the numbers engaged. On the Na-tional side the total loss was 1,604, of which 1,196 were in Slocum's command. Among them was General Fearing, who was severely wounded in his charge upon the Con-federate centre. Of the Confederates, 267 dead and 1,625 prisoners fell into Sherman's hands. Johnston states the number of his wounded at 1,467, but puts the dead and missing at only 876, which is 1,000 less than the number in our possession. A similar discrepancy is found in the statements of numbers engaged. Johnston states Slocum's force in the battle on the 19th as 35,000, and his own at about 14,100 infantry and artillery. Slocum's troops on the field during the action of the 19th, were two out of three divisions of Davis's corps, and two brigades of Williams's. The casualty lists show that none others arrived in time to take part in the fight. Their numbers were therefore about 1,000 less than those of the whole Fourteenth Corps, which numbered 13,000 when it left Savannah, infantry and artillery. Johnston's official report for 31st March shows 22,000 of these arms present, besides 5,500 cavalry. As the army was freshly assembled, his sick who were present when this report was made up must represent his wounded men ; and when his trains were parked, most of his " extra-duty" men must be supposed to be at the breastworks. Letting the dead and prisoners in our hands offset the detachments which joined him afterward, and it would appear that about 22,000 men, besides the cavalry, will fairly represent the force with which he attacked Slocum's 12,000.

In Slocum's disposition of his troops the only point open to criticism is suggested by the question, whether it was wise to deploy both of Davis's divisions upon the line of the advanced brigade when it came in contact with an intrenched infantry line, and when the best information showed all of Johnston's army present. It would seem to be better to have placed Morgan's division and two of Carlin's brigades upon the line near the Morris house, where Carlin's men rallied in the afternoon, and to have withdrawn Hobart's brigade to the same point. Johnston would then have had to move in line over a mile of swamps and thickets, to be

---

[1] See Appendix E, III.

received at a barricade which would by that time have been strong, while his own attack would be disjointed by such a march. To rush against an unknown line, without full reconnoissance, is always full of risk, and in such a marshy wilderness is much like falling into an ambuscade. Johnston had intrenched to receive an attack, and would have been somewhat slow to move out in the presence of an active skirmishing reconnoissance. This would have gained time, both for intrenching Davis's rear line and for Williams to approach. The situation, however, was full of difficulty, and the left wing came off with honors of which it had a right to be proud.

CHAPTER XII.

STONEMAN'S AND WILSON'S CAVALRY EXPEDITIONS.

BEFORE resuming the narrative of the closing events of the war in North Carolina, let us go back to the portion of Sherman's territorial command which General Thomas was now directing, and trace briefly the current of events there, so that the general relation of the final movements may be clearly understood.

It had been part of the plan, both of Grant and of Sherman, that the battle of Nashville should be followed by an active winter campaign in Mississippi and Alabama, pressing the defeated army of Hood and giving it no rest or time to reorganize. The natural plan of this campaign would have been for Thomas to march through Alabama as Sherman had done through Georgia, reaching Mobile as Savannah had been reached, and uniting forces with Canby, who would have been prepared to establish a new base of supplies upon the Gulf. The belief of General Thomas that his army was not prepared for this work brought General Grant to the conclusion that the plan which promised results most nearly equal, would be to send General A. J. Smith's corps with Knipe's division of cavalry to reinforce General Canby at New Orleans for a decisive campaign against Mobile, to transfer Schofield to the seaboard, and to limit the aggressive movements of Thomas's department to cavalry expeditions to be made by Generals Stoneman and Wilson, one from East Tennessee into the Carolinas, and the other from Florence and Tuscumbia into Central Alabama. In any event, the purpose was to maintain such activity in all portions of the theatre of war as to allow no reinforcement of the Confederate armies in the east because of lack of active and incessant occupation for the troops the enemy still had in the Gulf States.

Before the Department of the Ohio had been consolidated with that of the Cumberland by Schofield's transfer to North Carolina, the latter (acting under Thomas), had directed General Stoneman, commanding in East Tennessee, to drive out the forces with which Breckenridge had been making a diversion in favor of Hood. Stoneman started from Knoxville on December 9th with two brigades of mounted men under Generals Gillem and Burbridge, and quickly cleared East Tennessee of the enemy. Following up his advantage promptly, he penetrated Virginia, ascending the valley of the Holston to Abingdon, Wytheville, and Saltville. At the latter place he destroyed the salt works, which were of great value to the Confederacy, and which had been the coveted object of many a raid before. At Marion, extensive iron works were burned, and the lead works of Wythe County were ruined. Two railway trains were captured, the railway bridges along many miles of road were burned, and large amounts of military stores were also taken. Ten pieces of field artillery and two hundred prisoners were also captured. Breckenridge was forced to escape by a rapid retreat into North Carolina, and at the end of December Stoneman returned to East Tennessee.

In accordance with the policy of activity already stated, Grant directed Thomas on February 6th to send Stoneman with his cavalry through the Great Smoky Mountains

into South Carolina, to interrupt railway communication between Columbia and Charlotte, N. C., and by occupying the attention of part of the Confederate forces in
that region, assist the movement of Sherman.   Delays
occurred in preparation, and it was not till March 22d,
when Sherman had already reached his new communications with the North Carolina coast, that this column was
ready to start.   The great progress of the Eastern campaign changed its object somewhat, and Stoneman was directed toward Lynchburg, Va., with the purpose of increasing the damage done by him to the Virginia and Tennessee
Railway in December, and making it useless as a line of
retreat for Lee's army, if Richmond should be evacuated.
Thomas was ordered to send also the infantry of the Fourth
Corps into East Tennessee to oppose and delay Lee if he
should escape from Virginia by that route.   The troops now
at Stoneman's disposal were Gillem's division of cavalry,
which consisted of the three brigades of Brown, Palmer,
and Miller.

The upper valley of the Holston had been reoccupied by
a small Confederate force under General Jackson, and the
local militia and reserves were out.   Railway bridges had
been rebuilt in anticipation of Lee's probable necessities.
On the 26th, Stoneman was with the division at Jonesboro,
in the extreme northeast corner of Tennessee.   Here he
took the valley of the Watauga River, following the moun-
tain gorges through which it flows, to Boone, in North Carolina.   He now crossed the Blue Ridge to the upper waters of
the Yadkin, and turning northward reached New River and
Wytheville by a long detour, in which he had turned all the
hostile positions of Jackson's forces.   At Wytheville a
dépôt of supplies for the Confederate army was destroyed,
and detached parties burned the railway bridges along

ninety miles of road, and within fifty miles of Lynchburg.
This work was continued on April 6th and 7th, when Lee,
who had retreated from Petersburg in the night of tho
2d, had already been anticipated by Grant's forces on the
Danville road at Burke's Station, had thus been cut off from
the supplies accumulated in depots on that line, and was
shut up to the Lynchburg route as his last resource. The
speed with which Grant's columns surrounded him at Appomattox gave the *coup-de-grace* to his valiant army, but the
knowledge he had for a day or two before, that Stoneman
was destroying his railway and stores beyond Lynchburg,
must have added to his despair. On the 9th, Stoneman reassembled his brigades in the edge of North Carolina, and
struck southward for the Danville and Charlotte road, which
was the line by which Lee would have united his forces
with Johnston had he succeeded in evading Grant at the
Burkesville Junction. He passed southward through Ger-
manton toward Salisbury, sending detachments right and
left to destroy factories of clothing and the like. One of
these columns narrowly missed capturing Davis and his
Cabinet at Greenesboro. On the 12th he captured Salisbury,
after a brisk skirmishing engagement, in which the local
troops made but a feeble resistance, being manifestly dis-
heartened by the surrender of Lee, which had occurred on
the 9th. The captures at Salisbury were enormous, and had
Stoneman been fully aware of the situation in Virginia and at
Goldsboro, it is possible they might have been preserved;
but he acted wisely according to the information he had,
and destroyed them. The Confederate forces under Gardi-
ner and Pemberton were routed, and 1,300 prisoners were
captured. Eighteen pieces of artillery, 10,000 stands of
small arms, and vast stores of ammunition, provisions, clothing and blankets which had been accumulated as a reserve

stock for Lee's army fell into Stoneman's hands. From
Salisbury, after destroying the railway bridges for many
miles he retired toward East Tennessee, learning, on the
way, of the armistice which resulted in Johnston's surrender.

The expedition into Alabama was led by General Wilson,
and was of much larger proportions. It also was much later
in starting than General Grant had intended, his directions
being that it should march as soon after February 20th as
possible. Wilson had four divisions of cavalry in canton-
ments at Gravelly Springs, nine miles below Florence on the
Tennessee River, where they had been refitting and drilling
since the retreat of Hood in the beginning of January. One
of these, Hatch's, had been dismounted to furnish horses to
Knipe's division, which had been sent to Vicksburg to move
inland from that point, in co-operation with Canby and with
the movement Wilson himself was preparing. The other three
divisions were commanded by Generals Long, Upton, and
McCook. All these subordinate campaigns were too late to
hold any part of Hood's infantry in Alabama, for the remnants of the Confederate Army of Tennessee had already
fought with Schofield at Kinston, and with Sherman at Bentonville, before Wilson's columns moved southward on March
23d. But General Richard Taylor was assembling the reserves and the militia under the conscription laws of the
Confederacy, and Forrest, who had also been busy in recruiting and refitting his cavalry corps, had four divisions under
his command, and was confident of his ability to defeat any
mounted force Wilson could lead into Alabama or Mississippi.
Taylor had to detach some brigades from these to watch
Canby's movements and to assist General Maury at Mobile,
but this did not detract from Forrest's faith that in the campaign with Wilson he could "get there first with the most

men," to use a pithy saying of his own in which he embodied the essence of the art of war.[1]

But "to get there first" it is necessary that detachments should be nearest the threatened point, and this was not now the case with Forrest. Selma was the one remaining great manufacturing arsenal of the Confederacy. It is upon the north bank of the Alabama River, about a hundred and fifty miles above Mobile, in the heart of the richest part of the State, the "cane-brake region." The river is navigable, and it had, besides, railway connection with the coast through Demopolis (on the Tombigbee River), and with Talladega to the northeast. On the latter railway, about fifty miles north, is Montevallo, which was then, as now, a centre for the manufacture of iron of a superior quality. Forrest's men were a good deal scattered through the central and eastern region of Mississippi, collecting remounts, bringing in deserters and enforcing the conscription. Jackson's division had headquarters at West Point, on the Mobile and Ohio Railway, and Chalmers's near Columbus, Miss. Two of Roddey's brigades were near Mobile, but Roddey himself, with the remaining one, was picketing North Alabama. Buford's division had not been fully re-organized since the campaign of Nashville, and Crossland's brigade was the only part of it which seems to have taken part in this campaign. One of Chalmers's brigades (Wirt Adams's) was on the march from Jackson, Miss., to Columbus, but it was ordered to remain upon the line of the Mobile and Ohio Railway as a guard. Seven or eight thousand men would therefore be all the cavalry Forrest could hope to have in hand to meet Wilson's twelve thousand.

The winter had been well spent by Wilson in organizing, and his train of two hundred and fifty wagons was carefully

---

[1] Taylor's Destruction and Reconstruction, p. 200.

selected and packed with a view to rapid movement. The 'small rations' and ammunition had the preference, as the country would be foraged for meat and bread. A pontoon train of thirty canvas boats accompanied the column, and the wheel vehicles were guarded by fifteen hundred dismounted men. The three divisions started southward on separate roads, but united at Jasper, about eighty miles southeast of Tuscumbia. From information he here received, Wilson felt the need of haste, so filling his men's haversacks he left the train behind and pushed hard for Montevallo. Roddey's brigade began to make some opposition at Elyton, but it hardly amounted to delay. McCook was ordered to detach Croxton's brigade and send it to Tuscaloosa to destroy stores and public property there, including a military school. A railway bridge at Hillsboro was seized before it could be destroyed, and the column crossed upon it, flooring it with plank from the covering of the sides of the structure. Montevallo was reached on the 31st, Roddey's brigade and a militia force under General Daniel Adams retreating before the advance of Upton's division. In the vicinity five iron furnaces and as many collieries were destroyed; but Wilson felt that hours were precious and hurried southward. Crossland's brigade had joined Roddey, and Forrest was hastening in person to them, but the heavy National columns gave them no rest, charging them without hesitation when they formed and hurrying them back toward Randolph, fourteen miles, during the first of April. Next day Randolph was reached, and a lucky capture of a courier gave Wilson knowledge of his adversary's positions and moves. He learned from the captured despatches that Forrest had now joined in person the force in front of him, but that Jackson's division was harassed by Croxton's brigade at Trion, thirty miles northwest, between the Cahawba and Black Warrior Rivers

He also learned that Chalmers's division was at Marion, about as far to the southwest, and was marching toward Selma, in-tending to cross the Cahawba near his present position. Croxton also sent word that he should follow Jackson and bring him to an engagement. Wilson had evidently "got there first," and with the most men. He at once sent Mc-Cook with the rest of his division to co-operate with Crox-ton by attacking Jackson in front, crossing the Cahawba at Centreville, fifteen miles west of Randolph, for this purpose. McCook drove off a militia guard from the Centreville bridge and advanced toward Trion, but finding that Croxton was no longer fighting Jackson, and that the latter greatly outnum-bered him, he retired to the bridge and burned it, after cross-ing to the east bank. The river was unfordable, and as Jackson must go nearly to Marion to get over, Wilson was relieved of any fear of his joining Forrest north of Selma. He accordingly advanced with increased vigor against For-rest, who had selected an excellent defensive position six miles north of Plantersville. Fortune here favored Wilson again, as she usually does the bold, for by a mistake in tele-graphing Forrest had supposed that Chalmers was on the Selma road behind him, and had ordered him to move on Randolph. This dispatch being forwarded to Chalmers from Selma, that officer, who was upon the west side of the Ca-hawba, took the direct road up the river, separating himself from his commander instead of going to his assistance. This accident kept Forrest's force down to the two brigades of cavalry and the militia under General Adams, besides the battalion of his escort; but he was a host in himself.[1] Wil-

---

[1] Wilson's report says that Armstrong's brigade from Chalmers had joined Forrest; but the authors of Forrest's Campaigns (pp. 666 and 671) are so explicit in stating the contrary that, without access to Chalmers's official report, I feel obliged to yield to their authority.

son had, for ease of marching, put Upton's and Long's divisions upon separate roads at Randolph, and these converged near the enemy's position. Long was up first and allowed no delay. His advanced guard pushed forward on foot and broke the first line of Roddey's brigade, and he then sent a battalion of the Seventeenth Indiana mounted, with drawn sabres, to charge the retreating foe. Roddey's men were thrown into confusion, but Forrest advanced in person with his escort, their repeating carbines proved too much for the sabres, and Roddey and Adams succeeded in reforming their lines.[1] Colonel White had ridden with his Indianians over the guns, crushing the wheel of one of them by a blow which crushed the breast of a horse as well, but turning to the left he cut his way out. A gallant man, however, Captain Taylor, did not hear the order in the mêlée, and, followed by his company, rode straight at Forrest, his men falling at every step. Forrest used only his pistols, warding and firing, but he received several sabre cuts, and finally broke loose by a great bound of his horse in answer to the spur, and killed Taylor by a fatal shot before he could reach him again.

Upton's men had come up on Long's right and all dashed forward together, when Forrest's lines gave way and crowded in a confused rout toward Selma. Three guns and some two hundred prisoners fell into Wil on's hands. About midnight Forrest found Armstrong's brigade and hurrying it to Selma sent urgent orders to Chalmers to march the rest of his division instantly in the same direction.[2]   Wilson's movements

---

[1] It is an interesting fact that Forrest, whose experience was equal to that of any one, had reached the conclusion that repeating fire-arms were the proper weapons for mounted troops, and that he rejected sabres, using his force, by preference, as a mounted infantry.

[2] Forrest's biographers suggest (Campaigns, p. 671) that the hospitality of his reception at Marion had made Chalmers forget the need of haste in the previous movements.

are an admirable proof of the value of time in such a campaign. After fighting and chasing till late in the night of
April 1st, making twenty-four miles of progress during
the day, he marched at dawn of the 2d, and closed in upon
Selma early in the afternoon, in time to prevent Chalmers
and Jackson from entering the city. Forrest, covered with
the blood and dust of the battle, had a hurried conference
with General Taylor, the department commander, and the
latter quickly left for Demopolis on the Western Railway, to
see what resources he could gather to assist his heroic but
badly worsted lieutenant. The locomotive on which he went
had hardly passed beyond the city when Wilson's lines advanced, and these sent a volley after Taylor, who, however,
sped on his way unhurt.

Forrest now disposed his little garrison as best he could,
though they made but a thin line in the long parapet,
and the militia, composed of old men and young boys, were
so demoralized that he placed no reliance on them. The
works were strong and carefully built, with good ditch and
palisade, and many heavy guns were in position. Steamboats
and trains had worked hard to carry away the ordnance and
stores which were worth their weight in gold to the Confederacy now ; but these had all steamed away and the city was
left to its fate.

Wilson placed Long on the right and Upton on the left,
but despite their utmost exertions, it was near evening when
their lines had been established and the works reconnoitred.
The plan had been to pick the way through swamps on the
left, where Upton thought he could reach a less guarded part
of the fortifications, but Long heard that a force was threatening his rear and sending a regiment to protect his pack
train and led horses, he pushed headlong at the works. The
noise of his attack was the signal for the rest, the audacity

of the thing confounded the already demoralized Confederates, and after a short struggle, the lines were carried every-
where, and Wilson's men entered the town on all sides amid
a scene of indescribable confusion. Forrest had again exposed himself like a trooper in the line ; but it was of no
use, and with a mere handful of the best of his men and
some of his principal officers, he cut his way out by the
Montgomery road to the east. During the night he made
the circuit of the National Army by the north and reached
Plantersville in the morning, the scene of his hasty retreat
the day before. Resting here a few hours, he led his men
toward Marion, but was soon confronted by McCook's division, marching to rejoin Wilson at Selma. Skirmishing to
gain time, he again evaded by the left, and by another night
march crossed the Cahawba River and joined Chalmers and
Jackson at Marion, on the morning of the 4th.

Wilson's prize was an enormous one, and it had been most
skilfully won. His rapid movements, his prompt attacks,
his untiring pursuit had made his preponderance of force of
double value. He had always anticipated his adversary in
time and overpowered him in strength, so that for once in
his career the doughty Forrest had his own tactics completely turned upon him, and had been thoroughly beaten
in detail. Forty guns, twenty-seven hundred prisoners, and
great stores of material of war were captured ; but the sever-
est loss to the Confederacy was the destruction of their great
manufacturing arsenal.

Wilson laid a pontoon bridge across the Alabama River
with great difficulty, for the stream was deep and swift.
After destroying the workshops and public stores, he determined to move on Montgomery and thence into Georgia,
with the ultimate purpose, he says, of using the discretion
allowed him, to march through the Carolinas to the armies in

the east. The militia and reserves made but feeble resistance, the evacuation of Richmond and surrender of Lee
were soon rumored through the country, and the march to
Macon had none of the military significance of the brilliant
and instructive campaign against Forrest. In a strategic
point of view, it was a departure from the sound principles
which had guided the preceding part of the campaign. Two-
thirds of Forrest's corps was still intact between the Cahawba
and Tombigbee Rivers, and Mobile was not yet taken. His
true objectives were west and south, not east and north.
But the exhausted Confederacy was collapsing from all sides,
its President was fleeing for his life, as he thought, and it
was the fortune of a detachment of Wilson's command to
arrest him in the far southern part of Georgia, near the
Florida line. Mobile soon fell, and Forrest, sore with his
wounds, but more sore with the chagrin of terminating his
military career with so great a defeat, gave his parole, dis-
banded his hardy troopers, and like most of the good soldiers
of the South, taught the people by word and by example to
submit without reserve to the triumphant National Government.

CHAPTER XIII.

GOLDSBORO TO RALEIGH.—SURRENDER OF JOHNSTON'S ARMY.

UPON assembling his army at Goldsboro, the first work demanding Sherman's attention was to supply with clothing and shoes the four corps which had become nearly naked and barefoot in the march from Savannah. Colonel Wright had worked so industriously upon the Neuse River Railway that a train reached Goldsboro the day of Sherman's arrival there; but the line was so poorly stocked with locomotives and cars that it could not be depended upon to supply the army. Kinston was therefore made a secondary base for a time, steamboats carried stores there from Beaufort, More-head City, and Newbern, and the army trains were kept busy between Kinston and Goldsboro. The Wilmington Railway was not badly damaged, and a few days sufficed to put its track in order, but it was bare of equipment. Loco-motives and cars could not be procured and shipped in a moment. Some interval must necessarily elapse before a new campaign could open, and after establishing his camps, Sherman left Schofield in command and made a swift jour-ney to City Point, where he had a personal consultation with General Grant, and plans for the final campaign were defi-nitely arranged. The position of the Army of the Potomac about Petersburg was such that Lee's army must necessarily follow the Danville and Charlotte line in retreat, or make its way by Lynchburg into the valley of East Tennessee. To meet the latter contingency, General Thomas had been ordered, as has already been noted, to send the Fourth Corps (Wood's) to Bull's Gap, fifty miles northeast of Knoxville, where it could hold the passes through which the principal routes ran, long enough to enable Grant to close upon the rear of Lee's army. To meet the first contingency, Sheridan was already ordered into position on the left flank of the Army of the Potomac, where he was soon to fight the series of brilliant engagements near Five Forks, and to get where he could beat Lee in the race for Danville when the forced evacuation of Richmond and Petersburg should take place. In this final combination, Sherman's part was to move his whole army a little north of Raleigh and thence to Weldon on the Roanoke River, unless changes in the situation should induce General Grant to modify the orders.

Sherman also had the fortune to meet President Lincoln at City Point, and in an unreserved conversation upon the situation, he learned that that great man's heart was set upon restoring peace without more bloodshed, if that were possible ; the only terms which he demanded being submission to the National Constitution, disbanding of Confederate armies and governments, acknowledgment of the abolition of slavery, and the speedy resumption of the relations of the States to the Federal Government, the existing State governments continuing to act *de facto* till necessary legislation by Congress could be had. A general amnesty would follow such submission, but he hoped to be relieved of embarrassment as to the political chiefs, by the voluntary expatriation of Mr. Davis and a few of the most prominent.

Sherman returned to Goldsboro on March 30th, with authority for some changes in his army organization which were essential to its easy administration. His left wing, under Slocum, was formally constituted the Army of Georgia; the centre remained the Army of the Ohio, under Schofield, including the divisions under General Terry, which were permanently organized as the Tenth Corps; and the right wing retaining the organization it had as Army of the Tennessee. These were not merely nominal distinctions, but were necessary, under the laws, to give the commanders of these three grand divisions the power to relieve Sherman of the details of business administration of the whole. The only change in the commanders of corps was the assignment of Major-General Mower to the Twentieth Corps. The accumulation of supplies and refitting of the troops had so far progressed that, on April 5th, confidential instructions were issued, ordering the new campaign to open on the 10th. But next day came the news that Richmond was evacuated, Lee was struggling to reach Danville, and Sherman's line was accordingly changed to Raleigh, with Greensboro and Charlotte as his objective points beyond.

The march began on the 10th, and on the 11th, at Smithfield, the army was electrified by the announcement that Lee had surrendered at Appomattox on the 9th. The day was a warm and bright spring day; the columns had halted for the usual rest at the end of each hour's march; the men were sitting or lying upon the grass on either side the road, near Smithfield, when a staff officer was seen riding from the front, galloping and gesticulating in great excitement, the men cheering and cutting strange antics as he passed. When he came nearer he was heard to shout, "Lee has surrendered!" The soldiers screamed out their delight; they flung their hats at him as he rode; they shouted, "You're the man we've been looking for these three years!" They turned somersaults like over-excited children. They knew the long Civil War was virtually over. Another phase of

the universal rejoicing in the land was quite as well illustrated by the roadside. A Southern woman had come to the
gate with her children, to ask of a corps commander the
usual protection for her family while the column was passing, and as she caught the meaning of the wild shout, she
looked down upon the wondering little ones, while tears
streamed down her cheeks, saying to them only, " Now father
will come home."

From this time the march had military importance only
as it led to the quickly approaching end. The skirmishing
of advance and rear guards continued, but Johnston was
only delaying Sherman's movements till he could communicate with the Confederate President, who, with some of
his Cabinet and the more important archives of the dissolv-
ing Government, was upon a railway train at Greensboro.
Raleigh was occupied on the 13th, and on the next day a
flag of truce from General Johnston opened the final negotiations for surrender. It was on the evening of that day
that President Lincoln was assassinated. The conjuncture of
events was one of the strangest that the strange current of
human history has ever presented, and we puzzle our brains
in the vain effort to conjecture how the destiny of the country might have been modified if that horrible murder had
not been committed.

Sherman met Johnston at Durham Station in the spirit of
the lenient policy Lincoln had indicated to him a fortnight
before, and an outline of a convention was arranged before
he knew of the President's death. Knowing the danger
that the war would take a more revengeful and destructive
form if the campaign were continued, and deeply impressed
by the dismay and sorrow with which General Johnston received the terrible news of the assassination, he felt that
this was only a new reason for ending the strife before it de-

generated into one of extermination on the one side, and despair on the other. Both generals recognized the uselessness of any further destruction of human life, and agreed in regarding it as criminal. Johnston and the prominent men with him were explicit in admitting the abolition of slavery as an accomplished fact, but the negotiating parties made the error of failing to see that the embodiment of such a statement in the terms of the convention would have increased greatly the chances of its approval by the National Administration.

The history of the armistice and of its disapproval are part of the political history of the country rather than of the military campaign. It is enough to say here that the agreement reached Washington when the members of the Administration and the leaders in Congress were under the influence of a panic resulting from the belief that the Confederate leaders, conscious of the desperation of their cause, had organized a plot for the murder not only of the President, but of all his Cabinet and the principal generals of the army. We now know that the leading southern men felt Lincoln's murder to be the most grievous misfortune that could then have befallen them; and Sherman was influenced by the conviction of this, as he saw it involuntarily expressed in the countenances of General Johnston and the men about him. But panic is unreasoning, and the Secretary of War, whose position at the moment was a dominant one in the Government, seems to have rushed to the conclusion that Sherman was ready to betray the cause he had so greatly served, and acted accordingly.

No trait of Sherman's character was more marked than his loyal subordination to his superiors in army rank or in the State. Full of confidence in his own views, and vigorous in urging them, he never complained at being overruled, and

instantly adapted his military conduct to the orders he received when once debate was closed by specific directions
from those in authority.   He had shown this in the Vicksburg campaign and at Savannah; and, hurt and humiliated
as he now was, his conduct as an officer was the same,
though he resented the personal wrong.   He had not known
that General Grant had been directed to have no negotiations with Lee except for the military surrender of his army,
and he overestimated the importance, as a guard against
anarchy, of having a formal agreement of submission made
in the name of all the Southern people.   His armistice and
convention with Johnston was subject to confirmation or re-
jection.   He had given to his Government the opportunity
of doing either, or of taking the negotiation into the control
of civil officers and modifying it.   Had President Johnson
simply said to him that the arrangement was inadmissible,
and that he must resume the campaign unless the Confederate General made an unconditional surrender, he would
have obeyed, not only without protest, but without any
thought of complaint.

Instead of this, the Secretary of War published the agreement as if he were proclaiming a discovered treason and
were appealing to the country to sustain the Government
against a formidable enemy in its own camp.   General
Grant was hurried to Raleigh to supervise Sherman in the
control of his army and to take away his responsibility,
leaving only the nominal command.   Even this would perhaps have been taken from him had not the same un-
founded fears made the authorities do the army the injustice
of supposing it, too, might rebel.   Grant's practical, cool
judgment made him turn his presence at Raleigh into an
apparent visit of consultation with Sherman, who had
promptly given the stipulated notice of the termination of

the armistice before Grant's arrival, and soon after received
the final surrender of the Confederate army. When the
panic was over, the Secretary of War gave public evidence
of his sorrow for the offensive incidents in the course pursued, but Sherman could not at once forgive the imputation
upon his personal loyalty to the Government.

The duty of receiving the arms of the late Confederates
and of issuing the paroles was committed to General Schofield, and was performed at Greenesboro, in close neighborhood of the battlefield of Guilford Court House, where, in
the War of the Revolution, General Greene had won laurels
in an important engagement with Lord Cornwallis. General Hardee met Schofield and a small detachment of the
Twenty-third Corps on the railway near Hillsboro, and conducted him to Johnston's headquarters in a grove in the
edge of Greenesboro. The Confederate General had declined
the use of a house for his headquarters, and a few war-worn
tents sheltered him and his staff. Hampton, still irreconcil-
able, had refused to bring in the cavalry for surrender,
and these were scattering over the country, making their
way home as they might. Some four thousand horsemen,
and nearly or quite as many of the infantry, had deserted
since the beginning of the armistice, fearing it might end in
their being held as prisoners of war.[1] Those who remained
found the advantage of having a respected and responsible
head to represent them, for, after receiving their paroles,
they were furnished with transportation on the railways, and
with rations from the National stores. Johnston scrupu-
lously distributed to each officer and man a coined dollar
out of a small sum of money he had received from the Confederate treasury, and, with this token of the unpaid ser-

---

[1] Johnston's Narrative.

vices they had given to the lost cause, the men in gray scattering on different routes, took up the journey home-ward—to many of them a long and weary one—to begin anew the struggle of life in an almost universal impoverish-ment. The National columns marched northward with flying colors and swell of martial music, full of hope and enthusiasm, to take part in the memorable review at Wash-ington, where their sorrow that Lincoln could not have returned their salute from the front of the White House was a representative sorrow for all the comrades who could not answer to that morning's roll-call.

APPENDIX A.

FORCES OF THE OPPOSING ARMIES IN TENNESSEE.

I.—*Forces "present for duty" under the immediate command of* MAJOR-GENERAL GEORGE H. THOMAS, *October* 31, *November* 20 *and* 30, *and December* 10, 1864, *as reported by the returns on file in the office of the Adjutant-General, Washington, D. C.*

COMMANDS.	OCT. 31ST.		NOV. 20TH.		NOV. 30TH.		DEC. 10TH.	
	Commiss'd officers.	Enlisted men.	Commiss'd officers.	Enlisted men.	Commiss'd officers.	Enlisted men.	Commiss'd officers.	Enlisted men.
Fourth Corps	719	11,612	775	13,940	766	16,200	686	14,415
Twenty-third Corps [1]....	461	10,163	455	9,903	494	10,033	496	9,781
Cavalry	227	5,364	[2]252	5 551	[3]431	10,453	[4]566	14,133
District of Tennessee [5] ..	748	17,913	792	19,141	704	16,911	653	15,850
Unassigned Detachments	248	7,111	......	......	......	....	......	....
District of Etowah	....	....	193	6,238	210	6,864	237	7,612
Reserve Brigade, Chatta-nooga	......	......	29	891	25	880	25	753
Unassigned Infantry ...	......	......	28	1,047	30	1,122	30	1,060
" Artillery....	......	......	7	268	7	262	3	115
Signal Corps, Chattan'ga.	......	......	11	63	11	60	12	57
Veteran Reserve Corps, Nashville............	......	......	3	327	15	493	15	522
Det. Army of Tennessee [6].	......	......	......	......	483	8,843	581	11,345
Reserve Artillery, Chatta-nooga	......	......	......	......	......	......	8	463
Total present for duty...	2,403	52,163	2,545	57,369	3,176	72,121	3,312	76,106
Present for duty equipped	2,293	51,122	2,509	57,025	3,129	68,323	3,092	67,180

[1] Second and Third Divisions.

[2] Consisted of Hatch's Division, Croxton's and Capron's Brigades, and Fourth U. S. Cavalry.

[3] Consisted of Hatch's and Johnson's Divisions, Croxton's Brigade and Fourth U S. Cavalry, and several independent cavalry commands not specifically enumerated. Of these 2,272 are reported " present for duty," but not " present for duty equipped " (dismounted).

[4] Composed of McCook's, Hatch's, Johnson's, and Knipe's Divisions, and Fourth U. S. Cavalry. Of these 6,460 are reported " present for duty," and not " present for duty equipped " (dismounted).

[5] See abstract in detail.

[6] General A. J. Smith's divisions.

II.—*Forces "present for duty," as reported to the Adjutant-General of the Army, Washington, D. C., by the Commandant of the District of Tennessee, November 20 and 30, and December 10, 1864.*

COMMANDS.	STATIONS.	Commiss'd officers. Nov. 20th.	Enlisted men.	Commiss'd officers. Nov. 30th.	Enlisted men.	Commiss'd officers. Dec. 10th.	Enlisted men.
Fourth Division Twentieth Corps	Nashville, Tenn.	172	3,916	474	10,390	424	9,210
Post Forces	" "	178	4,698	60	2,000	61	1,969
"	Springfield, Tenn.	6	380	8	376	12	539
"	Fort Donelson, Tenn.	2	108	3	106	2	109
"	Clarksville, Tenn.	3	60	3	109	3	111
"	Gallatin, Tenn	39	907	4	144	4	145
Troops on N. & N. W. R. R.	Johnsonville, Tenn.	96	2,617	63	1,964	....	....
District of N. Alabama	Decatur, Ala.	3	....	....	....	...	....
Post Forces	" "	106	2,285	....	....	....	....
"	Larkinsville, Ala.	24	493	....	....	....	....
Troops on T. & A. R. R.	Pulaski. Tenn.	1	....	....	....	....	....
Post Forces	Columbia, Tenn.	35	810	....	....	....	....
Defences N. & C. R. R.	Tullahoma, Tenn.	¹52	1,028	5	83	4	90
Post Forces	Stevenson, Ala.	3	128	2	124	2	122
"	Decherd, Tenn	32	703	..	....	...	...
"	Murfreesboro', Tenn.	40	1,008	70	1,361	65	1,348
District of N. Alabama	Stevenson, Ala.	....	....	3	....	3	....
Battery F. First Ohio Artilery	" "	....	....	4	120	5	117
Troops on T. & A. R. R.	Nashville, Tenn.	....	....	1	....	1	...
Twenty-first Indiana Volunteer Battery	" "	....	....	4	134	4	126
Troops on N. & N. W R. R.	" "	....	....	....	....	63	1,964
Total "present for duty"		792	19,141	704	16,911	653	15,850

¹ Post of Tullahoma included.

III.—*Forces "present for duty," as reported to the Adjutant-General of the Army, Washington, D. C., by the Commandant of the District of Etowah, December 10, 1864.*

COMMANDS.	STATIONS.	Commiss'd officers.	Enlisted men.
F rst Separate Div. Different Corps.	Chattanooga, Tenn.	101	3,939
Fourteenth U. S. Colored Troops	Nashville, Tenn.	16	594
Sixteenth " "	" "	26	655
Eighteenth " "	Bridgeport, Ala.	11	353
Forty-second " "	Chattanooga, Tenn.	20	399
Forty-fourth " "	Nashville, Tenn.	14	198
Artillery	Chattanooga, Tenn.	49	1,474
Total "present for duty"		237	7,612

IV.—*Abstract of officers and men "present," taken from* GENERAL J. B. HOOD'S *return of December* 10, 1864.

	PRESENT FOR DUTY.		SICK.		EXTRA DUTY.		IN ARREST.		AGGREGATE PRESENT.
	Officers.	Men.	Officers.	Men.	Officers.	Men.	Officers.	Men.	
General and Staff......	13	.....	....	....	....	....	....	....	13
Lee's Corps :									
Staff	19								19
Johnson's Division...	219	2,530	9	87	56	777	5	5	3,688
Stevenson's Division [1]	246	2,664	7	177	31	736	...	8	3,969
Clayton's Division ...	254	2,053	3	127	44	684	3	7	3,175
	838	7,247	19	391	131	2,197	8	20	10,851
Stewart's Corps :									
Staff	9								9
Loring's Division ...	252	2,625	52	516	26	723	3	8	4,205
French's Division [2]...	88	602	1	87	21	215	...	2	1,016
Walthall's Division...	160	1,476	21	296	33	624	3	8	2,621
	509	4,703	74	899	80	1,562	6	18	7,851
Cheatham's Corps :									
Staff	12								12
Cleburne's Division [3].	274	2,539	9	246	41	794	3	17	3,923
Cheatham's Division, (Brown)...........	267	2,730	12	215	51	754	3	10	4,042
Bate's Division	191	1,659	15	216	46	530	....	6	2,663
	744	6,923	36	677	138	2,078	6	33	10,640
Engineer Battalion.....	11	377	...	16	4	76	....	....	484
Escorts......	44	272	...	11	2	52	....	....	381
Jackson's Div. Cavalry.	197	2,344	18	62	43	476	4	8	3,152
	241	2,616	18	73	45	528	4	8	3,533
Artillery :									
Lee's Corps..........	42	726	....	15	3	122	1	....	909
Stewart's Corps......	52	801	....	22	1	82	....	....	958
Cheatham's Corps....	39	730	....	1	2	108	....	....	880
Jackson's Cav. Div...	13	247	...	11	2	44	...	4	321
	146	2,504	....	49	8	356	1	4	3,063

[1] Palmer's brigade not included
[2] Sears's and Cockrell's brigades not included.
[3] Mercer's brigade not included.

	Present for Duty.		Sick.		Extra Duty.		In Arrest.		Aggregate Present.
	Officers.	Men.	Officers.	Men.	Officers.	Men.	Officers.	Men.	
Summary :									
Gen. Hood and Staff..	13	.....	....	......	.....	......	....	.....	13
Lee's Corps..........	838	7.247	19	391	131	2.197	8	20	10,851
Stewart's Corps......	509	4,703	74	899	80	1,562	6	18	7,851
Cheatham's Corps....	744	6,928	36	677	138	2,078	6	33	10,640
Cavalry	241	2.616	18	73	45	528	4	8	3,533 [1]
Artillery	146	2.504	....	49	8	356	1	4	3,068
Engineers...........	11	377	....	16	4	76	....	......	484
	2,502	24,375	147	2,105	406	6,797	25	83	26,440 [2]

On the original return are the following remarks :

"Palmer's brigade of Lee's corps, French's (Mercer's) brigade of Cheatham's corps, and Sears's and Cockrell's brigades of Stewart's corps, are on detached service and not herein included."

"A return of the cavalry under Major-General Forrest has not been furnished, and consequently not included. The last field return of the division of cavalry commanded by Brig.-General Jackson (of November 6, 1864), is included."

The numbers of the cavalry corps of General Forrest, given in the text, page 12, are taken, as there stated, from his official return made just before entering upon this campaign, and are the only ones accessible. While, therefore, the foregoing table should be increased by the numbers of Sears's brigade to give the aggregate force of Hood in the battle of Nashville, Forrest's cavalry must also be added, and the three other infantry brigades, to show the whole of his army in Tennessee.

The abstract of Hood's forces at the opening of the campaign (November 20th), as given in the text, is also made up from official returns in the War Records Office, and need not be repeated here.

---

[1] Error in original, which reads 3,532.
[2] Original return erroneously footed 34,439.

APPENDIX B.

ORGANIZATION OF OPPOSING ARMIES IN TENNESSEE.

I.—*Organization of U. S. forces commanded by* MAJOR-GENERAL GEORGE H. THOMAS *at the Battle of Nashville, Tenn., December 15 and 16, 1864.*[1]

FOURTH ARMY CORPS.

BRIGADIER-GENERAL THOMAS J. WOOD.

FIRST DIVISION.

BRIGADIER-GENERAL NATHAN KIMBALL.

First Brigade.	*Second Brigade.*	*Third Brigade.*
Col. ISAAC M. KIRBY.	Brig.-Gen. WALTER C. WHITAKER.	Brig.-Gen. WM. GROSE.
21st Illinois.	96th Illinois.	75th Illinois.
38th Illinois.	115th Illinois.	80th Illinois.
31st Indiana.	35th Indiana.	84th Illinois.
81st Indiana.	21st Kentucky.	9th Indiana.
90th Ohio.	23d Kentucky.	30th Indiana.
101st Ohio.	45th Ohio.	36th Indiana (detach't).
	51st Ohio.	84th Indiana.
		77th Pennsylvania.

SECOND DIVISION.

BRIGADIER-GENERAL WASHINGTON L. ELLIOTT.

First Brigade.	*Second Brigade.*	*Third Brigade.*
Col. EMERSON OPDYCKE.	Col. JOHN Q. LANE.	Col. JOSEPH CONRAD.
36th Illinois.	100th Illinois.	42d Illinois.
44th Illinois.	40th Indiana.	51st Illinois.
73d Illinois.	57th Indiana.	79th Illinois.
74th Illinois.	28th Kentucky.	15th Missouri.
88th Illinois.	26th Ohio.	64th Ohio.
125th Ohio.	97th Ohio.	65th Ohio.
24th Wisconsin.		

---

[1] Compiled from the Records of the Adjutant-General's Office.

THIRD DIVISION.

Brigadier-General SAMUEL BEATTY.

First Brigade.	*Second Brigade.*	*Third Brigade.*
Col. ABEL D. STREIGHT.	(1) Col. P. SIDNEY POST.[1]	Col. FRED. KNEFLER.
89th Illinois.	(2) Lt.-Col. ROBT. L. KIMBERLY.	79th Indiana.
51st Indiana.	59th Illinois.	86th Indiana.
8th Kansas.	41st Ohio.	13th Ohio.
15th Ohio.	71st Ohio.	19th Ohio.
49th Ohio.	93d Ohio.	
	124th Ohio.	

ARTILLERY BRIGADE.

MAJOR WILBER F. GOODSPEED.

Indiana Light Artillery, 25th Battery.
Kentucky Light Artillery, 1st Battery.
1st Michigan Light Artillery, Batt'y E.
1st Ohio Light Artillery, Battery G.

Ohio Light Artillery, 6th Battery.
Pennsylvania Light Artillery, Battery B
4th U. S. Artillery, Battery M.

TWENTY-THIRD ARMY CORPS.

Major-General JOHN M. SCHOFIELD.

SECOND DIVISION.

Major-General DARIUS N. COUCH.

First Brigade.	*Second Brigade.*	*Third Brigade.*
Brig.-Gen. JOS. A. COOPER.	Col. ORLANDO H. MOORE.	Col. JOHN MEHRINGER.
130th Indiana.	107th Illinois.	91st Indiana.
26th Kentucky.	80th Indiana.	123d Indiana.
25th Michigan.	129th Indiana.	50th Ohio.
99th Ohio.	23d Michigan.	183d Ohio.
3d Tennessee.	111th Ohio.	
6th Tennessee.	118th Ohio.	

ARTILLERY.

Indiana Light Artillery, 15th Battery.   Ohio Light Artillery, 19th Battery.

THIRD DIVISION.

Brigadier-General JACOB D. COX.

First Brigade.	*Second Brigade.*	*Third Brigade.*
Col. CHAS. C. DOOLITTLE.	Col. JOHN S. CASEMENT.	Col. ISRAEL N. STILES.
12th Kentucky.	65th Illinois.	112th Illinois.
16th Kentucky.	65th Indiana.	63d Indiana.
100th Ohio.	124th Indiana.	120th Indiana.
104th Ohio.	103d Ohio.	128th Indiana.
8th Tennessee.	5th Tennessee.	

ARTILLERY.

Indiana Light Artillery, 23d Battery.   1st Ohio Light Artillery, Battery D.

---

[1] Wounded.

DETACHMENT OF ARMY OF THE TENNESSEE.

Major-General ANDREW J. SMITH.

FIRST DIVISION.

Brigadier-General JOHN McARTHUR.

First Brigade.	*Second Brigade.*	*Third Brigade.*
Col. WM. L. McMILLEN.	Col. LUCIUS F. HUBBARD.	(1) Col. S. G. HILL (killed).
Illinois Lt. Artillery, Cogs-	Iowa Light Artillery, 2d	(2) Col. WM. R. MARSHALL.
well's Battery.	Battery.	12th Iowa.
114th Illinois.	5th Minnesota.	35th Iowa.
93d Indiana.	9th Minnesota.	7th Minnesota.
10th Minnesota.	11th Missouri.	33d Missouri.
72d Ohio.	8th Wisconsin.	2d Missouri Light Artillery,
95th Ohio.		Battery I.

SECOND DIVISION.

Brigadier-General KENNER GARRARD.

First Brigade.	*Second Brigade.*	*Third Brigade.*
Col. DAVID MOORE.	Col. JAMES I. GILBERT.	Col. EDWARD H. WOLFE.
119th Illinois.	58th Illinois.	49th Illinois.
122d Illinois.	Indiana Lt. Art., 3d Bat.	117th Illinois.
89th Indiana.	27th Iowa.	2d Illinois Lt. Art., Bat. G.
Indiana Lt. Art., 9th Bat.	32d Iowa.	52d Indiana.
21st Missouri.	10th Kansas.	178th New York.

THIRD DIVISION.

Colonel JONATHAN B. MOORE.

First Brigade.	*Second Brigade.*	*Artillery.*
Col. LYMAN M. WARD.	Col. LEANDER BLANDEN.	
72d Illinois.	81st Illinois.	Indiana Lt. Art., 14th Bat.
40th Missouri.	95th Illinois.	2d Missouri Light Artillery,
14th Wisconsin.	44th Missouri.	Battery A.
33d Wisconsin.		

PROVISIONAL DETACHMENT (District of the Etowah).

Major-General JAMES B. STEEDMAN.

PROVISIONAL DIVISION.[1]

Brigadier-General CHARLES CRUFT.

First Brigade.	*Second Brigade.*	*Third Brigade.*
Col. BENJAMIN HARRISON.	Col. JOHN G. MITCHELL.	Lt.-Col. C. H. GROSVENOR.
		Artillery.
Second Brigade (Army Tenn.)	68th Indiana Infantry.[2]	20th Indiana Battery.
Col. ADAM G. MALLOY.	18th Ohio Infantry.[2]	18th Ohio Battery.

---

[1] Composed mainly of detachments belonging to the Fourteenth, Fifteenth, Seventeenth, and Twentieth Army Corps, which had been unable to rejoin their proper commands serving with General Sherman's army, on the march through Georgia.

[2] Attached to Third Brigade.

First Colored Brigade.
Col. THOMAS J. MORGAN.
14th U. S. Colored Troops.
16th U. S. Colored Troops.[1]
17th U. S. Colored Troops.
18th U. S. Colored Troops (battalion).
44th U. S. Colored Troops.

Second Colored Brigade.
Col. CHARLES R. THOMPSON.
12th U. S. Colored Troops.
13th U. S. Colored Troops.
100th U. S. Colored Troops.

POST OF NASHVILLE.
BRIGADIER-GENERAL JOHN F. MILLER.

SECOND BRIGADE, FOURTH DIVISION, TWENTIETH ARMY CORPS.
COLONEL EDWIN C. MASON.

142d Indiana.
45th New York.

176th Ohio.
179th Ohio.

182d Ohio.

UNATTACHED.

3d Kentucky.
28th Michigan.

173d Ohio.
78th Pennsylvania.
45th Wisconsin.

Veteran Reserve Corps.
44th Wisconsin.

GARRISON ARTILLERY.
MAJOR JOHN J. ELY.

Indiana Light Artillery, 2d Battery.
Indiana Light Artillery, 4th Battery.
Indiana Light Infantry, 12th Battery.
Indiana Light Artillery, 21st Battery.
Indiana Light Artillery, 22d Battery.
Indiana Light Artillery, 24th Battery.

1st Michigan Light Artillery, Battery F.
1st Ohio Light Artillery, Battery E.
Ohio Light Artillery, 20th Battery.
1st Tennessee Light Artillery, Battery C.
1st Tennessee Light Artillery, Battery D.
2d U. S. Colored Lt. Artillery, Battery A.

QUARTERMASTER'S DIVISION.[2]
COLONEL JAMES L. DONALDSON.

CAVALRY CORPS.
BREVET MAJOR-GENERAL JAMES H. WILSON.

ESCORT.
4th United States.

FIRST DIVISION.[3]
First Brigade.
Brigadier-General JOHN T. CROXTON.
Illinois Lt. Art., Board of Trade Bat.   8th Iowa.   2d Michigan.
4th Kentucky (mounted infantry).   1st Tennessee.

FIFTH DIVISION.
BRIGADIER-GENERAL EDWARD HATCH.

First Brigade.	*Second Brigade.*	*Artillery.*
Col. ROBERT R. STEWART.	Col. DATUS E. COON.	1st Illinois, Battery I.
3d Illinois.	6th Illinois.	
11th Indiana.	7th Illinois.	
12th Missouri.	9th Illinois.	
10th Tennessee.	2d Iowa.	
	12th Tennessee.	

[1] Detached with pontoon train.
[2] Composed of quartermaster's employés.
[3] The Second and Third Brigades of this division, under the division commander, Brigadier-General E. M. McCook, were absent on an expedition into Western Kentucky.

SIXTH DIVISION.
Brigadier-General RICHARD W. JOHNSON.

First Brigade.	Second Brigade.	Artillery.
Col. Thomas J. Harrison.	Col. James Biddle.	4th United States, Bat'y I.
16th Illinois.	14th Illinois.	
5th Iowa.	6th Indiana.	
7th Ohio.	8th Michigan.	
	3d Tennessee.	

SEVENTH DIVISION.
Brigadier-General JOSEPH F. KNIPE.

First Brigade.	Second Brigade.	Artillery.
Col. J. H. Hammond.	Col. G. M. L. Johnson.	Ohio Lt. Art., 14th Battery
9th Indiana.	12th Indiana.	
10th Indiana.	13th Indiana.	
19th Pennsylvania.	6th Tennessee.	
2d Tennessee.		
4th Tennessee.		

The forces under Major-General L. H. Rousseau at Murfreesboro are not included in the foregoing.

II.—*Organization of the Army of Tennessee (Confederate), commanded by* General John B. Hood, *for the period ending December* 10, 1864.

LEE'S ARMY CORPS.
Lieut.-General S. D. LEE Commanding.

DIVISION.
Major-General ED. JOHNSON.

Deas's Brigade.
Brig.-Gen. Z. C. Deas Commanding.
19th, 22d, 25th, 39th, and 50th Alabama.

Manigault's Brigade.
Lieut.-Col. W. L. Butler Commanding.
10th and 19th South Carolina.
24th, 28th, and 34th Alabama.

Sharp's Brigade.
7th, 9th, 10th, 41st, and 44th Mississippi.
Sharpshooters, Mississippi.

Brantley's Brigade.
24th, 34th, 27th, 29th, and 30th Mississippi and dismounted Cavalry.

DIVISION.
Major-General C. L. STEVENSON.

Cumming's Brigade.
Colonel E. P. Watkins Commanding.
34th, 36th, 39th, and 56th Georgia.

Pettus's Brigade.
20th, 23d, 30th, 31st, and 46th Alabama.

Brown and Reynolds's Brigade.
Colonel J. B. Palmer Commanding.
3d, 18th, 23d, 26th, 32d, and 45th Tennessee, 54th and 63d Virginia,
60th North Carolina.

DIVISION.
Major-General H. D. CLAYTON.

Stovall's Brigade.
Brig.-Gen. M. A. Stovall Comd'g.
40th, 41st, 42d, 43d, and 52d Georgia.

Gibson's Brigade.
Brig.-Gen. R. L. Gibson Commanding.
1st, 4th, 13th, 16th, 19th, 20th, and 30th Louisiana.
Austin's battalion and 25th Louisiana.

Holtzclaw's Brigade.
18th, 36th, 38th, 32d, and 58th Alabama.

4th battalion, Louisiana.

STEWART'S ARMY CORPS.
LIEUT.-GENERAL A. P. STEWART COMMANDING.

DIVISION.
MAJOR-GENERAL W. W. LORING.

Featherston's Brigade.

Col. I. B. PALMER Commanding.
1st, 3d, 22d, 31st, 33d, 40th Mississippi.
1st Mississippi Battalion.

Adams's Brigade.

Col. R. LOWRY Commanding.
6th, 14th, 15th, 20th, 23d, 43d Miss.

Scott's Brigade.

Col. JOHN SNODGRASS Commanding.
12th Louisiana, 55th, 57th, and Consolidated Alabama.

DIVISION.
MAJOR-GENERAL S. G. FRENCH.

Ector's Brigade.

Col. D. COLEMAN Commanding.
9th Texas Infantry.
10th, 14th, 32d Texas Dism'd Cavalry.
29th and 39th North Carolina.

Cockrell's Brigade.

Col. FLOURNOY Commanding.
1st, 2d, 3d, 4th, 5th, and 6th Missouri
Infantry.
1st and 3d dismounted Missouri Cav'ry.

Sears's Brigade.

4th, 35th, 36th, 39th, and 46th Miss.   7th Battalion, Mississippi.

DIVISION.
MAJOR-GENERAL E. C. WALTHALL.

Quarles's Brigade.

Brig.-Gen. GEO. D. JOHNSON Comd'g.
42d, 46th, 48th, 49th, 53d, 55th Tennessee, and 1st Alabama.

Canty's Brigade.

Brig.-Gen. C. M. SHELLEY Comd'g.
17th, 26th, 29th Alabama, and 37th Mississippi.

Reynolds's Brigade.

1st, 2d, 4th, 9th, and 25th Arkansas.

CHEATHAM'S ARMY CORPS.
MAJOR-GENERAL B. F. CHEATHAM COMMANDING.

CHEATHAM'S DIVISION.
BRIG.-GENERAL M. P. LOWRY COMMANDING.

Gist's Brigade.

Lieut.-Col. B. L. WATERS Comd'g.
16th and 24th South Carolina.
2d, 5th, and 8th Georgia Battalions.
46th Georgia.

Maney's Brigade.

Colonel H. R. FIELD Commanding.
1st. 6th, 8th, 9th, 16th, 27th, 28th, and
50th Tennessee.
4th Confederates.

Strahl's Brigade.

Colonel A. J. KELLER Commanding.
4th, 5th, 19th, 24th, 31st, 33d, 38th, 41st,
and 44th Tennessee.

Vaughn's Brigade.

Colonel WATKINS Commanding.
11th, 12th, 13th, 29th, 47th, 51st, 52d,
and 154th Tennessee.

CLEBURNE'S DIVISION.
BRIGADIER-GENERAL J. H. SMITH, COMMANDING.

Smith's Brigade.

Colonel C. H. OLMSTEAD Comd'g.
1st, 54th, 57th, and 63d Georgia.

Lowry's Brigade.

3d Battalion, 5th, 8th, and 32d Miss.
16th, 33d, and 45th Alabama.

Govan's Brigade.

Brig.-Gen. D. C. GOVAN Comd'g.
1st, 2d, 5th, 13th 15th, and 25th Ark.
6th, 7th, 8th, and 19th Arkansas.

Granberry's Brigade.

Captain E. T. BROUGHTON Comd'g.
6th, 7th, 10th, 15th, 17th, 18th, 24th, and
25th Texas.
5th Confederate, 35th Tennessee, and
Nutt's Cavalry company.

BATE'S DIVISION.

MAJOR-GENERAL WILLIAM B. BATE COMMANDING.

Tyler's Brigade.

Brig.-Gen. T. B. SMITH Commanding.
2d, 10th, 20th, and 37th Tennessee.
37th Georgia and 4th Ga. Sharpshooters.

Finley's Brigade.

Major J. A. LUSH Commanding.
1st, 3d, 4th, 6th, and 7th Florida.

Jackson's Brigade.

1st Confederate. 25th, 29th, 30th, and 66th Georgia, and 1st Ga. Sharpshooters.

ARTILLERY.

LEE'S CORPS.—Commanded by MAJOR J. W. JOHNSTON.

Douglass's Battery.
Dent's   "
Garrity's   "

Fenner's Battery.
Eufaula   "
Stanford's   "

Rowan's Battery.
Corput's   "
Marshall's   "

STEWART'S CORPS.—Commanded by LIEUT.-COLONEL S. C. WILLIAMS.

Selden's Battery.
Tarrant's   "
Lumsden's   "

Bonanchord's Battery.
Cowan's Battery.
Darden's   "

Haskin's Battery.
Guibor's   "
Kalk's   "

CHEATHAM'S CORPS.—Commanded by COLONEL M. SMITH.

Turner's Battery.
Phelan's   "
Perry's   "

Bledsoe's Battery.
Key's   "
Goldthwaite's Battery.

Slocumb's Battery.
Ferguson's   "
Phillips's   "

CAVALRY CORPS.

MAJOR-GENERAL N. B. FORREST COMMANDING.

DIVISION.

BRIGADIER-GENERAL JAMES R. CHALMERS.

Rucker's Brigade.

Col. E. W. RUCKER Commanding.

McCulloch's Brigade.

Col. ROBT. MCCULLOCH Commanding.

Neely's Brigade.

Col. J. J. NEELY Commanding.

DIVISION.

BRIGADIER-GENERAL A. BUFORD.

Bell's Brigade.

Brig.-Gen. T. H. BELL Commanding.

Crossland's Brigade.

Col. EDWARD CROSSLAND Commanding

DIVISION.

BRIGADIER-GENERAL WILLIAM H. JACKSON.

Ross's Brigade.

Brig.-Gen. ROSS Commanding.

Armstrong's Brigade.

Brig.-Gen. F. C. ARMSTRONG Comd'g.

DIVISION.

BRIG.-GENERAL P. D. RODDEY.

APPENDIX C.

CONFEDERATE STRAGGLERS.

THE assertion has been so often and so persistently made in the South, since the war, that devastation of property was only practised by the National troops, that it is well to preserve for reference such extracts from their newspaper press as the following:

Extracts from a letter to the Confederate Secretary of War, published in the Charleston *Courier* of January 10, 1865, and in the Charleston *Mercury* (tri-weekly) of January 11th:

"I cannot forbear appealing to you, in behalf of the producing population of the States of Georgia and South Carolina, for protection against the destructive lawlessness of members of General Wheeler's command. From Augusta to Hardeeville, the road is now strewn with corn left on the ground unconsumed. Beeves have been shot down in the fields, one quarter taken off, and the balance left for buzzards. Horses are stolen out of wagons on the road, and by wholesale out of stables at night. . . . . Within a few miles of this neighborhood, Wheeler's men tried to rob a young lady of a horse while she was on a visit to a neighbor's, but for the timely arrival of a citizen, who prevented the outrage being perpetrated. It is no unusual sight to see these men ride late into camp with all sorts of plunder. Private houses are visited; carpets, blankets, and other furniture they can lay their hands on are taken by force in the presence of the owners," etc.

In an editorial of a column in length *apropos* to the above, the editor of the *Mercury* says: "There must be radical reform. It is folly to talk of red-tape now. We want *the thing;* we must have it: reform—shooting—cashiering—order—subordination—soldiers—not runaways, ragamuffins, ruffians."

The following is from the Savannah *Republican* of October 1, 1864: "It is notorious that our own army, while falling back from Dalton, was even more dreaded by the inhabitants than was the army of Sherman. The soldiers, and even the officers, took everything that came in their way, giving the excuse that if they did not, the enemy would. Subsequently, stragglers from our own army almost sacked the stores in Atlanta. Now, complaints loud and deep come up from that portion of Georgia in the neighborhood of our army, telling of outrages committed by straggling squads of cavalry, and of insults offered to the families of the best and most patriotic citizens."

The following is from the Richmond *Whig*, being part of a letter of a correspondent of that paper, soon after Sherman marched north from Columbia. Republished in *Army and Navy Journal*, March 18, 1865. Speaking of the Confederate evacuation of Columbia, S. C., the writer says: "The worst feature of the entire scene occurred on the day of which I write. A party of Wheeler's cavalry, accompanied by their officers, dashed into town, tied their horses, and as systematically as if they had been bred to the business, proceeded to break into the stores along Main Street, and rob them of their contents. Under these circumstances, you may well imagine that our people would rather see the Yankees, or old Satan himself, than a party of the aforesaid Wheeler's cavalry. The barbarities committed by some of them are represented to be frightful."

The Richmond *Enquirer* of October 6, 1864, contained the following, with reference to Early's command in the Valley of Virginia. After speaking of the drunkenness habitual among them, from the chief downward, its correspondent says: "The cavalry forces that had been operating in the Valley, and flitting hither and thither along the Potomac and Shenandoah were already demoralized, and since their last visit to Maryland, they have been utterly worthless. They were in the habit of robbing friend and foe alike. They have been known to strip Virginia women of all they had—widows whose sons were in our army—and then to burn their houses. At Hancock, in Western Maryland, they stopped a minister of the Gospel in the street on the Sabbath day, and made him stand and deliver his money. These monstrous truths are stated in the official report of the officer commanding a part of these cavalry forces, and which I have read."

APPENDIX D.

BATTLE OF FRANKLIN.

THE following are copies of the orders referred to in the text, taken from the files in the Adjutant-General's office, viz. :

HEADQUARTERS ARMY OF THE OHIO,
FRANKLIN, TENN., November 30, 1864.

GENERAL KIMBALL:

The Commanding General directs that you report with your command to Brig.-Gen. J. D. Cox for position on the line to-day.

Very respectfully,
J. A. CAMPBELL,
Major and A. A. G.

———

HEADQUARTERS ARMY OF THE OHIO,
FRANKLIN, TENN., November 30, 1864.

CAPT. BRIDGES:

The Commanding General directs that you report four (4) batteries from your command to Brig.-Gen. J. D. Cox, for position on the line.

Very respectfully,
J. A. CAMPBELL,
Major and A. A. G.

———

The order to General Wagner does not appear to be preserved in the Adjutant-General's files; but General Schofield and General Stanley are both perfectly in accord with the writer as to its tenor.

———

The interest attaching to the subject makes it desirable to give in full the correspondence between Generals Thomas and Schofield on the 28th, 29th and 30th November, so far as the same has been preserved in the Adjutant-General's office. It is as follows:

(Telegram.) HEADQUARTERS ARMY OF THE OHIO,
NEAR COLUMBIA, TENN., November 28, 1864—8.45 A.M.

MAJOR-GENERAL THOMAS, Nashville:

GENERAL—My troops and material are all on the north side of Duck River. The withdrawal was completed at daylight this morning without serious difficulty. Cox holds the ford in front of Columbia, and Ruger the R. R. bridge, which I partially destroyed. Stanley is going into position a short distance in rear of Cox. I think I can now stop Hood's advance by any line near this, and meet in time any distant movement to turn my position. I regret extremely the necessity of withdrawing from Columbia, but believe it was absolute. I will explain fully in time. Reinforcements will have to march from Spring Hill or Thompson's Station.

(Signed) J. M. SCHOFIELD,
Major-General.

(Telegram.)   HEADQUARTERS ARMY OF THE OHIO,
NEAR COLUMBIA, TENN., November 28, 1864—9 A.M.

MAJOR-GENERAL THOMAS, Nashville:

GENERAL—I am in doubt whether it is advisable, with reference to future operations, to hold this position, or to retire to some point from which we can move offensively. Of course we cannot secure the river here. I could easily have held the bridge-head at the R. R., but it would have been useless, as we could not possibly advance from that point. Please give me your views and wishes.

(Signed)   J. M. SCHOFIELD,
Major-General.

(Telegram.)   HEADQUARTERS ARMY OF THE OHIO,
NEAR COLUMBIA, TENN., November 28, 1864—9.10 A.M.

MAJOR-GENERAL THOMAS, Nashville:

GENERAL—I have all the fords above and below this place well watched, and guarded as far as possible. Wilson is operating with his main force on my left. The enemy does not appear to have moved in that direction yet to any considerable distance. I will probably be able to give you pretty full information this evening. Do you not think the infantry at the distant crossings below here should now be withdrawn, and cavalry substituted? I do not think we can prevent the crossing of even the enemy's cavalry, because the places are so numerous. I think the best we can do is to hold the crossings near us and watch the distant ones.

(Signed)   J. M. SCHOFIELD,
Major-General.

(Telegram.)   NASHVILLE, November 28, 1864—10 A.M.

MAJOR-GENERAL SCHOFIELD, Columbia *via* Franklin:

The following just received from Lieut.-General Grant: "City Point, Nov. 27, 9 P.M.—Savannah papers just received state that Forrest is expected in the rear of General Sherman, and that Breckenridge is already on his way to Georgia from East Tennessee." If this proves true, General Grant wishes me to take the offensive against Hood, and destroy the railroad into Virginia with Stoneman's force now beyond Knoxville. General Smith will certainly be here in three days, when I think we will be able to commence moving on Hood, whether Forrest goes to Georgia or remains with Hood.

(Signed)   GEO. H. THOMAS,
Major-General U. S. Vols., Com'dg.

(Telegram.)   HEADQUARTERS ARMY OF THE OHIO,
NEAR COLUMBIA, TENN., November 28, 1864.

MAJOR-GENERAL THOMAS, Nashville:

The enemy was crossing in force a short distance this side of the Lewisburg Pike at noon to-day, and had driven our cavalry back across the river and the Pike at the same time. The force is reputed to be infantry, but I do not regard it as very probable. Wilson has gone with his main force to learn the fact, and drive the enemy back, if practicable.

(Signed)   J. M. SCHOFIELD,
Major-General.

(Telegram.)   NASHVILLE, November 28, 1864.
MAJOR-GENERAL SCHOFIELD, near Columbia:
Your despatch of 3.30 is just received. If General Wilson cannot succeed in driving back the enemy, should it prove true that he has crossed the river. you will necessarily have to make preparations to take up a new position at Franklin, behind Harpeth, immediately, if it becomes necessary to fall back.
          (Signed)   GEO. H. THOMAS,
                                  Major-General U. S. Vols., Comd'g.

(Telegram.)   HEADQUARTERS ARMY OF THE OHIO,
                    FRANKLIN PIKE, TENN., November 28, 1864.
MAJOR-GENERAL GEORGE H. THOMAS, Nashville, Tenn.
GENERAL—I am informed the wagon bridge at Franklin has been carried away. Would it not be well to replace it by pontoon bridge during the rainy season?
          (Signed)   J. M. SCHOFIELD,
                                           Major-General,

(Telegram.)   NASHVILLE, November 28, 1864.
MAJOR-GENERAL SCHOFIELD :
You can send some of the pontoons you used at Columbia to Franklin, to lay a bridge there. I will answer your other telegrams in a few moments.
          (Signed)   GEO. H. THOMAS,
                                  Major-General U. S. Vols., Comd'g.

(Telegram.)   NEAR COLUMBIA, November 28, 1864—6 P.M.
MAJOR-GENERAL THOMAS, Nashville :
The enemy's cavalry in force has crossed the river on the Lewisburg Pike, and is now in possession of Rally Hill. Wilson is trying to get on the Franklin Pike ahead of them. He thinks the enemy may swing in between him and me and strike Spring Hill, and wants Hammond's brigade to halt there. Please give it orders if you know where it is. Also, I think, it would be well to send A. J. Smith's force to that place.
          (Signed)   J. M. SCHOFIELD,
                                           Major-General.

(Telegram.)   HEADQUARTERS ARMY OF THE OHIO,
                    NEAR COLUMBIA, TENN., November 28, 1864—9 P.M.
MAJOR-GENERAL THOMAS :
If Hood advances on the Lewisburg and Franklin Pike, where do you propose to fight him ? I have all the force that is necessary here, and A. J. Smith's troops should be placed with reference to the proposed point of concentration.
          (Signed)   J. M. SCHOFIELD,
                                           Major-General.

(Telegram.)   NASHVILLE, November 28, 1864—8 P.M.
MAJOR-GENERAL SCHOFIELD :
If you are confident you can hold your present position I wish you to do so until I can get General Smith here. After his arrival we can withdraw gradually, and invite Hood across Duck River and fall upon him with our whole force, or wait until Wilson can organize his entire cavalry force, and then withdraw from

your present position. Should Hood then cross the river we surely can ruin him. You may have the fords at Centreville, Beard's Ferry, Gordon's Ferry, and Williamsport thoroughly obstructed by filling up all the roads leading from them with trees, and then replace your infantry by cavalry. Send an intelligent staff officer to see that the work is properly done. As soon as relieved concentrate your infantry. The cavalry will be able to retard if not prevent Hood from crossing after the roads are thoroughly obstructed, if they do their duty. The road leading from Centreville to Nashville should be thoroughly obstructed. I am not sure but it would be a good plan to invite Hood across Duck River if we can get him to move toward Clarksville. Is there no convenience for unloading beyond Thompson's Station?

                    (Signed)   GEO. H. THOMAS,
                                           Major-General U. S. Vols., Com'd'g.

(Telegram.)   NASHVILLE, November 29, 1864—3.30 A.M.
MAJOR-GENERAL SCHOFIELD, near Columbia:
    Your despatches of 6 P.M. and 9 P.M. yesterday are received. I have directed General Hammond to halt his command at Spring Hill and report to you for orders, if he cannot communicate with General Wilson, and also instructing him to keep you well advised of the enemy's movements. I desire you to fall back from Columbia and to take up your position at Franklin, leaving a sufficient force at Spring Hill to contest the enemy's progress until you are securely posted at Franklin. The troops at the fords below Williamsport, etc., will be withdrawn and take up a position behind Franklin. General A. J. Smith's command has not yet reached Nashville; as soon as he arrives I will make immediate disposition of his troops and notify you of the same. Please send me a report as to how matters stand upon your receipt of this.

                    (Signed)   GEO. H. THOMAS,
                                           Major-General U. S. Vols., Com'd'g.

(Telegram.)   NASHVILLE, November 29, 1864.
MAJOR-GENERAL SCHOFIELD, near Columbia *via* Franklin:
    I have a report from the N. W. R. R. that four regiments of Forrest's cavalry have crossed Duck River below Williamsport. Have you any such information?
                    (Signed)   GEO. H. THOMAS,
                                           Major-General U. S. Vols., Com'd'g.

(Telegram.)   HEADQUARTERS ARMY OF THE OHIO,
                    FRANKLIN PIKE, TENN., November 29, 1864—8.20 A.M.
MAJOR-GENERAL THOMAS, Nashville:
    The enemy's cavalry has crossed in force on the Lewisburg Pike, and General Wilson reports the infantry crossing above Huey's Mill, about five miles from this place. I have sent an infantry reconnoissance to learn the fact. If it proves true I will act according to your instructions received this morning. Please send orders to General Cooper at Centreville. It may be doubtful whether any messenger from here will reach him.

                    (Signed)   J. M. SCHOFIELD,
                                                   Major-General.

(Telegram.)   FRANKLIN PIKE, TENN., November 29, 1864—1 P.M.
MAJOR-GENERAL THOMAS, Nashville:
Please have pontoons put down at Franklin at once.
                    (Signed)   J. M. SCHOFIELD,
                                                     Major-General.

(Telegram.)   NASHVILLE, November 29, 1864—2.30 P.M.
MAJOR-GENERAL SCHOFIELD, Franklin:
Your despatch of 8 A.M. received. I have sent orders to General Cooper as you
requested, but think it would be well for you to send a second messenger to him
to make sure that he receives his orders.
                    (Signed)   GEO. H. THOMAS,
                                               Major-General U. S. Vols., Comd'g.

(Telegram.)   NASHVILLE, November 29, 1864—11 P.M.
MAJOR-GENERAL SCHOFIELD, Franklin:
General Wilson telegraphed me very fully the movements of the enemy yesterday and this morning. He believes Forrest is aiming to strike this place, whilst
the infantry will move against you and attempt to get on your flank. If you dis-
cover such to be his movement you had better cross Harpeth at Franklin, and
then retire along the Franklin Pike to this place, covering your wagon train and
the railroad. I directed General Cooper in accordance with your wishes yesterday, to withdraw from Centreville by the Nashville road, crossing Harpeth at
Widow Dean's, and report to you from that place for further orders. You had
better send orders to meet him.
                    (Signed)   GEO. H. THOMAS,
                                               Major-General U. S. Vols., Comd'g.

(Telegram.)   FRANKLIN, November 30, 1864—5.30 A.M.
MAJOR-GENERAL THOMAS, Nashville:
I hope to get my troops and material safely across the Harpeth this morning.
We have suffered no material loss so far. I shall try to get Wilson on my flank
this morning. Forrest was all around us yesterday, but we brushed him away
during the evening, and came through. Hood attacked in front and flank, but
did not hurt us.
                    (Signed)   J. M. SCHOFIELD,
                                                     Major-General.

(Telegram.)   FRANKLIN, November 30, 1864—9.50 A.M.
MAJOR-GENERAL THOMAS, Nashville:
My trains are coming in all right. Half the troops are here, and the other half
about five miles out, coming on in good order, with light skirmishing. I will
have all across the river this evening. Wilson is here, and his cavalry on my
flank I do not know where Forrest is. He may have gone east, but no doubt
will strike our flank and rear again soon. Wilson is entirely unable to cope with
him. Of course, I cannot prevent Hood from crossing the Harpeth whenever he
may attempt it. Do you desire me to hold on here until compelled to fall back?
                    (Signed)   J. M. SCHOFIELD,
                                                     Major-General.

(Telegram.)   NASHVILLE, November 30, 1864.

MAJOR-GENERAL SCHOFIELD, Franklin:

Your despatches of 5.30, 5.50, and Wilson's despatch, forwarded to you, have been received. It will take Smith quite all day to disembark, but if I find there is no immediate necessity to retain him here, will send him to Franklin or Brentwood, according to circumstances. If you can prevent Hood from turning your position at Franklin, it should be held; but I do not wish you to risk too much. I send you a map of the environs of Franklin.

         (Signed)   GEO. H. THOMAS,
                              Major-General U. S. Vols., Comd'g.

(Telegram.)   FRANKLIN, November 30, 1864—12 M.

MAJOR-GENERAL THOMAS, Nashville:

Your despatch of 10.25 A.M. is received. I am satisfied that I have heretofore run too much risk in trying to hold Hood in check, while so far inferior to him in both infantry and cavalry. The slightest mistake on my part, or failure of a subordinate, during the last three days, might have proved disastrous. I don't want to get into so tight a place again. Yet I will cheerfully act in accordance with your views of expediency, if you think it important to hold Hood back as long as possible. When you get all your troops together, and the cavalry in effective condition, we can whip Hood easily, and, I believe, make the campaign a decisive one. Before that, the most we can do is to husband our strength and increase it as much as possible. I fear the troops which were stationed on the river below Columbia will be lost. I will get my trains out of the way as soon as possible, and watch Hood carefully. Possibly I may be able to hold him here, but do not expect to be able to do so long.

         (Signed)   J. M. SCHOFIELD,
                              Major-General.

(Telegram.)   NASHVILLE, November 30, 1864.

MAJOR GENERAL SCHOFIELD, Franklin:

General Smith reported to me this morning that one division of his troops is still behind. We must therefore try to hold Hood where he now is until these troops can get up and the steamers return. After that we will concentrate here, reorganize our cavalry, and try Hood again. Do you think you can hold Hood at Franklin for three days longer? Answer, giving your views; and I should like to know what Wilson thinks he can do to aid you in holding Hood.

         (Signed)   GEO. H. THOMAS,
                              Major-General U. S. Vols., Comd'g.

(Telegram.)   FRANKLIN, November 30, 1864—3 P.M.

MAJOR-GENERAL THOMAS, Nashville:

I have just received your despatch asking whether I can hold Hood here three days. I do not believe I can. I can doubtless hold him one day, but will hazard something in doing that. He now has a large force, probably two corps, in my front, and seems prepared to cross the river above and below. I think he can effect a crossing to-morrow in spite of all my efforts, and probably to-night, if he attempts it. A worse position than this for an inferior force could hardly be found. I will refer your question to General Wilson this evening. I think he can do very little. I have no doubt Forrest will be in my rear to-morrow, or doing some greater mischief. It appears to me that I ought to take position at

Brentwood at once. If A. J. Smith's division and the Murfreesboro garrison join me there, I ought to be able to hold Hood in check for some time. I have just learned that the enemy's cavalry is already crossing three miles below. I will have lively times with my trains again.

(Signed)   J. M. SCHOFIELD,
                                        Major-General.

(Telegram.)   NASHVILLE, November 30, 1864.
MAJOR-GENERAL SCHOFIELD, Franklin:

Your despatch of 3 P.M. is received. Send back your trains to this place at once, and hold your troops in readiness to march to Brentwood, and thence to this place as soon as your trains are fairly on the way, so disposing your force as to cover the wagon train. Have all R. R. trains sent back immediately. Notify General Wilson of my instructions. He will govern himself accordingly. Relieve all garrisons in blockhouses, and send back by railroad trains last over the road. Acknowledge receipt.

(Signed)   GEO. H. THOMAS,
                                        Major-General U. S. Vols., Comd'g.

(Telegram.)   HEADQUARTERS ARMY OF THE OHIO,
                                  FRANKLIN, TENN., November 30, 1864.
MAJOR-GENERAL GEO. H. THOMAS, Nashville, Tenn.:

GENERAL—Please send A. J. Smith's division to Brentwood early to-morrow morning. Also please send to Brentwood to-morrow morning one million rounds of infantry ammunition, 2,000 rounds three-inch and 1,000 rounds light twelve artillery.

(Signed)   J. M. SCHOFIELD,
                                        Major-General.

(Telegram.)   FRANKLIN, November 30th—7.10 P.M.
MAJOR-GENERAL THOMAS, Nashville:

The enemy made a heavy and persistent attack with about two corps, commencing at 4 P.M. and lasting until after dark. He was repulsed at all points, with very heavy loss—probably 5,000 or 6,000 men. Our loss is not probably more than one-fourth that number. We have captured about 1,000 prisoners, including one brigadier-general. Your despatch of this P.M. is received. I had already given the orders you direct, and am now executing them.

(Signed)   J. M. SCHOFIELD,
                                        Major-General.

(Telegram.)   NASHVILLE, November 30, 1864.
MAJOR-GENERAL SCHOFIELD, Franklin:

Your telegram is just received. It is glorious news, and I congratulate you and the brave men of your command. But you must look out that the enemy does not still persist. The courier you sent to General Cooper at Widow Dean's could not reach there, and reports that he was chased by rebel cavalry on the whole route, and finally came into this place. Major-General Steedman, with five thousand men, should be here in the morning. When he arrives, I will start General A. J. Smith's command and General Steedman's troops to your assistance at Brentwood.

(Signed)   GEO. H. THOMAS,
                                        Major-General U. S. Vols., Comd'g.

APPENDIX E.

STRENGTH OF OPPOSING ARMIES IN THE CAROLINAS.

I.—*National Army under* GENERAL W. T. SHERMAN *on entering the Campaign, February* 1, 1865.

COMMANDS.	Infantry.	Cavalry.	Artillery.	Total.
Fifteenth Army Corps......	15,358	16	381	15,755
Seventeenth "	11,686	47	264	11,997
Right Wing	27,044	63	645	27,752
Fourteenth Army Corps....	13,968	......	452	14,420
Twentieth "	12,911	......	523	13,434
Left Wing.............	26,879	......	975	27,854
Cavalry Division	. ..	4,375	98	4,473
Aggregate.............	53,923	4,438	1,718	60,079

The Same, April 10, 1865.

RIGHT WING—ARMY OF THE TENNESSEE—MAJOR-GENERAL O. O. HOWARD.

COMMANDS.	Infantry.	Cavalry.	Artillery.	Total.
Fifteenth Army Corps	15,244	23	403	15,670
Seventeenth "	12,873	30	261	13,164
Aggregate.............	28,117	53	664	28,834

LEFT WING—ARMY OF GEORGIA—MAJOR-GENERAL H. W. SLOCUM.

Fourteenth Army Corps....	14,653	......	445	15,098
Twentieth "	12,471	......	494	12,965
Aggregate.............	27,124	......	939	28,063

CENTRE—ARMY OF THE OHIO—MAJOR-GENERAL J. M. SCHOFIELD.

COMMANDS.	Infantry.	Cavalry.	Artillery.	Total.
Tenth Army Corps...	11,727	......	372	12,099
Twenty-third Army Corps..	14,000	......	293	14,293
Aggregate.............	25,727	......	665	26,392

CAVALRY—BREVET MAJOR-GENERAL J. KILPATRICK.

Cavalry Division	......	5,484	175	5,659
Grand aggregate.......	80,968	5,537	2,443	88,948
Total number of guns..	......	......	......	91

II.—Confederate forces available to resist Sherman's march through the Carolinas.

Although exact data are not easily to be got, we are not wholly without evidence as to the means which General Beauregard had at his command when Sherman's movement began. In the "Historical Sketch of the Chatham Artillery," Colonel C. C. Jones, Jr., who was Hardee's Chief of Artillery, gives the following as a foot-note to p. 206. His authority is certainly conclusive as to the conference and the estimates made at it:

"At a conference held on the second day of February, 1865, at Green's Cut Station, on the Augusta and Waynesboro Railroad, in Burke County, Georgia, at which General Beauregard, Lieut.-General Hardee, Major-General D. H. Hill, and Major-General G. W. Smith were present, the following was the estimated strength of the forces in and about Augusta and in the State of South Carolina, which it was thought could be relied on as effective to resist the advance of General Sherman:

General Hardee's Regular Infantry, P. A. C. S.................	8,000	
" Militia and Reserves	3,000	
		11,000
" Light Artillery	2,000	
Butler's division, half only now available....................	1,500	
		3,500
Total under command of General Hardee in S. Carolina........		14,500
Major-General Smith's Georgia Militia	1,200	
Colonel Browne's Georgia Reserves...........................	250	
		1,450
Lieut.-General Lee's corps........ { Only about half of which	4,000	
Lieut.-General Cheatham's corps . { were reported for ac-	3,000	
Lieut.-General Stewart's corps.... { tive duty.	3,000	
		10,000
Artillery, Army of Tennessee...............		800
General Wheeler's Cavalry		6,700

RECAPITULATION.

Total Infantry 22,450
Light Artillery 2,800
Cavalry, mounted and dismounted 8,200
                                                         _____

Grand Total............ 33,450

" Cheatham's corps had not arrived. The head of Cheatham's corps was ex-pected to arrive in Augusta on the 4th or 5th inst., and the head of Stewart's on the 10th or 11th."

In the text to which the above is a foot-note, the same writer says : " General Hardee, with his *eighteen thousand* Confederate troops at detached points along the Carolina coast and elsewhere, composed in large measure of reserves and State forces recently brought into and unaccustomed to the hardships of actual service, and of artillerists drawn from fixed batteries, who for the first time were taking the field as infantry, was incapable of offering effectual resistance," etc.

On March 1, 1865, General Beauregard, then at Charlotte, N. C., submitted to General J. E. Johnston, at the same place, a plan of operations against Sherman, in which he estimated their effective force of infantry and artillery then available at 26,000, as follows :

" Hardee's corps (infantry and artillery)........ 10,000
Army of Tennessee............................. 6,000
Bragg's forces........ 10,000
                                                          _____

Infantry and Artillery.. .... 26,000 "

The full plan is published in " The Land we Love," a monthly magazine, Charlotte, N. C., Vol. I., p. 188 (1866). In it Beauregard distinctly states that the 6,000 are then at Charlotte. Detachments from the Army of the Tennessee continued to arrive much later, Cheatham himself reaching Johnston with part of his corps after the battle of Bentonville, March 19th and 20th (see Johnston's " Narrative," p. 393). A reinforcement of about 2,000 joined on the 20th and 21st.

Jefferson Davis, in his " Rise and Fall of the Confederate Government," Vol. II., p. 632, says, on this subject : " General Johnston's force, according to his estimate, when he took command, amounted to about 16,000 infantry and artillery and 4,000 cavalry ; if to this be added the portion of the Army of Tennessee, about 2,500 men, under command of General Stephen D. Lee, which afterward joined the Army at Smithfield, N. C., and that of General Bragg's command at Goldsboro, which amounted to about 8,000, the aggregate would be about 30,500 men of all arms."

As bearing upon this question, see also the table of paroles issued to Johnston's army upon its surrender, p. 243, *infra.*

III.—*Abstract from return of the Army*, GENERAL J. E. JOHNSTON, *Commanding, for period ending March* 31, 1865, *Headquarters, Smithfield, N. C.*

COMMAND.	PRESENT FOR DUTY.		Effective total present.	Aggregate present.	Aggregate present and absent.	PRISONERS OF WAR.	
	Officers.	Men.				Officers.	Men.
General Staff....	15	....	....	15	15		
Hardee's Army Corps: [1]							
Staff.......................	11	....	....	11	14		
McLaw's division............	274	2,592	2,533	3,685	10.145		
Taliaferro's "	93	1,556	1.534	1,907	4,257		
Hoke's [2] "	409	4,217	4,091	5,287	16,672	179	3,353
Total......................	787	8,365	8,158	10,890	31,088	179	3,353
Army of Tennessee:							
Staff.......................	5	.....	....	5	11		
Lee's corps....	503	3,779	3,589	5,201	24,711	371	6,666
Cheatham's corps	300	2,386	2,273	3,266	24,124	410	5,390
Stewart's corps..............	129	951	883	1,544	10,139	100	1,027
Total	937	7,116	6,745	10,016	58,985	881	13,083
Total Infantry	1,739	15,481	14,903	20,921	90,088	1,060	16,436
Artillery: [3]							
Hardee's corps..............	36	716	697	847	1,035		
Army of the Tennessee.......	3	98	96	112	152	....	4
Total Artillery.......... ..	39	814	793	959	1,187	....	4
Pioneer Regiment (Tucker's Confederate) [4]....	25	326	318	398	621		
Grand total, without cavalry. [5]	1,803	16,621	16,014	22,278	91,896	1,060	16,440

[1] The return of Hardee's troops, from which this is prepared, is dated March 27th, that of the Army of Tennessee April 1st.

[2] The Sixty-eighth and Sixty-seventh Regiments, North Carolina (State) troops, and the First North Caroli. a Battalion (State), operating on the enemy's communications with Newberne are not reported.

[3] The artillery of the Army of Tennessee has not yet arrived from Mississippi. The larger portion of the artillery of the Departments of North Carolina and South Carolina, Georgia and Florida, has been sent to the rear for reorganization, and no report has been received.

[4] and [5]. See next page.

IV.—*Army of Tennessee, and other forces under* GENERAL JOHNSTON'S *command, paroled at Greensboro', N. C., May* 1 *and* 2, 1865.

COMMANDS, ETC.	Officers.	Men.	Aggregate
Generals Johnston and Beauregard and staffs.....	275	533	808
Stewart's corps.............	739	8,145	8,884
Lee's corps......................................	550	4,426	4,976
Hardee's corps	961	8,101	9,062
Reserve Artillery .... ,...... ..,,,..	61	1,191	1,252
Cavalry corps ..... ,.............................	175	2,331	2,506
Detachments....................................	212	1,033	1,245
Naval Brigade.............	106	197	303
Medical officers, attendants, and patients in hospital	135	867	1,002
General Cooper and Brig.-Gen. Colquitt and staff...	7	......	7
Total.............	3,221	26,824	30,045
Paroled at Salisbury..............................	279	2,708	2,987
" Charlotte..............................	386	3,629	4,015
Total.................................	665	6,337	7,002
Grand Total....................	3,886	33,161	37,047

General Johnston, in his "Narrative," p. 410, says the apprehension of being made prisoners or war "caused a great number of desertions between the 19th and 24th of April—not less than four thousand in the infantry and artillery, and almost as many from the cavalry ; many of them rode off artillery horses and mules belonging to the baggage trains." If this estimate of eight thousand be added to those paroled at Greensboro', the number of his troops will be raised to about 45,000.

⁴ Companies A and D, Engineer Regiment, are on detached service and not included, as no report has been received from them. Effective total (about) 80.

⁵ A formal return of the cavalry has not yet been furnished. Effective total, April 1, 5,105. Total present, 6,587. Aggregate present, 7,042.

At the time of the above report nearly all Johnston's artillery was at Hillsboro, N. C., refitting. Colonel Jones says ("Chatham Artillery," p. 215): "Of thirty light batteries there concentrated—the most of them being unfit for field service—ten were to be chosen and furnished at the expense of the others, with the best battery animals and equipments." Thirty batteries would make, say 2,500 men.—J. D. C.

APPENDIX F.

ORGANIZATION OF OPPOSING ARMIES IN THE CAROLINAS.

I.—*Organization of the Armies under the Command of* MAJOR-GEN W. T. SHERMAN, *April*, 1865.

ARMY OF THE TENNESSEE.

MAJOR-GENERAL O. O HOWARD, COMMANDING.

FIFTEENTH ARMY CORPS.

MAJOR-GENERAL JOHN A. LOGAN COMMANDING.

FIRST DIVISION.

INFANTRY.

BREVE* MAJOR-GENERAL C. R. WOODS.

First Brigade.	Second Brigade.	Third Brigade.
Brevet Brig-Gen. W. B. WOODS.	Col. R. F. CATTERSON.	Col. G. A. STONE.
27th Missouri.	40th Illinois.	4th Iowa.
12th Indiana.	46th Ohio.	9th "
76th Ohio.	103d Illinois.	25th "
26th Iowa.	6th Iowa.	30th "
31st Missouri.	97th Indiana.	31st "
32d Missouri.	26th Illinois.	
	100th Indiana.	

SECOND DIVISION.

MAJOR-GENERAL WILLIAM B. HAZEN.

First Brigade.	Second Brigade.	Third Brigade.
Colonel T. JONES.	Colonel W. S. JONES.	Brig.-Gen J. M. OLIVER.
6th Missouri.	37th Ohio.	15th Michigan.
55th Illinois.	47th "	70th Ohio.
116th "	53d "	48th Illinois.
127th "	54th "	90th "
30th Ohio.	83d Indiana.	99th Indiana.
57th "	111th Illinois.	

THIRD DIVISION.

BREVET MAJOR-GENERAL J. E. SMITH.

First Brigade.

Brig.-Gen. W. T. CLARK.
18th Wisconsin.
59th Indiana.
63d Illinois.
48th Indiana.
93d Illinois.

Second Brigade.

Colonel J. E. TOURTELLOTTE.
56th Illinois.
10th Iowa.
80th Ohio.
17th Iowa.
Battalion 26th Missouri.
Battalion 10th "
4th Minnesota.

FOURTH DIVISION.

BRIGADIER-GENERAL E. W. RICE.

First Brigade.

Col. N. B. HOWARD.
2d Iowa.
7th "
66th Indiana.
52d Illinois.

Second Brigade.

Col. R. N. ADAMS.
12th Illinois.
66th "
81st Ohio.

Third Brigade.

Col. F. J. HURLBUT.
7th Illinois
39th Iowa.
50th Illinois.
57th "
110th U. S. colored

DETACHMENTS.
Artillery Brigade.

Lieut.-Col. WILLIAM H. ROSS.

H, 1st Illinois.
12th Wisconsin Battery.

H, 1st Missouri.
B, 1st Michigan.

29th Missouri Infantry.
Signal Detachment.

SEVENTEENTH ARMY CORPS.

MAJOR-GENERAL F. P. BLAIR, COMMANDING.

FIRST DIVISION.

INFANTRY.

BRIGADIER-GENERAL M. F. FORCE.

First Brigade.

Brig.-Gen. J. W. FULLER.
18th Missouri.
27th Ohio.
39th "
64th Illinois.

Second Brigade.

Brig.-Gen. J. W. SPRAGUE.
25th Wisconsin.
35th New Jersey.
43d Ohio.
63d "

Third Brigade.

Lt.-Col. J. S. WRIGHT
10th Illinois.
25th Indiana.
32d Wisconsin.

THIRD DIVISION.

BREVET MAJOR-GENERAL M. D. LEGGETT.

First Brigade.

Brig.-Gen. CHARLES EWING.
16th Wisconsin.
45th Illinois.
31st "
20th "
30th "
12th Wisconsin.

Second Brigade.

Brig.-Gen. R. K. SCOTT.
20th Ohio.
68th "
78th "
19th Wisconsin.

FOURTH DIVISION.

Brevet Major-General G. A. Smith.

First Brigade.
Brig.-Gen. B. F. Potts.
23d Indiana.
32d Ohio.
53d Indiana.
14th Illinois.
53d   "
15th   "

Third Brigade.
Brig.-Gen. W. W. Belknap.
11th Iowa.
13th   "
15th   "
16th   "
32d Illinois.

DETACHMENTS.

Artillery Brigade.

Major Frederick Welker.

C, 1st Michigan Artillery.
1st Minnesota Battery.
15th Ohio Battery.

9th Illinois Mounted Infantry.
G Company, 11th Illinois Cavalry
Signal Detachment.

ARMY OF GEORGIA.

Major-General H. W. SLOCUM, Commanding.

FOURTEENTH ARMY CORPS.
Brevet Major-General J. C. DAVIS Commanding.

FIRST DIVISION.
Infantry.
Brigadier-General C. C. WALCUTT.

First Brigade.
Bvt. Brig.-Gen. Hobart.
21st Wisconsin.
33d Ohio.
94th   "
42d Indiana.
88th   "
104th Illinois.

Second Brigade.
Bvt. Brig.-Gen. Buell.
21st Michigan.
13th   "
69th Ohio.

Third Brigade.
Colonel Hambright
21st Ohio.
74th   "
38th Pennsylvania.
79th   "

SECOND DIVISION.
Brigadier-General J. D. MORGAN.

First Brigade.
Brig.-Gen. Wm. Vandever.
10th Michigan.
14th   "
16th Illinois.
60th   "
17th New York.

Second Brigade.
Brig.-Gen. J. G. Mitchell.
121st Ohio.
113th   "
108th   "
98th   "
78th Illinois.
34th   "

Third Brigade.
Lt.-Colonel Langley.
85th Illinois.
86th   "
110th   "
125th   "
52d Ohio.
22d Indiana.
37th   "   (det.)

THIRD DIVISION.

BREVET MAJOR-GENERAL A. BAIRD.

First Brigade.	*Second Brigade.*	*Third Brigade.*
Colonel M. C. HUNTER.	Lt.-Colonel DOAN.	Brig.-Gen. GEO. S. GREENE.
17th Ohio.	2d Minnesota.	14th Ohio.
31st "	105th Ohio.	38th "
89th "	75th Indiana.	10th Kentucky.
92d "	87th "	18th "
82d Indiana.	101st "	74th Indiana.
23d Missouri (det).		
11th Ohio.		

DETACHMENTS.
Artillery Brigade.
Major CHARLES HOUGHTALING.

Battery I, 2d Illinois.	5th Wisconsin Battery.
" C, 1st "	19th Indiana "

TWENTIETH ARMY CORPS.
MAJOR-GENERAL J. A. MOWER COMMANDING.

FIRST DIVISION.
INFANTRY.
BREVET MAJOR-GENERAL A. S. WILLIAMS.

First Brigade	*Second Brigade.*	*Third Brigade.*
Colonel J. L. SELFRIDGE.	Colonel WM. HAWLEY.	Brig.-Gen. J. S. ROBINSON.
4th Pennsylvania.	2d Massachusetts.	31st Wisconsin.
5th Connecticut.	3d Wisconsin.	61st Ohio.
123d New York.	13th New Jersey.	82d "
141st "	107th New York.	82d Illinois.
	150th "	101st "
		143d New York.

SECOND DIVISION.
BREVET MAJOR-GENERAL JOHN W. GEARY.

First Brigade.	*Second Brigade.*	*Third Brigade.*
Bvt. Bg.-Gen. N. PARDEE, Jr.	Col. P. H. JONES.	Bvt. Brig.-Gen. BARNUM.
5th Ohio.	33d New Jersey.	29th Pennsylvania.
29th "	73d Pennsylvania.	111th "
66th "	109th "	60th New York.
28th Pennsylvania.	119th New York.	102d "
147th "	134th "	137th "
Detachment K. P. B.	154th "	149th "

THIRD DIVISION.
BREVET MAJOR-GENERAL W. T. WARD.

First Brigade.	*Second Brigade.*	*Third Brigade.*
Col. H. CASE.	Col. DANIEL DUSTIN.	Bvt. Brig.-Gen. COGGSWELL.
70th Indiana.	19th Michigan.	20th Connecticut.
79th Ohio.	22d Wisconsin.	26th Wisconsin.
102d Illinois.	33d Indiana.	33d Massachusetts.
105th "	85th "	55th Ohio.
129th "		73d "
		136th New York.

DETACHMENTS.
Artillery Brigade.

Captain C. E. WINEGAR.

Battery I, 1st New York. Battery O, 1st Ohio.
" M, 1st "   " E, Independent Pennsylvania.
Pontoiners, 58th Indiana Veterans.
Mechanics and Engineers, 1st Michigan.

ARMY OF THE OHIO.

MAJOR-GENERAL JOHN M. SCHOFIELD COMMANDING.

TENTH ARMY CORPS.

MAJOR-GENERAL A. H. TERRY COMMANDING.

FIRST DIVISION.

INFANTRY.

BREVET MAJOR-GENERAL H. W. BIRGE.

First Brigade.	*Second Brigade.*	*Third Brigade.*
Col. H. D. WASHBURN.	Col. HARVEY GRAHAM.	Col. N. W. DAY.
8th Indiana,	159th New York.	38th Massachusetts.
18th "	13th Connecticut.	156th New York.
9th Connecticut.	22d Iowa.	128th "
14th New Hampshire.	131st New York.	175th "
12th Maine.	28th Iowa.	176th "
14th "		24th Iowa.
75th New York.		

SECOND DIVISION.

BREVET MAJOR-GENERAL A. AMES.

First Brigade.	*Second Brigade.*	*Third Brigade.*
Col. R. DAGGETT.	Col. J. S. LITTELL.	Col. G. F. GRANGER.
3d New York.	47th New York.	4th New Hampshire.
112th "	48th "	9th Maine.
117th "	203d Pennsylvania.	13th Indiana.
142d "	97th "	115th New York.
	76th "	169th "

THIRD DIVISION.

BRIGADIER-GENERAL C. J. PAINE.

First Brigade.	*Second Brigade.*	*Third Brigade.*
Bvt. Brig.-Gen. D. BATES.	Bvt. Brig.-Gen. S. DUNCAN.	Col. J. H. HOLMAN.
1st U. S. Colored Troops.	4th U. S. Colored Troops.	5th U. S. Colored Troops
30th " "	6th " "	27th " "
107th " "	39th " "	37th " "

DETACHMENTS.

Brigade (not numbered).

Brevet Brigadier-General J. C. ABBOTT.

3d New Hampshire Infantry. 6th Connecticut Infantry.
7th " " 7th " "
16th New York Heavy Artillery (six companies).
16th " Independent Battery.
22d Indiana Battery.
Light Company E, 3d U. S. Artillery.
Co. A, 2d Pennsylvania Heavy Artillery.
Cos. E and K, 12th New York Cavalry.
Detachment Signal Corps.

TWENTY-THIRD ARMY CORPS.

MAJOR-GENERAL J. D. COX COMMANDING.

FIRST DIVISION.

INFANTRY.

BRIGADIER-GENERAL THOMAS H. RUGER.

First Brigade.	Second Brigade.	Third Brigade.
Bvt. Bg.-Gen. I. N. STILES.	Col. J. C. McQUISTON.	Col. M. T. THOMAS.
120th Indiana.	123d Indiana.	8th Minnesota.
124th "	129th "	174th Ohio.
128th "	130th "	178th "
180th Ohio.	28th Michigan.	

Battery Elgin, Illinois Artillery.

SECOND DIVISION.

MAJOR-GENERAL D. N. COUCH.

First Brigade.	Second Brigade.	Third Brigade.
Col. O. H. MOORE.	Col. J. MEHRINGER.	Col. S. A. STRICKLAND.
25th Michigan.	23d Michigan.	91st Indiana.
26th Kentucky.	80th Indiana.	183d Ohio.
	118th Ohio.	181st "
	107th Illinois.	50th "
	111th Ohio.	

19th Ohio Battery.

THIRD DIVISION.

BRIGADIER-GENERAL S. P. CARTER.

First Brigade.	Second Brigade.	Third Brigade.
Col. O. W. STERL.	Brevet Brig.-Gen. J. S.	Brevet Brig.-Gen. T. J.
8th Tennessee.	CASEMENT.	HENDERSON.
12th Kentucky.	103d Ohio.	112th Illinois.
16th "	177th "	63d Indiana.
100th Ohio.	65th Indiana.	140th "
104th "	65th Illinois.	

Battery D, 1st Ohio Light Artillery.

CAVALRY DIVISION, M. D. M.

BREVET MAJOR-GENERAL JUDSON KILPATRICK.

First Brigade.	Second Brigade.	Third Brigade.
Brevet Brig.-Gen. THOS. J.	Brevet Brig.-Gen. S. D.	Col. GEO. E. SPENCER.
JORDAN.	ATKINS	5th Kentucky.
9th Pennsylvania.	92d Illinois Mounted Inf.	5th Ohio.
2d Kentucky.	10th Ohio.	1st Alabama.
3d "	9th "	
3d Indiana.	1st Ohio Squadron.	
8th "	9th Michigan.	

10th Wisconsin Battery.

II.—*Organization of the Army near Smithfield, N. C., Commanded by* Gen. Joseph E. Johnston, *March* 31, 1865.

HARDEE'S ARMY CORPS.

Lieut.-General WILLIAM J. HARDEE Commanding.

MAJOR-GENERAL L. McLAWS'S DIVISION.

Brigades—Blanchard's, Harrison's, Kennedy's, Fizer's.

BRIGADIER-GENERAL W. B. TALIAFERRO'S DIVISION.

Brigades—Elliott's, Rhett's.

MAJOR-GENERAL R. F. HOKE'S DIVISION.

Brigades—Clingman's, Hagood's, Colquitt's, Kirkland's, Nethercutt's Junior Reserves.

ARMY OF THE TENNESSEE.

STEWART'S, LEE'S, and CHEATHAM'S CORPS.

(These corps are reported as having the same organization as when with Hood, both as to divisions and brigades, except that Anderson's Division of Lee's Corps was under command of Major-General D. H. Hill, and the whole of Stewart's Corps was under the command of Major-General E. C. Walthall.)

ARTILLERY ATTACHED TO HARDEE'S CORPS.

Batteries—Abelle's, Anderson's, Brooks's, Maxwell's (section), Atkins's, Parvis's, Detachment 10th North Carolina Battalion, Le Garden's, Stuart's.

ARTILLERY ATTACHED TO ARMY OF TENNESSEE.

Battery—Kanapaux's. For memorandum as to other artillery of the Army of the Tennessee, see Appendix E, III.

CAVALRY CORPS.

Lieut.-General WADE HAMPTON Commanding.

Wheeler's Cavalry. Butler's Cavalry. Divisions and brigades not given.[1]

---

[1] It is regretted that it has not been practicable to procure the list of regiments in Hardee's Corps, or the Cavalry.

INDEX.

Other DA CAPO titles of interest